"Jeff Roper takes the timeless word of God t
truths for all who wish to become better le;
his Bible study on Proverbs, and this book fu
earlier teachings."

—**DANIEL BROWN**, author of *The Other Side of Pastoral
Ministry: Using Process Leadership to Transform Your Church*

"Ancient wisdom can be relevant today! I love how my friend, Jeff Roper,
leans into the depth and breadth of his lifetime of experience and global
journey in order to bring this insightful gift to us. Jeff's transparency, applied to his experience and scholarly wisdom, is refreshing and strikes an
easy reading tone. I am enriched by the relevancy of the timeless wisdom
of Proverbs as illuminated and amplified in this book. It's a win that you
will enjoy as well."

—**TED VAIL**, vice president of global
operations, The Foursquare Church

"Jeff Roper mines out treasures found along the path of lifelong development. He provides a fresh framework to lift the gaze of the weary and
re-envision leaders to the character formation for sustainable ministry
efficacy. Jeff's insights point us inward so the expansion can happen
outwardly—a must-read."

—**WENDY NOLASCO**, senior director of US
mission, The Foursquare Church

"Digging primarily into the book of Proverbs and integrating insights
from theologians as well as leading contemporary leadership constructs,
Jeff Roper's book presents today's leaders with well-synthesized frame-
works and approaches for leading well. The discussion questions for each
chapter provide a platform for leadership evaluation and application. I
highly commend and recommend this book."

—**REMI LAWANSON**, professor of leadership
studies, Life Pacific University

"*Following Wisdom, Leading Wisely* takes the Bible seriously! It's a well-written, well-researched book that invites us into a season of reflection on the profound influence of godly character. It's designed to help the reader become the kind of person people gladly follow."

—**STEVE SCHELL**, author of *The Promise of the Father: Understanding and Receiving the Baptism in the Holy Spirit*

# Following Wisdom, Leading Wisely

# Following Wisdom, Leading Wisely

## Proverbs as Ancient Wisdom for Today's Leader

Jeff Roper

*Foreword by Tammy Dunahoo*

WIPF & STOCK · Eugene, Oregon

FOLLOWING WISDOM, LEADING WISELY
Proverbs as Ancient Wisdom for Today's Leader

Wipf & Stock
An Imprint of Wipf and Stock Publishers
199 W. 8th Ave., Suite 3
Eugene, OR 97401

www.wipfandstock.com

PAPERBACK ISBN: 979-8-3852-0583-7
HARDCOVER ISBN: 979-8-3852-0584-4
EBOOK ISBN: 979-8-3852-0585-1

VERSION NUMBER 02/19/24

To Debbie

# Contents

# Foreword

I was about twelve years old when I realized my religious home was actually quite dysfunctional and that parenting one's parent is not the normal responsibility of a preteen. I did not know that my mother's "fearful faith" was not God's plan for his children nor that my worthiness was not found in her approval of my performance. It was in that same age that I heard a pastor talk about the book of Proverbs and I was immediately intrigued. Being a Sunday School-Bible-Quiz-kid, I was drawn to scripture even though I had no idea how to interpret or apply it. What made sense to me was the simple rhyme, "A Proverb a day keeps foolishness away!" I discovered there are thirty-one chapters so I began my lifelong practice of reading a chapter a day. I knew enough to know that if I were going to grow up healthy and live well, I needed something from those pages to teach me a different way of being. I began praying, "God, give me wisdom beyond my years and experience." Where would a twelve-year-old gain the wherewithal to pray such a prayer? The abiding Holy Spirit had taught me to pray, even as I questioned and wrestled with what I was seeing at home and experiencing in the church. Little did I know that reading those pages over and again and praying those words would become a sculpting tool for my heart, mind and soul.

Considering the meaning of the wisdom literature year after year cultivated a desire in me for knowledge, understanding, wisdom, discernment and discretion. It was more than intellectual stimulation, it was the formation of my inner life. I kept reading how these are to be searched for like great treasure. They were described as jewels adorning one's life. They were portrayed as guardians, keepers of the soul. Why knowledge, wisdom, understanding, discernment and discretion? Think about the riches found within these words. New knowledge challenges our current mindsets, which is essential for growth and keeps us from becoming fixed, small-minded. We are instructed to grow in knowledge coupled with grace. Understanding moves that knowledge from head to heart to hand where wisdom applies that knowledge to all of life. Discernment teaches us the mind and ways of Christ and informs what we are to do and know. Discretion is the way wisdom shows up in every situation. The right way, the right thing, the right word, at the right time. That twelve-year-old girl needed this treasure in abundance!

Through the years, I learned our deepest pain and challenges early in life can turn into strengths and, if processed well, equip us for the assignments ahead. I began to understand Romans 8:28 and how "in all things God works for the good of those who love him, who have been called according to his purpose." Unfolding within me was the understanding of what God calls good, his purpose of maturing his people (wisdom), which is made clear in verse 29, "For those God foreknew he also predestined to be conformed to the image of his Son, that he might be the firstborn among many brothers and sisters." I was growing to understand that this maturing of God's people, this forming of Christ in us, is for the sake of the world. That our transforming lives become the story they read to know God, to experience his great love, to know they are created in His image to be his daughters and sons, with our Elder Brother's resemblance, his ways becoming our own. This is the work of wisdom!

I am now in my sixties, and after forty years of pastoral ministry and twenty years of denominational leadership serving pastors and churches, I still pray that childhood prayer with the pages of Proverbs written in my heart. So, when my friend, Jeff Roper, asked if I would write the forward to his book about wisdom for leaders, I did not hesitate for two main reasons. First, I know Jeff. I know his deep devotion to God and that he has grown in and lives the words he has written. I know he loves leaders and gives his life to serve their well-being. Second, after so many years in denominational and pastoral ministry, I am more convinced than ever that this is one of the greatest needs of the hour, as Jeff so aptly describes in his opening chapter.

Our world is crying out for maturing, healthy, adaptive, self-differentiated spiritual leaders who exude a non-anxious presence. This is what wisdom looks like. It is portrayed in humility, grace, a life of repentance, the fruit of the Spirit, guided by prayer and spiritual practices. Influential charisma, communication gifts, astute organizational skills, and technological savviness are added tools to be used as directed, but not as a substitute. They will not reorder loves, form Christ's character, or express the true mission of God in today's world. In fact, much damage is done to the lives of the people we are influencing when we prioritize these external tools as substitutes for spiritual formation. Proverbs paints many startling and sad pictures of lives without wisdom, and they are all the more weighty when those lives lead others. We have all seen them, maybe we have been them. May we humbly turn from our human wisdom and ask from the One who gives heavenly wisdom liberally to those who ask. May we apply our hearts to wisdom.

Jeff has masterfully highlighted core issues in a leader's life through the Proverbs.

I ask you to read each page slowly, dig for the riches, and excavate with a heart of openness, discovery, application, and repentance. Ask the Holy Spirit to be the active teacher and guide through every word. Then be faithful and pass on to others what you have learned and lived. Oh, and enjoy the treasure hunt!

Dr. Tammy Dunahoo
Executive Dean
Portland Seminary of George Fox University

# Acknowledgments

I AM DEEPLY GRATEFUL to my daughter, the Reverend Elizabeth Horn, for converting the original sermon notes into a rough outline that became this book. To Bob Hunt of Foursquare Missions Press for your original encouragement to write this book. To my editor, Joya Stevenson, your exceptional skills and profound biblical insights are truly remarkable. To Wipf and Stock Publishers for making this book a reality.

To my ministry team, Brandon and Marcie Brazee, Steve and Kim Cecil, Gary and Joy Peiss, and Tim and Dhana Wimberly. You have carried the weight of our shared ministry, provided invaluable feedback and insight, and been a safe harbor and true friends. You folks are amazing. I am a better follower of Jesus because of you. Tim, I am so grateful for your help in developing the questions at the end of this book. To the leadership of The Foursquare Church and Foursquare Missions International. Your humility and faithfulness continue to model what it means to follow wisdom and lead wisely.

To my children and grandchildren. You continue to teach me the joy and richness of life and the power of family.

Most of all, I am thankful to my wife, Debbie. I have no words to describe how much you have taught me. The words written in this book were first written on my heart by you. You are the personification of beauty and wisdom in my life. This book is a testament to your profound influence, and I dedicate it wholeheartedly to you.

# 1

# A Book for Leaders

Without wise leadership, a nation falls.

—Proverbs 11:14 NLT

John Maxwell claims, "Everything rises and falls on leadership."[1] If this is true, then we are in trouble. A recent survey conducted by the World Economic Forum discovered that a startling 86 percent of respondents believe we have a leadership crisis in the world today. The study encompassed leadership in multiple fields, including business, government, the nonprofit sector, and religion. Nonprofit and business leaders ranked highest in terms of public confidence. Government leaders ranked very low. The only leaders to rank lower than government leaders were religious leaders.[2] More than half of the respondents lacked confidence that religious leaders were actively dealing with global problems. A separate international study conducted by the Barna Group discovered that 82 percent of people between the ages of 18 and 35 believe "society is facing a crisis of leadership because there are not enough good leaders right now."[3] Society in general, and the church in particular, exhibit all

1. Maxwell, *Developing the Leader Within You,* ix.
2. World Economic Forum, "Outlook on the Global Agenda: 2015," Trend 3.
3. Barna, "Leadership Crisis," para. 1.

1

the signs of a crisis in leadership: war on the truth, factionalism, societal breakdown, moral corruption, abuse of power, sexual harassment, financial corruption, demonization of opponents, and the cult of personality. These are all indicators of a culture in the throes of a leadership crisis.

The leadership crisis is not driven by an absence of leaders. Everywhere you look, you find strategic leaders, charismatic leaders, transformational leaders, visionary leaders, empowering leaders, motivational leaders, and even servant leaders. Leaders are everywhere, yet we still have a leadership crisis. Nor is this crisis caused by a lack of leadership training. Who can keep up with the flood of books, seminars, and training programs offering the latest trends and best thinking on leadership? Colleges and universities are riding this leadership wave by offering graduate and doctoral programs in strategic, organizational, or global leadership. It seems everyone is either looking for or selling the secret sauce of great leadership. And yet, we still have a leadership crisis.

Don't get me wrong. I am all for visionary, charismatic, servant leaders who motivate and empower others for transformational living. I am all for the "Seven Habits of Highly Effective People"[4] and "Getting Things Done."[5] I am all for training and education. I want leaders to sharpen their skills and improve their tactics. But something more is needed. For while the world is looking for better leadership methods, God is looking for better leaders.

When the World Economic Forum asked, "What skills do our leaders need to win back the confidence of their populations?" respondents revealed that leaders must possess specific skills, such as a global interdisciplinary perspective; long-term empirical planning; strong communication skills; and collaboration. More important, leaders must also possess character virtues such as empathy, courage, morality, and prioritizing social justice and well-being over financial growth. As these respondents show, the solution to our crisis is leaders who are trusted for their skillful competence and virtuous character.

The World Economic Forum discovered something that the book of Proverbs has proclaimed for a few thousand years: We need wise leaders. The crisis of our times calls for men and women who will follow wisdom and lead wisely. What use, after all, is getting things done, or even servant leadership, without wisdom?

4. Covey, *7 Habits*, 2020.

5. Allen, *Getting Things Done*, 2015.

# A Book for Leaders and Those Who Will Become Leaders

Wise leadership is so important that the Bible dedicates an entire book to the subject. The book of Proverbs served ancient Israel as a training regimen in character formation for social and political leaders.[6] The book is presented as the writing of Solomon to his sons.[7] Presumably, one of the sons would eventually become king, and as such, he would need to lead wisely. This literary device served the purpose of the book. While anyone can benefit from Proverbs, its purpose is to teach insight to the inexperienced leader, knowledge and discretion to the young leader, and understanding to the mature leader (Prov 1:4). So, whether you are an inexperienced novice just getting started, a journeyman leader in the trenches, or an "old hand" at the height of your influence, you will benefit from Proverbs. It is eternal wisdom from an ancient book for today's leader.

As the implied author, Solomon is renowned as a wise leader. However, like every human leader, Solomon was flawed. Indeed, God did give Solomon incredible wisdom in answer to prayer (1 Kgs 3:3–15). The breadth of his knowledge, aptitude, skill, perception, and wisdom was world renowned (1 Kgs 4:34; 10:1–13, 24). He is remembered as the prolific author of 3,000 Proverbs and 1,005 songs (1 Kgs 4:32). Though Solomon left an enduring legacy of wisdom, his glory was but for a moment. He brought prosperity and grandeur to Israel until his later years, when his disobedience caught up with him.

Solomon's astounding wisdom did not prevent him from ruining his life. Solomon, you see, was obsessed with women (1 Kgs 11:1). Contrary to the word of God (Exod 34:16), he took wives from the lands of Egypt, Moab, Ammon, Edom, Sidon, and Hittite. A vast multitude, seven hundred wives and three hundred concubines surrounded this once-great king. As Solomon advanced in years these wives, foreign and forbidden, turned his heart to worship gods foreign and forbidden; Ashtoreth of the Sidonians, Chemosh of Moab, Molech and Milcom of the Ammonites (1 Kgs 11:1–8). This monarch deemed the wisest among men ended his days as an old fool (1 Kgs 4:29–34). As the sun sets upon his reign, we witness the lamentable sight of Solomon's reign tarnished by the weight of his choice to abandon wisdom and pursue folly.

6. Brown, "The Pedagogy of Proverbs," 150–82, and Dunham, "Structure," 361–88.

7. Prov 1:1; 10:1; 25:1. Though other authors are also named "the wise" (Prov 22:17; 24:23): Agur (Prov 30:1) and King Lemuel (Prov 31:1).

Sadly, the tragic story of Solomon's downfall is not an isolated occurrence. It is a lamentable tale we witness time and again as the destiny of leaders unravels. Whether it is the founder of the world's largest church brought low by embezzlement, a staggering sum of twelve million dollars misappropriated,[8] or influential leaders who make headlines as their institutions collapse, or the small church pastor whose moral shortcomings you will never hear about, failures in leadership are played out before our eyes on an almost daily basis. The traumatic toll of this crisis is paid by the multiple millions of individuals whose lives have been destroyed and whose faith has been shipwrecked.

Your calling, competency, charisma, and accomplishments will never substitute for what only your character shaped by wisdom can provide. Pursue your calling. Develop your competencies. Minister as God has gifted you. Ask great things of God. Attempt great things for God. And in all your getting, get wisdom. For no matter how gifted and fruitful you are, your character is your destiny. This is the meaning of Solomon's story and the message of the book of Proverbs.

## Some Essential Points About Genre and Literary Forms

Much of the Hebrew Bible is poetic in spirit and structure. Poetry uses language to ignite the imagination and stir the depths of emotion. The poetic use of figures of speech, metaphors, and hyperboles are woven throughout the prophetic writings[9] and the wisdom literature of the Hebrew Bible.[10] Even the historical books[11] contain fine examples of poetry. Some scholars estimate as much as one-third of the Hebrew Bible may be poetry.[12] Biblical Hebrew, with its simplicity of form combined with intensity of feeling and pictorial power, is an ideal instrument for poetic and imaginative speech.[13]

---

8. Moon, "Founder," para 1–3.

9. Isaiah through Malachi

10. Job, Psalms, Proverbs, Ecclesiastes, and Song of Songs

11. Joshua, Judges, Ruth, 1 & 2 Samuel, 1 & 2 Kings, 1 & 2 Chronicles, Ezra, Nehemiah

12. Myers, "Poetry," 837.

13. Elwell and Comfort, "Poetry, Biblical," 1060–1061.

Hebrew poetry is not like modern poetry.[14] Modern poetry often makes use of meter or rhyme. Hebrew poetry, in contrast, focuses on the rhyming of thoughts, not the rhyming of words. It accomplishes this "thought rhyme" through the mutual correspondence of sentences or clauses, called "parallelism." For example, in Proverbs 1:2, we read that the purpose of the book of Proverbs is: "For learning about wisdom and instruction, for understanding words of insight" (NRSV). Notice how the thoughts stand in harmony. "Learning" and "understanding" are synonyms, and the objects "wisdom," "instruction," and "words of insight" are all related and nearly synonymous. The words do not rhyme, but the thoughts do.

There are four main types of parallelism in Hebrew poetry.[15] The first is *synonymous parallelism*, where the thought expressed in the first part of the verse is repeated in the second part, in different but equivalent terms (Pss 2:4; 19:1; 36:1–2; 103:11–12; Prov 3:13–18). The second is *antithetic parallelism*, where contrasts take center stage. Here, the thought of the first part of the verse is contrasted with its opposite in the second (Ps 1:6; Prov 10:1–4, 16–18; 13:9). The third is *emblematic parallelism*, where one line is figurative and the other is literal, while together they form a simile with the word "like" or "as" introducing the figurative line (Prov 10:26; 11:22). The fourth is *synthetic parallelism*, where the verses are like steppingstones in which the idea expressed in the first line of a verse is developed and completed in the following lines (Pss 1:1; 3:5–6; 18:8–10; Prov 26:3). There are more complicated forms of parallelism, but these four are the most common.[16]

The normal unit of Hebrew verse is the couplet, consisting of two parallel lines. But this is not the only grouping of lines in Hebrew poetry. Units of three (Pss 1:1; 5:11; 45:1–2), four (Pss 1:3; 55:21; Prov 27:15–16), five (Ps 6:6–7; Prov 24:23–25), six (Ps 99:1–3; Prov 30:21–23), and even larger combinations of parallel lines occur.

The book of Proverbs employs a rich mosaic of poetry, parables, questions, short stories, and wise maxims to communicate nuggets of wisdom as proverbial sayings. A proverb is a short, pithy saying encapsulating a profound truth. It is a short sentence based on a long experience designed to stick in your mind. All nations and cultures have their own versions of these short, memorable sentences. Growing up in the

14. See Alter, *Biblical Poetry*, 2011.

15. Berlin, "Parallelism," 155–62.

16. Tucker Jr., "Psalms 1," 585–89.

American South, I was often counseled to be wary of my associations, for "If you lie down with dogs, you will get up with fleas." The Irish, too, offer their sage advice, reminding us that it is wiser to "pay the butcher than the doctor." It is their colorful way of saying that eating healthy is more expensive but worth it when you consider the long-term consequences. An American proverb tells us, "The longest distance between two points is a shortcut." I remind myself of this proverbial wisdom every time I am tempted to do things quickly rather than correctly. When it comes to matters of speech and action, the Apache proverb rings true, "It is better to have less thunder in the mouth and more lightning in the fist."

The Hebrew word for proverb (*mashal*) is also translated as "parable" and sometimes "allegory." Its basic meaning is "a comparison" because a proverb typically seeks to instruct by making a comparison. Many of Solomon's proverbs are comparisons or contrasts. The paired subjects include the wise and the foolish, wisdom and folly, and the righteous and the wicked. These comparisons are often indicated by the word "like." For example, Proverbs says a beautiful woman without discretion is like a gold ring in a pig's snout (Prov 11:22). Her beauty may be attractive, but her character is as ugly and unclean as a pig.[17]

Some Proverbs present these comparisons by using the word "better." For example, "Whoever is slow to anger is better than the mighty, and he who rules his spirit than he who takes a city" (Prov 16:32). God used this verse to recalibrate my focus when I was a young, ambitious pastor trying to "take my city for God." I had an anger problem that I conveniently ignored and justified in pursuit of my ambition. I so easily dismissed it, hiding it beneath a cloak of humor. I thought it was funny to joke, "I have never lost my temper. It has always been there when I needed it." But the truth was far from humorous. My anger was rooted in my thirst for control. I needed to learn gentleness toward others. My quest to control people and circumstances led me astray. People and circumstances were not my problem. I was my problem. I needed to learn to control myself. It was a formidable struggle, but as time passed, I learned that controlling myself was far better and more difficult than "taking my city."[18]

The world has changed a lot since the writing of Proverbs, but we humans have not. We are still in desperate need of God's wisdom, for it gives order and purpose to life, discernment for making decisions, and a

17. Other examples of comparisons and contrasts can be seen in Prov 25:25; 26:6–9.
18. See also Prov 15:16–17; 16:19; 17:1; 19:1.

sense of fulfillment—all to the glory of God. It keeps us in rhythm with the symphony of creation, attuned to the grand design of the Creator. It is not confined to lofty ideals, but rather, it is practical and all-encompassing, permeating every aspect of our existence. It equips us for life and leadership by teaching us God's character in the affairs of life.

The wisdom we encounter in Proverbs is not theoretical or ephemeral, nor is it dressed in a priestly ephod or a prophet's mantle. We do not find it hidden on a mountaintop or sequestered in a hermit's cave. Instead, the wisdom we encounter here is fiercely practical, dressed in work clothes, standing on busy streets and in messy houses, claiming all areas of life as spheres of her dominion. Wisdom walks straight into your disordered world and promises insight and skill, courage and success, purpose and destiny, if only you will listen to her voice, eat from her table, and walk on her path. She is not a distant stranger but a companion close at hand. She beckons you to partake in her bounty, offering the key to a life well-lived, abundant with meaning and direction, ready to guide you in the midst of your ordinary days and turbulent nights. She waits, ever eager, for you.

## How to Use This Book

This book is not a commentary on Proverbs.[19] It is my witness to lessons learned about life and leadership from reading Proverbs every day while doing ministry in a global context. My goal is to help provide answers to the leadership crisis we are facing. We have a problem, and God's word has the answer. If you are looking for help and longing for something more meaningful than success and more significant than popularity, this book is for you. If the next trendy thing will not satisfy your hunger for depth of meaning and skillfulness in life, then this book is for you. More importantly, the book of Proverbs is for you. So come, embark on this journey with me, as we explore what it means to follow wisdom and lead wisely.

I have two recommendations. First, use this book as part of your spiritual formation as a leader. While Proverbs offers practical insights into leadership tactics like long-term planning, its primary focus is on the character of leaders, not the tactics of leadership. This book focuses on ten major character issues discussed in Proverbs. This list is by no

---

19. If you want to dig deeper, you can consult commentaries such as Waltke, *Proverbs*, 2004, Waltke and De Silva, *Shorter Commentary*, 2021, and Longman, *Proverbs*, 2006.

means exhaustive. It is not intended to be. After more than thirty years of leadership development in multiple nations, one thing is clear to me: Leaders, regardless of their stature or accomplishments, never outgrow the need to be strong in these ten areas:

- Wisdom and Folly (chapter 2)
- Wise and Foolish Leaders (chapter 3)
- An Intoxicating Attraction (chapter 4)
- Husbands and Wives (chapter 5)
- Parents and Children (chapter 6)
- Friends, Foes, and Neighbors (chapter 7)
- The Lazy and the Diligent (chapter 8)
- The Wise Leader's Use of Money (chapter 9)
- The Wise Leader's Use of Words (chapter 10)
- Righteous and Wicked Leaders (chapter 11)

Take the time to read the scripture references in your own Bible. Do not settle for only reading my summaries of the book of Proverbs. That will never satisfy your desire for wisdom, any more than reading the ingredients of a meal will satisfy your hunger for food. Get into the word for yourself. If you use this book in a classroom setting or in mentoring and discipleship groups, I suggest a steady progression of studying one chapter per week over the span of twelve weeks. Allow these gatherings to blossom into lively discussions, where the collective wisdom of diverse minds coalesce and bring forth even more perspective and insight.

The discussion questions are provided to enhance your study. They invite reflection and present you with an opportunity to write your own portion of the book. Proverbs 16:20 tells us, "Whoever gives thought to the word will discover good." Take time to give thought to the word and discover good. Perhaps this will be the start of a lifelong habit of taking your pen and notebook with you, or whatever you use to take notes, every time you read Proverbs. You will always find something that speaks to your situation. It is there, but you must slow down and listen to hear the voice of wisdom.

My second recommendation is to make Proverbs part of your daily Bible reading. The easiest way to do this is to read the chapter number that corresponds to the day's date. For example, if the day is October 9, then read Proverbs 9. There are 31 chapters in Proverbs, and all months except February have 30 or 31 days. If you put this reading plan into practice, you will read through Proverbs every month.

Settle in for a long journey that knows no swift conclusion. Wisdom is not gained in a day, but it is gained daily through a lifetime of humble love and obedience to God. You will make mistakes and stumble along the way. That is OK if you get up, dust yourself off, learn from your mistakes, and start walking again. It is comforting to know that imperfection is not fatal, for by embracing our shortcomings and acknowledging our need for growth, we embark upon a path of constant renewal. This is when Wisdom goes to work upon her hidden loom to weave together the warp and woof of human frailty and divine providence as a seamless tapestry that, when unfurled, can only be called the glory of God.

So, let your journey begin with a heart of endurance. As you progress, remember that wisdom is woven through the fabric of a lifetime, a steadfast companion to those who humbly seek it. Embrace each day, for it bears the promise of wisdom's unfolding, and with each step, you draw closer to the source of all wisdom—the divine hand that guides your way.

The key lies not in dwelling on the past or pondering the distant future but in starting now, right where you are. Waste no time in hesitating, for Wisdom beckons you to listen to her whisper, to savor the morsels she lays before you, and to embark on the path she lays out. It is in these small yet significant actions that Wisdom takes root, weaving her way into the very fabric of your character. Do this every day for the rest of your life and you will become wise.[20]

## A Note Regarding Gender and Gender Language

Proverbs was written from a male orientation and perspective, as was most literature of the time. The patriarchal context of the biblical writers presents multiple challenges for today's reader.[21] The biblical texts can too easily be read as demonizing and degrading to women, which results in legitimating their oppression and trivializing their experience.[22] Unfortunately, Christian history is littered with examples of well-meaning

20. See Heb 5:14

21. For a fascinating study of the Bible and women, see Bellis, *Helpmates, Harlots, and Heroes,* 2007.

22. Schneiders, *The Revelatory Text,* 182.

Bible believers equating cultural norms with biblical standards. The subjugation of women, sexism, nationalism, slavery, polygamy, and genocide have all been justified by mistakenly equating cultural norms or evil behavior recorded in the Bible with biblical standards of piety and justice. God's word, in truth, never demeans or enslaves but instead shows us how we are to treat others, ethically and theologically, regardless of gender, ethnicity, nationality, or class.

If gender in the Bible isn't complicated enough, we can throw in the challenges of translating its original languages of Hebrew, Aramaic, and Greek into modern languages. For example, the English language is biased towards the masculine gender. This bias often restricts or obscures the meaning of the original text. Semitic languages such as Hebrew and Aramaic are often more gender-inclusive than a literal translation would convey.[23] With this in mind, I will endeavor to use inclusive language as much as possible. However, when the constraints of language force me to use gendered language, please read it as a limitation of language and not a restriction based on gender.

As contemporary readers of biblical texts, we must contextualize the material to make the text meaningful for our experience. For example, I am neither a beautiful woman nor the queen of an empire; yet I can read the book of Esther with great benefit by contextualizing its message and adapting myself to its story. We may lament the gender biases reflected in the cultural contexts of the biblical world, but we must deal with the literature that we have and the society it reflects. The ultimate point of Proverbs is the gaining of wisdom, and this is a gender-neutral activity.[24]

I admit it. Reading and understanding the Bible can be messy.[25] I cannot deny that the Bible can be read as though it were written by members of the "He-man Womanhaters' Club."[26] However, with careful and faithful reading, we will discover what Karl Barth called "the strange new world within the Bible."[27] The Bible has liberated souls from the darkness of sin and ignorance and brought them into the light of God's grace and

---

23. Mojola, "Bible Translation," 4.

24. Bellis, et al., *Proverbs*, xlviii–l.

25. Four helpful books for the serious Bible student: McKnight, *The Blue Parakeet*, 2018; Enns, *How the Bible Actually Works*, 2020; Fee and Stuart, *How to Read the Bible*, 2014; and Schneiders, *The Revelatory Text*, 1999.

26. Depending on your age and nation of origin, you may need to do a Google search for this cultural reference to "The Little Rascals" television show.

27. Barth, *Word of God*, p. 28.

truth in Jesus Christ. The transformative message of the Bible has em-powered people to confront injustice, relieve suffering, fight oppression, overthrow slavery, and strive for human rights, equality, and dignity. While the Bible was misused to justify slavery, it was also the Bible that transformed John Newton (1725–1807) from a vicious slave trader to a minister of the Gospel devoted to ending slavery. Abolitionists around the world were motivated by his example and strengthened through his hymns of praise. Today, multitudes are still moved to tears when they sing his most famous hymn that begins, "Amazing Grace, how sweet the sound that saved a wretch like me."

Christian leadership is not merely a quest for ever-growing minis-tries and budgets. Christian leadership is about unleashing the power of the word of God in whatever arena of influence you have been granted. And let's be very clear about this: You do not make the Bible relevant; the Bible makes you relevant. Proverbs is an invitation for you to unleash the power of the Bible in your leadership. Whatever your cause, however high your ambitions or wide your vision for a world transformed by the Gospel, there is rich wisdom to assist you in the book of Proverbs. Let this ancient book mold your character and guide your leadership.

# 2

# Wisdom and Folly

ALLOW ME TO SHARE a candid story of my own journey in ministry. I started out as a young, overconfident know-it-all determined to do church leadership "the right way." My heart brimmed with hubris, convinced everyone else was doing it wrong. A few years passed, and I found myself so beaten and defeated that I didn't think I could drop a rock and make it hit the ground. The pride that had propelled me was crushed by what I perceived as failure. I came to learn it was something else altogether. My once prideful heart lay broken, its arrogance humbled, wounded by his love and now open to his grace. It was then that a profound healing process began.

In desperation, I cried out to God, "Lord, if you will help me survive this, I promise I will do whatever I can to help other leaders avoid the terrible mistakes I have made." This cry from my brokenness opened me to God's wholeness. It was transformational for my life and a turning point in my ministry. I had a long way to go to strip away my hubris, but I was heading in the right direction. I had reached the end of myself, and it was there that I found God. He was waiting for me, welcoming me, embracing me, and healing me. During this experience, I began a journey from foolishness to wisdom. God ceased being a distant relation I chased but never caught. He became the Father who walks with me in the cool of the day and in the heat of the battle. Throughout this critical time, Proverbs became life-giving.

Through reading Proverbs, I learned that the wisdom of God is freely available if I pursued it with my whole heart. Lady Wisdom calls, "O simple ones, learn prudence; O fools, learn sense" (Prov 8:5). In the busy streets she cries out, on the highest points she stations herself and calls out, and she lifts her voice in front of the city gates. She says to those on the busy streets, "Slow down to listen to me." She speaks to those who are trying to find their way, "Walk on my path." To those who are empty, she invites, "Come feast at my table" (Prov 8:1–36). Anyone may come and learn from Lady Wisdom. She only requires humility, fear of the Lord, and discipline.

Not only is Lady Wisdom there to guide you, but Woman Folly is there to lead you astray.[1] Woman Folly is always there, calling out, inviting you to listen to her voice, to eat from her table, and to walk on her paths. Discipline is what keeps you safe from her (Prov 25:28). When I was growing up, my mother would say in exasperation, "Boy, do you want me to whip the fool out of you?" I realize that kind of language isn't appropriate today. Plus, I don't want you to get the wrong impression of my mother. She was the gentlest person I have ever known. Her objective in asking me this question was not to punish but to discipline me. I did not understand it then. I understand it now, for folly is locked in our hearts from childhood, and only discipline will drive it out (Prov 22:15). This struggle with folly is lifelong. The only thing that changes between childhood and adulthood is who does the discipline. As adults, we are responsible for disciplining ourselves. This is what growing up is all about. We outgrow our need for mother or father to discipline us, or at least we should outgrow it. Becoming wise requires growing up, not just growing old. Growing old is inevitable; growing up is a choice.

## Wisdom in Proverbs

The Hebrew Bible contains a treasure trove of words for wisdom, each illuminating facets of understanding, perception, and discernment. The exquisite richness of this vocabulary reflects the importance of wisdom in scripture. Pregnant with meaning, they beckon us to a deeper intimacy with God, opening the gates to a life of deeper comprehension, understanding, knowledge, discernment, and self-discovery.

---

1. Murphy, *Proverbs*, 277–87.

The primary word, *ḥokma* (from the stem *ḥkm*), generally refers to practical skill or special expertise, ranging from technical skills to shrewdness, discernment, or understanding. It can refer to the practical skills of craftsmanship (Exod 28:3; 31:6; 36:1, 2; 1 Kgs 7:14) or the skills of sound judgment and discernment in navigating the situations of life (2 Sam 20:22; 1 Kgs 2:6), or to the wisdom of the godly (Ps 90:12) and God's wisdom (1 Kgs 3:28; 2 Sam 14:20; Deut 34:9). The practical sense is evident with Hiram, who had the necessary skills to do all the bronze work for Solomon's temple, turning raw elements into sacred beauty (1 Kgs 7:14).

Most of the occurrences of *ḥkm* are found in the wisdom literature of Job, Psalms, Proverbs, and Ecclesiastes. It is typically presented as something of supreme value to pursue at any cost (Prov 4:5–7). The Psalms celebrate the inherent worth of *ḥkm* in guiding ethical and religious conduct. Like a compass for the soul, it points the way to righteous paths and virtuous deeds (Pss 37:30; 90:12; 111:10). But it is in the Proverbs that *ḥkm* unveils its true splendor, calling us to heed its counsel like a wise mentor guiding our steps. With an insistent voice, it summons us to embrace its teachings, to be molded into skillful beings—ones distinguished by excellence, virtue, righteousness, and justice. Integrous in who we are and what we do. Wisdom, in other words, is God's character in the affairs of life and the iridescent mark of a life well-lived.

Other Hebrew words for wisdom include *śēkel*: "to understand, have insight, behave wisely." It refers to prudent, thoughtful, and insightful action. It is a term that transcends mere knowledge, ascending into the realm of understanding and insight. To "*śēkel*" is to grasp the essence of things, to have the keenness of perception that distinguishes the wise from the thoughtless. The word occurs most frequently in the book of Proverbs, urging the reader to seek prudence, thoughtfulness, and insightful action. The one who wields this virtue is often described as "prudent" (Prov 10:5) or as one who "acts wisely" (Prov 14:35), walking the path of discernment with every step. The noun derived from *śēkel* breathes life into the concept of "insight, prudence, understanding" and generally refers to those possessing good sense and discretion.

First Samuel 25 offers a poignant illustration of this idea when we see the foolishness of Nabal (1 Sam 25:25) in stark contrast to the "good sense" (*ṭôbat-śekel*) of his wife Abigail. Their story is one of folly and wisdom, pride and humility. Nabal, a man of wealth, surly and mean, is a striking figure of self-indulgence. His name aptly describes his character, for Nabal means fool. It is a name he lives up to. His heart is stubborn, impervious to reason or wisdom, and his actions are marked by arrogance and disdain. As David's emissaries approach seeking hospitality and kindness, Nabal's response exemplifies his folly, offering derision instead of graciousness. His unyielding pride and selfishness set him on a path to destruction, for he fails to recognize the significance of the moment and the implications of his actions. In contrast to Nabal's imprudence, Abigail stands as a figure of understanding and discernment. Her heart is not encumbered by the weight of wealth and power. Beautiful and clever, she embodies the goodness of understanding and the brilliance of discernment (1 Sam 25:3). When she hears of Nabal's folly, she does not falter or cower but takes it upon herself to intervene. With insight and understanding, she discerns the gravity of the situation and acts with wisdom. With gifts and words, she pleads with David to withhold his wrath and desist from avenging the offense. The ancient wisdom of Proverbs holds true, "Wise warriors are mightier than strong ones and those who have knowledge than those who have strength" (Prov 24:5, NRSVue).

We have yet to exhaust the treasury of words for wisdom. *Bîn* (Prov 7:7) is to perceive with clarity by unraveling the intricacies of life through keen observation. *Bînâ*, another word in this treasury, refers to "the applied use of understanding." It asks us to wield our understanding with artistic skill, for it is through the application of knowledge that its true value emerges. As a skilled artisan molds clay into art, so *bînâ* molds understanding into practical use (Prov 2:1–5; 4:5; 7:4). *Tĕbûnâ*, understanding with competence, is the ability to navigate life's intricacies and challenges, applying understanding with grace and efficacy (Prov 2:1–2; 3:19; 5:1). *Tûšiyyâ* is the light of wisdom that comes from clear thinking that results in effective action. It is like a master architect whose blueprints materialize into awe-inspiring buildings (Prov 2:6–7; 3:21; 8:14). Finally, *da'at*, the very essence of knowledge, understanding, skill, and discernment, encompasses the wisdom seeker's journey. It is the capacity to grasp the deeper truths of existence, the skill to wield knowledge with finesse, and the discernment to choose wisely in the myriad paths life unfolds (Prov 1:22, 29).[2]

Considering both the splendor of the Hebrew Bible's teaching and the richness of its vocabulary with respect to wisdom, we begin to see why Proverbs vividly portrays wisdom as a *woman*, a *feast*, and a *path*.

---

2. Nettelhorst, "Wisdom," 2014.

Those who listen to her find life (Prov 1:20–33; 8:1–36); those who feast at its table gain understanding (Prov 9:1–6); and those who walk on its path are safe (Prov 2:9; 4:18; 12:28; 15:19, 24; 23:19). It is no wonder then that the highest priority of those entrusted with leadership is to gain a heart of wisdom.

Wisdom resides as an attribute intrinsic to God, eternal and uncreated. Yet, there is a paradox, for wisdom is also created (Prov 8:22–36). Before the creation of the heavens and the earth, God brought forth Wisdom into being. "The LORD created me at the beginning of his work, the first of his acts of long ago" (Prov 8:22, NRSVue). The opening verse of the Bible declares, "In the beginning, God created the heavens and the earth" (Gen 1:1), yet here in Proverbs it proclaims wisdom as the beginning of God's creation. This has led some interpreters to wonder since wisdom is called the beginning of God's work, might the word "beginning" itself be used elsewhere in the Bible as a shorthand reference to the very first thing God created.[3] Thus, Genesis 1:1 may not solely indicate the outset of creation but rather the context and framework of creation itself, for "In wisdom God created the heavens and the earth." Wisdom, then, is the grand design underlying all creation. It unveils the profound plan woven into the fabric of existence, revealing the divine purpose that permeates every element of the cosmos.

Wisdom as the beginning of creation, consequently, includes the natural, biological, and social sciences, as well as mathematics, logic, history, and literature. These are not to be thought of as "secular" categories. They are domains of knowledge and understanding of creation, and here too, Wisdom frolics around, rejoicing in the handiwork of God. Wisdom invites us to understand God through his creation, just as she invites us to understand God through scripture as his revelation. Understanding Wisdom in this way guards against the dangers of both a world-denying Manicheism that asserts the material world is an evil from which we must flee and the rampant secularism that seeks a world disenchanted and deprived of God.

When God reveals his presence, we know this as the glory of God. When God reveals his way, we know this as the wisdom of God. When God reveals his ability, we know this as the power of God. This glory-wisdom-power of God is revealed when Creator and creation are in joyous harmony and perfect union. It is the divine presence we sense but cannot

---

3. Philo, *Works*, 29.

see. It is that sense of awe you experience when enraptured by beauty. It is the radiant splendor of wonder experienced in the meeting of divine love and humanity, of communion with the One who is wholly Other, unveiling a vision of God worthy of prayer. It is this Wisdom and Glory and Power of God that was revealed when the Word became flesh and dwelt among us, and we beheld his glory, full of grace and truth. This same trifecta is at work within us, repristinating the tarnished image-bearers of God, and there is Wisdom, the joyful one, frolicking in the works of God and delighting in the human race (Prov 8:30–31).

In the embrace of God's wisdom, we find our calling, beckoned by the Spirit to partake in the divine nature as the people of God. We seek the guiding light of God's wisdom each time we pray, "Your kingdom come. Your will be done." It is this wisdom to which you are summoned. Let it infuse your soul with its essence. And when you rise to lead others, lead with the gentleness born of that very wisdom. For in this wisdom lies the heart of genuine leadership—leadership that is simple yet profound, guiding with the quiet force of a seasoned humility. "Oh, the depth of the riches and wisdom and knowledge of God! How unsearchable are his judgments and how inscrutable his ways!" (Rom 11:33).

## Wisdom will Protect, Direct, and Perfect Your Path

Wisdom will *protect* your path (Prov 2:1–22). Wisdom's protection hinges upon a fundamental condition: You must be desperate for wisdom and unsatisfied with anything else. Notice the key actions mentioned in vv. 1–8, in the form of a conditional (if/then) construction: *If you will* accept my words, store up my commands within you, turn your ear to wisdom, apply your heart to understanding, call out for insight, cry aloud for understanding, look for it as for silver, and search for it as for hidden treasure—*then you will* understand righteousness, justice, equity, and every good path, for wisdom will come into your heart and knowledge will be pleasant to your soul. Discretion will watch over you, and understanding will guard you against a twofold danger: 1) the evil man, who with perverse words promises that you will *gain something* if you join him, and 2) the strange woman, whose flattering words promise that you will *be something* if you follow her (vv. 9–19). Protected by wisdom, you shall find yourself walking in the way of the good, treading the path of the righteous, and standing firm when the wicked reap the harvest of their folly (vv. 20–22).

Wisdom will also *direct* your path (Prov 3). Listen well to Wisdom's voice, for she will direct you to a contented life, graced by favor with God and others, with the hand of God guiding you along the way. Soak up this wisdom; let it seep into your very bones, instilling in you the virtue of humility, the fear of the LORD, and an instinct to flee evil. As you walk this path, a transformation takes place: Strength and vitality grow within you, creating character that is both robust and sturdy.

Not only does wisdom *protect* and *direct* your path, but wisdom will *perfect* your path (Prov 4). The Hebrew words for "perfect" (*kālâ* and *tāmam*) express the idea of bringing a process to completion and wholeness.[4] Following wisdom will bring to completion the good work God has started in you. The process unfolds like this: As you *learn* God's word (Prov 4:1–9), *trust* God's providence (Prov 4:10–19), and *obey* God's will (Prov 4:20–27), a transformation happens within you, leading to the fulness of the ever-renewing promise of wisdom: "The path of the righteous is like the light of dawn, which shines brighter and brighter until full day" (Prov 4:18).

## Folly in Proverbs

Folly, like wisdom, is portrayed in Proverbs as a *woman*, a *feast*, and a *path*. Those who listen to Woman Folly are destroyed (Prov 9:13–18; 7:11); those who feast at folly's table are doomed (Prov 9:17; 20:17); and those who walk upon folly's path are lost (Prov 4:14; 16:29; 28:10).

Folly, this brazen disregard of holy things,[5] is raucously loud, devoid of discipline, bereft of knowledge, and impervious to correction (Prov 9:13). Destructive and unyielding, it cannot be bargained with; it knowns no middle ground (Prov 16:22). It only grows in its intensity, unable to conceal its true nature (Prov 14:24). Endlessly chattering, ignorant of truth and devoid of knowledge, folly cannot be quiet (Prov 18:13). Unruly and uncontrollable, it defies attempts to tame its chaotic ways (Prov 9:13). Deceptive to its core, it cannot be trusted (Prov 14:8; cf. Jer 17:9). A blamer at heart, folly refuses to take responsibility for its own actions

---

4. Mounce, *Expository Dictionary*, 129.

5. Pss 38:6; 69:6; Prov 5:23; 12:23; 13:16; 14:1, 8, 17, 18, 24,29; 15:2, 14, 21; 16:22; 17:12; 18:13; 19:3; 22:15; 24:9; 26:4, 5, 11; 27:22

(Prov 19:3). These verses warn against the perils of folly. Proverbs teaches the discerning heart to listen closely, for by heeding Wisdom's voice, we avoid the traps of Folly's siren call.

Folly will beckon with enticing allure, leading you down paths of destruction paved with foolish decisions, squandered resources, and wasted fortunes (Prov 6:1–35; 13:11). Using her deceitful charm, she coaxes her followers into moral compromise, unethical shortcuts, and the perilous indulgence of idleness, leading to the very ruin of their labor and toil (Prov 6:6–11). The one descending into folly is branded *belial*, "a worthless person" (Prov 6:12–15). The Hebrew word *belial* is used to indicate worthlessness, baseness, and vulnerability to destruction—it is a state of being devoid of value and good for nothing. It is used in the scriptures to signify the domain of chaos, a spiritual power system of dominion and oppression set on destruction, wickedness, and evil (Deut 13:14; Nah 1:11; 2:1; Pss 18:5; 41:9; 101:3; Prov 6:12; 2 Cor 6:15).[6] In Proverbs, we see it personified in the foolish leader.

The worthless person—the foolish leader—ensnared in their own folly, resorts to crooked speech (Prov 6:12) and deceitful body language (Prov 6:13), while their wayward heart is constantly devising evil schemes (Prov 6:14). The consequences of discord and calamity are all too predictable (Prov 6:14–15). When these fools ascend to places of power, the very air thickens with arrogant pride, lies are so common that they become the norm, the innocent suffer, sinister plans are hatched to maintain and increase power, and society descends into chaos. Such is the fruit of the fool who becomes a leader (Prov 6:16–19). Brash, ignorant, and self-deceived, ensnared within the mirage of their own illusions, these leaders turn a deaf ear to discipline, stubbornly refusing to change their ways (Prov 9:13; 14:8; 16:22). Their rule bears nothing but folly's fruit (Prov 14:24). Because of their inflated self-importance, reason falls on deaf ears, for truth is a stranger to their hearts (Prov 18:13). In their imprudence, they sow the seeds of their own undoing, audaciously blaming God and others for the chaos they themselves have sown (Prov 19:3). No wonder Proverbs booms with resounding warnings against such treacherous leaders. We will explore this more in the next chapter.

If folly is so repugnant and destructive, why do people yield to its allure? Well, the answer is simple. Folly is a masterful seductress, ensnaring souls in her poisonous embrace. Proverbs overflows with warnings

---

6. Balz and Schneider, *Exegetical Dictionary*, 212.

against the dangers of sexual enticements, with Proverbs 7:1–27 standing as the most extensive among them. Though these warnings are to be heeded in their literal sense (as we shall explore in chapter four), they reach beyond mere cautionary tales of infidelity. These warnings are also to be understood as metaphors warning against the enticement to forsake wisdom and embrace folly.[7]

In Proverbs, both folly and wisdom assume the form of women engaged in a contest for the hearts of Solomon's sons. Lady Wisdom is beautiful, virtuous, and true. She stands as the cherished wife of one's youth. Woman Folly, presented in stark contrast, is loud, seductive, and flirtatious. She, like Lady Wisdom, cries out in the streets and squares (Prov 7:1–27), yet she is a monstrous predator who has slain multitudes in her wake. She entices the foolish young man with alluring promises of unrestrained pleasures, and he follows her like an ox to the slaughter (Prov 7:22). She offers pleasure without consequences, yet she delivers death and destruction (Prov 7:24–27). Proverbs 7 depicts not only the seduction of the body but also the seduction of the soul.

Countless is the number of leaders seduced by folly, who followed her to their own destruction. I saw this happen to Matthew, a gifted young man I once knew—a fervent church planter whose ministry touched countless lives. He held the power to shape a movement that could reshape his nation. But sadly, he walked down the treacherous path, succumbing to the charms of Woman Folly. Deluded, he convinced himself that his exceptional talent and divine calling exempted him from the moral character required of leaders. His response to questioning was anger, defensiveness, and abuse. Deaf to the counsel of others, no one could speak into his life. Jealousy and selfish ambition blinded his eyes and hardened his heart. Such selfish ambition is earthly, unspiritual, and demonic, inevitably breeding disorder and every kind of evil (see Jas 3:13–18). His ministry and legacy, once promising and inspiring, now lay victim. Such is the fate of leaders who follow folly.

## Wisdom and Folly Are Always Calling You

No one is born wise. Nope. Not one of us. We all commence life with folly fully entrenched, locked in our hearts. Thankfully, the path to wisdom lies open to all. She invites us all to pursue her through a life of disciplined

7. Waltke, *Proverbs, 1–15*, 38–50.

obedience to God and his ways. In this pursuit of wisdom, we are called to be vigilant custodians of our hearts (Prov 4:20–27), clinging to instruction and discipline with unyielding determination, for to loosen our grip is to wander from the words of knowledge (Prov 19:27). Wisdom, though freely given, does not come free. It demands an unwavering dedication, a disciplined spirit, and a commitment to listen, to learn, to grow—these are the dues to be settled on the path to wisdom.

Wisdom invites the simple, the fool, and the mocker to listen to her voice, feast at her table, and walk in her ways to become wise (Prov 1:22; 8:5; 9:4). She is persistent in her call to all to enjoy a secure salvation (Prov 1:8–33), true wealth (Prov 8:1–36), and real life (Prov 9:1–18). While generous and resilient in her invitation, Wisdom is also insistent and firm in her warnings of the consequences of not listening to her (Prov 1:20–33).

Folly also calls out to any who will listen. She calls for all to enjoy immediate satisfaction. She promises delights and pleasure. However, she promises more than she can deliver, and she deceptively fails to warn of the tragic consequences of listening to her voice, feasting from her table, and walking on her path. Those who choose folly will eat the fruit of their own way. In the end, they find only condemnation, bankruptcy, shame, destruction, and death (Prov 1:29–33).

## Folly is Attracted to Hubris and Repulsed by Humility

> Pride goes before destruction, and a haughty spirit before a fall.
>
> —PROVERBS 16:18

We can learn a lot about the theological nuances of the Bible by the choices of its early translators. Though Proverbs was originally composed in Hebrew, during the Hellenistic period, many Jews spoke Greek. According to tradition, seventy Jewish scholars were asked by Ptolemy the Great (285–46 BCE), the Greek Pharaoh of Egypt, to translate the Torah from Hebrew to Greek for inclusion in the Library of Alexandria. The remaining books of the Hebrew Bible were translated sometime in the second century BCE. This Greek translation of the Hebrew Bible is known as the Septuagint (from the Latin *septuaginta*, meaning "the seventy," and is often abbreviated in Roman numerals LXX). Most Old Testament quotations in the New Testament are from the Septuagint.[8]

The ancient Greek translation of the Hebrew Bible can reveal nuances of meanings in the biblical texts, otherwise hidden to us, given our historical, linguistical, and cultural distance. So, let's look at the Greek translations for the Hebrew vocabulary about "pride" in Proverbs. For instance, in Proverbs 16:18, the Septuagint translates "pride" as *hubris*. Hubris is a toxic combination of ambition, overconfidence, and arrogance; it's a kind of overweening pride that causes one to overstep one's rightful boundaries and invade the sphere of another with insolent force and the infliction of insult and injury.[9]

The Hebrew Scriptures have two major word groups for hubris *gā 'â* and *zîd*, which are often translated as "pride" (noun) or "proud" (adjective). The primary meaning of *gā 'â* is "to rise" (e.g., Job 22:29), and it denotes loftiness, arrogance, and pride.[10] This word is used in Ezek 16:49–50 to summarize the guilt of Sodom for its pride (*gā 'â*), excess of food, prosperous ease, and neglect of the poor and needy. Ezekiel's rebuke culminates in this stern declaration, "They were haughty and did an abomination before me. So I removed them, when I saw it" (Ezek 16:50). According to Ezekiel, Samaria and Jerusalem were equally guilty of the same behavior and now liable to the same judgement. Pride led Sodom, Samaria, and Jerusalem to their destruction.

The second Hebrew word for pride (*zîd*) is frequently used to refer to three specific aspects of pride.[11] The first characteristic is presumption. A person inflated with pride presumes too much in his or her favor, especially the perceived sense of authority. For example, a false prophet presumed to speak in the name of God and assumed the authority to do so without actually having been designated and called by God (Deut 18:20). The second characteristic of pride is rebellion or disobedience. The proud person asserts his or her own will to the point of rebelling against authority (Deut 1:43; Neh 9:16, 29). The third attribute of pride is self-will. Self-will is when you obstinately do what you want in spite of the wishes or instructions of others. When the Bible warns about being stiff-necked,[12] it is talking about self-will. Self-will is vividly portrayed

---

8. Law, *When God Spoke Greek*, 2013.

9. Bertram, "Ὕβρις, Ὑβρίζω, Ἐνυβρίζω, Ὑβριστής," 8:294–307.

10. Hamilton, "299 גָּאָה (gā 'â)." 143–44.

11. Wood, "547 זִיד (zîd), זוּד (zûd)," 239–40.

12. For example, Exo 33:3; Deut 9:13; Neh 9:16; Acts 7:51

in Isaiah's taunt against the king of Babylon (Isa 14:3–27). Five times the king boasted, "I will." He said, "I will ascend to heaven," "I will set my throne on high," "I will sit on the mount of the assembly," "I will ascend above the heights of the clouds," and "I will make myself like the Most High" (Isa 14:13–14). God's judgment fell on the king's self-will:

> "I will rise up against them," declares the Lord of hosts, "and will cut off from Babylon name and remnant, descendants and posterity," declares the Lord. "And I will make it a possession of the hedgehog, and pools of water, and I will sweep it with the broom of destruction," declares the Lord of hosts." (Isa 14:22–23)

Pride led the king of Babylon to his destruction.

King Uzziah displays another example of hubris (2 Chr 26:1–23). A dynamic and capable leader, King Uzziah conquered the Philistines and Arabians, subjugated the Ammonites, built great public works, organized and equipped the army, fortified Jerusalem, and was personally very successful. "His fame spread far, for he was marvelously helped, till he was strong" (2 Chr 26:15). Then his pride led to his downfall. Second Chronicles 26:16 tells us, "But when he was strong, he grew proud, to his destruction. For he was unfaithful to the LORD his God and entered the temple of the LORD to burn incense on the altar of incense." Entering the temple to burn incense was the job of the priests, not the king. The strength and greatness of Uzziah as king did not give him the right to overstep his boundaries as king and insolently invade the sphere of the priests (2 Chr 26:17–18). Uzziah's hubris in this act of worship was counted as unfaithfulness to the Lord. He was struck with leprosy and remained leprous until the day he died (2 Chr 26:19–21). Pride led Uzziah to his destruction.

Proverbs speaks extensively about the dangers of hubris in leadership because prideful arrogance and overstepping the boundaries of one's authority are easily justified with appeals to fruitfulness, calling, or leadership style. Fruitfulness does not give you permission to be abusive or unethical. Your calling does not authorize you to be arrogant or to make pronouncements on issues you are not qualified to speak on. Hubris is not a leadership style: It is a sin. It is to be rejected and renounced at every turn.

## Wisdom is Attracted to Humility and Repulsed by Hubris

> The effect of humility is fear of the Lord.
>
> —PROVERBS 22:4 NJPS

The apostle Peter tells us to "clothe ourselves with humility towards one another" (1 Pet 5:5). The phrase "be clothed with" is the translation of a word (*enkomboomai*) that speaks of tying or tucking in the long outer garments around the waist. The appeal is to put on humility as a working virtue that binds together all other Christian virtues. The other virtues, such as generosity, kindness, justice, and longsuffering, are acceptable and praiseworthy when saturated in humility; but they are almost intolerable when seen in a prideful person.

The word "humility" is a translation of a Greek word (*tapeinophrosynē*) that means "lowly." For example, it is used in one ancient document to speak of the Nile River in its low stage: "it runs low." The word means "not rising far from the ground."[13]

The English word "humility" comes to us through the Latin word *humilitas,* a noun related to the adjective *humilis,* which means "humble," but also "grounded," "from the earth," and "low." They have their root in the Latin word *humus,* meaning earth.

This is fascinating because the word *humus* refers to the naturally occurring layer of compost or mulch found on the soil's surface. This humus maintains healthy levels of soil life. It increases fertility by increasing the soil's ability to store nutrients and moisture. This increases the soil's capacity to withstand drought conditions. Humus also buffers excessive acid or alkaline. Thus, it helps prevent toxic substances from entering the broader ecosystem. Even the dark color of humus (usually black or dark brown) helps warm up the cold soils in springtime.

The soil is clothed with humus. In the same way, you are to clothe yourself with humility. Otherwise, your soul will become unhealthy, acidic, and unfruitful. While the world system teaches you to clamor for the top, the kingdom system teaches you to clamor for the bottom. While there may be little room at the top, there is plenty of room in the servant's quarters. The greatest among you shall be the servant of all.

---

13. Wuest, *Word Studies,* vol. 11, 128.

The way up is down in this upside-down kingdom. When you are slighted, neglected, rejected, or ignored, "put on humility as a garment" to protect the soil of your soul from bitterness, anger, self-righteousness, and self-pity. When you are not given the credit you may deserve, and thanks and appreciation are not expressed, "put on humility as a garment." When you are not treated with the respect you have earned, "put on humility as a garment." When you are tempted to speak beyond the measure of your authority or knowledge, "put on humility as a garment." The garment of humility will keep the soil of your soul from becoming acidic. It will help you retain moisture and nutrients in times of drought. Humility keeps you healthy. Humility is the Bible's secret to outrageous success.

You can finish well, or you can crash and burn. You can end your days like the apostle Paul, saying, "I have fought the good fight, I have finished the race, I have kept the faith." Or you can end your days, lamenting like King Saul, "I have sinned. I have played the fool and have erred exceedingly." You can choose humility and the way of wisdom, or you can choose hubris and the way of folly. Your destiny depends on which voice you listen to, which banquet you feast upon, and which path you walk upon.

# 3

# Wise and Foolish Leaders

Sensible people keep their eyes glued on wisdom, but
a fool's eyes wander to the ends of the earth.

—Proverbs 17:24 NLT

Where you start is not as important as where you finish. The Bible tells stories of people who began poorly yet ended well, like Saul of Tarsus, the persecutor of Christians who became Paul the apostle of Jesus Christ.[1] The Bible is also filled with people who started well and ended poorly. King Saul, Asa, and Hezekiah all started well, yet their ends were tragic.[2] The main difference between the two groups consists in the decisions they made along the way. It is the culmination of your choices, not fate, that determines if you finish well or not. We can move from folly to wisdom or from wisdom to folly. It's all in what we choose. When we choose wisdom with our heart, mind, and actions, these "wise choices will watch over you" (Prov 2:11 NLT).

Growing in wisdom requires the persistent choice of our minds. To become wise is not a matter of education or IQ; it is a matter of mental

1. Manasseh, 2 Chr 33; Saul the persecutor who Paul the apostle, Acts 9, cf. 2 Tim 4:7

2. 1 Sam 9–31; 2 Chr 14–16; 2 Chr 29–32

26

attitude and disposition. It is your chosen mental outlook not your mental capacity, that sets you on the path to wisdom. Plenty of geniuses have proven to be utter fools, while even the simplest among us have borne the grace of wisdom that enlightens all around them.

The path toward wisdom calls us to choose our actions as well as our attitudes. Wisdom is rooted in morality, not mentality. When we do the truth, we come to understand the truth. God promised through Isaiah, "If you are willing and obedient, you shall eat the good of the land" (Isa 1:19, NRSV). In other words, obedience is the organ of spiritual knowledge.

Jesus told us how to build a solid life:

> Everyone then who hears these words of mine and acts on them will be like a wise man who built his house on rock. The rain fell, the floods came, and the winds blew and beat on that house, but it did not fall, because it had been founded on rock. And everyone who hears these words of mine and does not act on them will be like a foolish man who built his house on sand. The rain fell, and the floods came, and the winds blew and beat against that house, and it fell—and great was its fall! (Matt 7:24–27 NRSV).

The wise and the foolish builder both heard the same message. They both built houses. Both experienced floods and winds that beat their homes. The difference between them is that the wise builder listened and acted on what Jesus said, while the foolish builder listened but did not act. In other words, "Be doers of the word, and not hearers only" (Jas 1:22).

Wisdom is for *anyone* who wants it. Wisdom calls out by name to the simple, the fools, and the mockers (Prov 1:22; 8:5; 9:4). Wisdom invites them by name to her feast, which is as free as the feast of folly. However, developing wisdom is costly. Its largesse is not scattered around but rather stored up for "the upright," for people of integrity (Prov 2:7–9). It comes by revelation and discipline and requires a daily and life-long pursuit. Those who refuse her call and choose instead to listen to folly become fools (Prov 1:20–33).

## The Foolish Leader

A fool in leadership destroys truth and trust, which unleashes chaos, discord, animosity, division, insurrection, tumult, and destruction. Therefore, avoid foolish leaders at all costs. Thankfully, Proverbs provides a detailed description so that you can spot foolish leaders and avoid them and the destruction they cause.

You will find three degrees of foolish leaders in Proverbs. Foolishness begins with "the simple," who become "fools" and eventually become "mockers." The simple are unfamiliar with or uncommitted to the truth. The simple in Proverbs are not necessarily immoral or anti-religious. Rather, they remain childish well beyond childhood. Their speaking, thinking, values, and behaviors stay in perpetual immaturity. They refuse to grow into adulthood in their reasoning or to put away childish ways.[3] The simple begin as gullible and naïve, yet if they do not commit to the truth, they end up feeding on folly and become fools (Prov 15:14). It is normal for children to think, speak, and behave like children. It is not normal for adults to do so. When one chooses to persist in childish ways, Proverbs calls this person "simple" (ESV). The Hebrew word (*pthiy*) refers to those who are easily deceived or persuaded, who show a lack of wisdom and understanding, and yet they have some capacity to change their condition (Prov 1:4, 22, 32; 7:7; 8:5; 9:4, 16; 14:15, 18; 19:25; 21:11; 22:3; 27:12). The Common English Bible translates this word at least six different ways: naïve (Prov 1:4; 7:7; 8:5; 9:4, 16; 14:15, 18; 19:25; 21:11); clueless (Prov 1:22), immature (Prov 1:32), simplistic (Prov 9:6), overly talkative (Prov 20:19), and simpleminded (Prov 22:3; 27:12).

When I first met Lawrence,[4] I thought he had real potential. People spoke well of him. He had a friendly disposition, a willingness to serve, and what seemed to be a child-like faith. Well, it ended up that what I thought to be child-like faith was a childish mind, locked in perpetual immaturity in its reasoning. Lawrence was not mentally deficient. His brain worked fine, but his mind was a mess. Lawrence, you see, went down the internet rabbit hole and came out believing a whole host of crazy ideas and conspiracy theories. To make matters worse, those beliefs were now guarded by an arsenal of pride. He heeded folly by his refusal to listen to anyone other than those who agree with him. He followed the path of folly. He learned her ways. What began as gullible and naïve thinking ended with Lawrence abandoning reason and reality for lies and conspiracies. Wisdom still calls out to Lawrence; I pray he answers her. Until then, he is one more gifted leader who is waylaid by folly.

---

3. 1 Cor 13:11

4. Some of the names and details have been altered to protect privacy.

The simple one has moved from being empty-headed to being wrongheaded, taking delight in things unproven and untrue. This spares him the ordeal of thinking for himself. It allows him to justify himself for not taking responsibility for his thoughts and actions (Prov 1:4, 22, 32; 7:7; 8:5; 9:4, 6, 16; 14:15, 18; 19:25; 20:19; 21:22; 22:3; 27:12). When the simple persists in his simple ways, he eventually becomes a fool.

The fool cannot be corrected because he is committed to his own truth, rendering him unteachable and unreceptive to any voice but his own (Prov 12:15). This foolish leader staunchly refuses to heed the counsel of others, be it parents, wise advisers, the educated and informed, or even God himself (Prov 13:1; 15:12; 1:7). He has no pleasure in understanding and no appetite for learning. He loves to feed on folly and hear himself speak (Prov 15:14; 18:2).

Despising discipline, his emotions are volatile, his impulses unrestrained, and his appetite unbridled (Prov 1:7; 12:16; 14:16,29; 29:11). He is big on words but small on deeds (Prov 10:8,10). He cannot, or will not, control his mouth (Prov 10:8, 10, 14). It will be his downfall, for his lips walk into a fight, and his mouth invites a beating. His mouth is his ruin, and his lips are a snare to his soul (Prov 10:14; 18:6–7). His words are foolish, rash, hasty, and full of lies and slander (Prov 10:8; 13:16; 15:2; 29:20). He carelessly blabs away, flaunting his folly (Prov 13:16; 29:11). He can't even walk down the road without revealing he is a fool (Eccl 10:3). His motto seems to be, "What is the point of being a fool if you cannot show it off?"

Filled with boundless arrogance, he is driven to meddle and stir up controversy (Prov 21:24; 28:26; 26:12). He is argumentative and combative. He creates problems and inflicts sorrow (Prov 10:1; 11:29; 15:20; 17:21; 27:3). He finds enjoyment in his folly; it is like a joke to him (Prov 10:23). He remains obstinate in his destructive behavior, despite the consequences (Prov 26:11; 27:22). Strife, quarrels, and insults are his stock in trade (Prov 22:10). It is better to meet a bear robbed of her cubs than this fool in his folly (Prov 17:12).

This foolish leader holds no regard for wisdom, discipline, or the moral life. He exalts himself as his own authority. Refusing to learn from his mistakes (Prov 26:11), he vehemently attacks any attempts at correction (Prov 9:7–8). When his plans fail, it is someone else's fault. When something goes wrong, it is because someone else "blew it." He is the victim of someone else's corruption or incompetence. He is a chronic blamer, consistently avoiding accountability for his actions and perpetually repeating the same mistakes and failures. He ruins his life through his own folly, yet he blames God and others for it (Prov 19:3). The reality is that the fool suffers because of his own choices (Prov 9:12; 14:3; 15:21; 26:3).

This foolish leader has wrapped himself so tightly in the cloak of arrogance and folly that even in his search for wisdom, he remains blind to its presence (Prov 14:6; 24:7). His mind lacks the focus needed to truly grasp the essence of wisdom (Prov 17:24). "It is senseless to pay to educate a fool since he has no heart for learning" (Prov 17:16, NLT). No matter the effort made, separating a fool from his folly is an impossible task. Even if one were to crush him in a mortar with a pestle, his foolishness would persist undeterred (Prov 27:22). Such is the pitiable state of the one entrenched in foolishness, unable to break free from its grip.

This leader recklessly wastes his resources and squanders precious opportunities (Prov 21:20; 29:3; 14:24; 19:10), making him unfit and unreliable for any responsibility (Prov 26:1,6,7,8,10). Despite putting on a facade of competence, in time, his folly will be exposed, laid bare for all to see the detestable nature of his actions (Prov 10:7; 24:9). He rebels against authority while relentlessly seeking power.[5] He rejects any form of restraint. Truth holds no value for him as he clings stubbornly to his own opinions. The folly of this leader's ways leaves a trail of chaos and disappointment in its wake.

If a fool persists in his foolishness, he eventually becomes a "mocker," sometimes translated as "scoffer." It is a term designating the most hardened apostates of wisdom, a more aggressive and hostile type of fool.[6] While both the fool and the mocker share the tragic quality of lacking wisdom and understanding, they differ by the degree to which folly has transformed them. "Fool" generally refers to those who, through their own choices and stubbornness, forsake wisdom and ignore counsel (Prov 1:7; 10:8). Nevertheless, there is still a glimmer of hope that they may yet change and seek wisdom if they open their hearts to listen and understand. However, the mocker, hardened and obstinate, shows no willingness to change or listen to reason and is given no such glimmer of hope (Prov 9:7–8).

If the simple are uncommitted to the truth and the fool is committed to his own truth, the mocker is committed against the truth. He stands in stark contrast to the wise (Prov 9:12; 13:1; 20:1; 21:4), for whom

---

5. See Ps 14:1

6. Hebrew (*lēṣ*) Prov 1:22; 3:34; 9:7–8; 13:1; 14:6; 15:12; 19:25, 29; 21:11, 24; 22:10; 24:9; 29:8

he harbors a deep hatred (Prov 9:7–8; 15:12). Because the mocker is committed against the truth, he refuses to listen to others (Prov 13:1), attacking and insulting any who try to correct him (Prov 3:34; 9:7–8). Since he will not listen to others or learn from his mistakes, he will suffer the consequences of his folly (Prov 9:12; 19:29).

Alongside fools (Prov 1:22; 3:34–35; 14:7–8; 19:29), the gullible (Prov 1:22), and the proud and haughty (Prov 21:24), the mocker embodies a spiritual problem deeply rooted in his excessive pride (Prov 21:24). His contemptuous arrogance blocks him from wisdom (Prov 14:6; 21:24).

Perhaps no person earns more universal contempt than the mocker. Bereft of the capacity for genuine loyalty and reverence, he harbors within himself a mission to erode the very values that form the bedrock of society (Prov 21:24; 22:10; 29:8). A loathsome figure, for sure.

When he opens his mouth, he seeks to inflame entire populations; it is what he lives for. He thrives on dividing people against one another (Prov 22:20; 29:8). While most can plainly see the harm he inflicts (Prov 24:9), his mastery of scornful and belittling language impresses those who are easily swayed. He is a master of exploiting anger to increase his power (Prov 19:25; 21:11). The fruit of his leadership is strife, quarrels, and insults (Prov 22:10;). To restore order, he must be driven out, and with him goes the strife, quarreling, and abuse he has unleashed (Prov 22:10; 24:9; 29:8). In any case, God himself ultimately scoffs at the scoffer, and so he, too, will disappear (Isa 29:20).[7]

Do yourself a favor. If you see a foolish leader, avoid him at all costs. "Leave the presence of a fool, for there you do not meet words of knowledge" (Prov 14:7). Do not hire him to do a job or entrust him with any responsibility because he will defile everyone (Prov 26:8, 10). If you have made the mistake of hiring or befriending a foolish leader, cut your losses and move on. Now that we are clear on what kind of leader we do not want to be let's turn our attention to how to become a wise leader.

## Becoming a Wise Leader

Every generation cries out for wise leaders.[8] The challenge in answering this cry is that no one is born wise. However, you can choose to become

---

7. Waltke, *Proverbs, 1–15*, 114.

8. Prov 1.5; Job 15:2; Ps 49:10

wise. If you choose to listen to wisdom and heed her voice by aligning your choices, thinking, and behavior, you will grow wise over time (Prov 9:1–12). Even the simple and foolish can become wise if they only choose the wisdom path (Prov 8:1–36). The key is to make an active decision to conform your life to the ways of wisdom. I have identified at least five choices in Proverbs that will transform your life, relationships, and leadership because they set you on the path toward wisdom. Let's explore them.

## Wise Leaders Choose the Fear of the Lord

The Hebrew word for fear, typically used in the expression "fear of the Lord" (*yir'at*, from the verb *yr'*), has a range of meanings, running from respect to horror. It is difficult to determine the exact English equivalent in each instance. In most occurrences, the "fear of God" is a virtue that is encouraged and leads to right behavior and good results. In some, the "fear of God" is negative (Gen 3:8–10; Amos 3:7). Consequently, it can be misleading to say that *yir'at* always means "fear" or "respect." It may be that the meaning falls somewhere in between. The meaning "respect" may not do justice to the gravity intended, though "fear" may suggest an unhealthy dread. The word "awe" is a good candidate for translation; for it encapsulates reverence, veneration, wonder, submission, and honor, all of which are owed to God as God. With this definition, we come close to understanding worship. The object of fear is the Creator of all, the one who is sovereign over creation. Isaiah's vision of the Lord (Isa 6:1–13) and the worship revealed in the book of Revelation (Rev 4–5; 15:2–8; 16:1–7; 19:1–10) are vivid examples of this overwhelming awe of the Lord.[9]

The fear of the Lord is mentioned at least seventeen times in Proverbs (Prov 1:7, 29; 2:5; 8:13; 9:10; 10:27; 14:2, 26, 27; 15:16, 33; 16:6; 19:23; 22:4; 23:17; 28:14; 31:30). It is the "beginning" of wisdom in that it is both the starting point and the controlling principle governing wisdom's pursuit. It means, first and foremost, that the wise leader has a strong, healthy relationship with the Creator of the Universe. This relationship with the Lord spans the beginning, middle, and end of the journey and involves this basic commitment: To love the Lord your God with all your heart, soul, mind, and strength (Deut 6:4; Matt 22:37; Mark 12:29; Luke 10:27). The fear of the Lord results in good judgment, wisdom, and humility and it is the pathway to true honor (Prov 9:10; 15:33). The God-fearing

9. Longman III, "Fear of the Lord," 201–3.

leader avoids self-promotion (Prov 25:6–7, 27), knowing that excellent character and superior skill are the best ways to gain promotion (Prov 22:29; 27:2). The fear of the Lord keeps you from being impressed by your own wisdom, and it teaches you to turn away from evil (Prov 3:7).

The wisdom of God is not a static and impersonal force of abstract ideas, nor is it a collection of theoretical principles. While the ancient Greek philosophers tended to reduce the gods and wisdom to principles derived from abstract ideas, the God of the Bible is far from abstract. He is the God who comes near, who acts, who speaks, and who calls us to draw near in awe. This is a fundamental distinction between the Hebrew and Greek worldviews. The Greeks learned in order to comprehend knowledge, and the Hebrews learned in order to revere God.[10] It is this deeply personal drawing near to God in reverence that nurtures wisdom in the heart. The prophet Jeremiah tells us,

> Let not the wise man boast in his wisdom, let not the mighty man boast in his might, let not the rich man boast in his riches, but let him who boasts boast in this, that he understands and knows me, that I am the Lord who practices steadfast love, justice, and righteousness in the earth. For in these things I delight, declares the Lord. (Jer 9:23–24)

When the fear of the Lord takes hold in the depths of the heart, it awakens the heart to see itself as it truly is: The image bearer of God, scarred by the ravages of sin yet brimming with untapped potential and deeply loved by God. In this awakening, a longing is kindled within us, a yearning to draw near to him. In our encounter with the God who is love itself, a transformation begins within us, igniting the flames of faith, hope, and love. A wellspring of devotion springs to life, inviting if not compelling us to pour out our hearts in prayer and worship, for we are drawn to him who loved us first. In this embrace of love, a divine partnership is formed. We are compelled to work together with him for our cleansing, healing, and sanctification. This is what happens when we choose the fear of the Lord (Prov 1:20–33).

As a young leader, I needed to grow in the fear of the Lord by "walking with the wise." Proverbs tells us, "Whoever walks with the wise becomes wise, but the companion of fools will suffer harm" (Prov 13:20; see also Prov 20:26). I needed a wise person who walked in the fear of the Lord to help me grow in this area. Steve, a pastor in a neighboring

---

10. Heschel, *Wisdom*, 221.

city, was such a man to me. I set up a lunch meeting with him and asked him every question I could think of about growing in the fear of the Lord. Steve pastored a very large church, but he made time for me when I was a struggling young pastor. I learned a lot from him, but it was more than intellectual. While we teach what we know, we reproduce what we are. Something in Steve was reproduced in me. I received more than a transfer of knowledge; I received an impartation of something deeper, something living. The best way I can describe it is to say that I caught something from Steve. Sometimes wisdom is more caught than taught. This is why walking with the wise is so important.

## Wise Leaders Choose to Guard Their Hearts

Humility and integrity of heart are essential for gaining wisdom. Proverbs 4:23 wisely instructs us to guard our hearts with all diligence because wisdom and pride cannot flourish in the same heart. It is impossible to be full of wisdom and full of yourself at the same time. Wise leaders are not impressed with themselves. In fact, anyone impressed with their self is a fool (Prov 26:12). Freed from the bondage of pride, wise leaders do not feel the need to prove themselves or impress people. They understand the folly of such pursuits (Prov 26:12). Instead, their desire is to honor the Lord by following his ways and turning away from evil (Prov 3:7; 26:12). They have intentionally chosen the way of humility (Prov 3:7; 26:12). This humility is woven into the fabric of every relationship and responsibility they undertake. Their humility becomes the wellspring of authenticity and strength, fostering bonds of trust and mutual respect.

This humility is essential for one who has a strong sense of a call from God because sometimes leaders interpret their calling as an entitlement to undue privileges. For example, I once worked with a person who had a strong sense of calling and determination. He had moved across the world and learned a new language to fulfill this calling. After a few years, he was frustrated and considering leaving the ministry assignment because the senior leader had not given him the leadership position he felt he deserved. While this young leader had clear evidence of a calling from God and had demonstrated commitment to the call, he also needed to develop characteristics like humility, patience, and trust earned through selfless service to others. His sense of calling had mistakenly created a sense of entitlement as well. A calling was not enough. Humility would be required to take his ministry to a deeper, more fruitful level.

## Wise Leaders Choose to Cry Out for Wisdom

Notice what Prov 2:1–5 says about gaining wisdom: "My son, *if you receive* my words and treasure up my commandments with you, making your ear attentive to wisdom and inclining your heart to understanding; yes, *if you call out* for insight and raise your voice for understanding, *if you seek* it like silver and search for it as for hidden treasures, *then you will* understand the fear of the Lord and find the knowledge of God" (emphasis mine). The acquisition of wisdom is an active pursuit. God delights in giving wisdom. However, you must cry out for it like you cry out for breath, for water, and for life itself (Prov 2:3). This kind of prayer is not a problem once you realize just how desperate you are.

The Psalmist states, "Behold, you desire truth in the innermost being, and in the hidden part you will make me know wisdom" (Ps 51:6, NASB ). The journey toward wisdom begins when you long for the truth of God more than your own truth, and you long for it in the deepest recesses of your heart. This longing for truth issues forth in a cry from the core of your being. The choice for wisdom begins in the heart as a longing beyond knowledge, ability, skill, and experience. It is the longing to know God. This is the holy ambition of all wise leaders, to forsake folly and follow Lady Wisdom back to the Father's house (Prov 2:1–15).

In the New Testament, the wisdom of God reaches its apex of revelation in Jesus Christ (John 1:1–18). In Christ are hidden all the treasures of wisdom and knowledge, for he is the wisdom of God, and he has "became wisdom from God for us" (Col 2:3; 1 Cor 1:24, 30). Please do not bypass this truth: Wisdom is personal. Growing in wisdom means growing in your relationship with God, drawing near to him in love, reverence, wonder, and awe.

## Wise Leaders Choose Self-Discipline

Wise leaders choose to control their words (Prov 10:19), their appetites (Prov 20:1; 23:1–3), and their emotions (Prov 29:11). They protect their hearts, ears, eyes, words, and path (Prov 4:20–27; 15:24), knowing that "a man without self-control is like a city broken into and left without walls" (Prov 25:28). In ancient days, walls protected cities from invaders. Someone without self-control is a victim of every wandering thought and random impulse. Self-control is the guardian of your soul, protecting you from yourself. You develop self-control through self-discipline. For example, I have had a lifelong struggle with an overactive mind. I could not control my thoughts. My mind was under a constant onslaught of unhealthy thoughts, vain imaginations, and uncontrolled ideas. I did not know how to make it stop. I tried. I prayed. I read the Bible. But still, my mind seemed to have a mind of its own. To gain self-control, I had to develop habits of self-discipline. I had to set boundaries around what I would allow myself to read, watch, or think about. I also started spending ten minutes each morning sitting in silence, just focused on breathing and being present. The exercise took work. My mind would wander, and my body would fidget. Slowly, I became better at this discipline. Eventually, this self-discipline was transformed into self-control. Mental struggles that plagued me for years were finally defeated. The self-discipline of calming my mind for ten minutes a day transformed into the self-control needed to protect my mind from the Blitzkrieg of uncontrolled thoughts that had plagued me my whole life. It was through self-disciple that the walls of protection had been rebuilt around my mind (Prov 16:32; 25:28).

There are two aspects of discipline. One part involves our self-discipline, how we train ourselves to be godly.[11] The second aspect involves the discipline of the Lord. Wise leaders embrace both self-discipline and the Lord's discipline (Prov 3:11; 5:12, 23). God's word is a lamp and a light, and even though the word disciplines us, these reproofs are the way to life (Prov 6:23). The wise choose to love discipline because it produces knowledge and life (Prov 12:1; 6:23). The wise choose the hard way of discipline, and the fool chooses the easy way of shunning discipline and avoiding reproof (Prov 15:10).

Self-discipline requires vigilance (Prov 8:13; 14:16). Leadership is stressful, but you must vigilantly avoid burying your stress in comfort food or drowning it in alcohol or distracting yourself through the clamor of social activities. Social events and sharing meals are central aspects of a leader's role. However, the wise leader is self-disciplined and vigilant even here to avoid the traps of excessive eating or alcohol (Prov 23:19–35). Ecclesiastes reminds us, "Happy are you, O land, when your king is the

---

11. 1 Tim 4:6–8

son of the nobility, and your princes feast at the proper time, for strength, and not for drunkenness!" (10:17).

Self-discipline teaches you the value of good planning, hard work, and high standards (Prov 10:5; 21:5). While fools squander everything they have (Prov 21:20), the wise choose to be diligent, careful, and resourceful with everything entrusted to them (Prov 12:11, 27; 14:1; 28:19). The temptation to cut corners, skip planning, and take shortcuts is ever present. The wise know "A slack hand causes poverty, but the hand of the diligent makes rich" (Prov 10:4) and "Whoever is slack in his work is a brother to him who destroys" (Prov 18:9). Lazy people excel at making excuses (Prov 22:13; 26:13), yet even lazy people can become wise if they choose diligent self-discipline (Prov 6:6; 10:5; 12:27; 21:20).

## Wise Leaders Choose to Listen and Learn

The wise leader chooses to listen to good advice and instructions, even when it is painful. (Prov 1:5; 8:33; 10:8; 12:15; 13:1; 19:20; 23:19; 25:12). Since the wise are teachable and treasure knowledge, they are always listening, learning, seeking, and hearing, no matter who the teacher is (Prov 10:14; 18:15; 21:11), knowing that even little ants can teach wisdom (Prov 6:6). The wise choose to be teachable and correctable (Prov 9:8, 9; 15:31; 19:25). To be correctable means choosing to listen to criticism (Prov 25:12). If you correct a fool, you will get abuse, but if you correct the wise, they will love you for it (Prov 9:8). If you listen to instruction and constructive criticism, you will be at home among the wise (Prov 15:31; 19:25; 23:19). The next time a wise person gives you healthy correction, say "Thank you." Do not argue your point or defend yourself. That is the way to wisdom. If a fool criticizes you, consider the source.

The biblical concept of "to listen" includes with it "to obey, or to heed." Your life is transformed through the small daily acts of obedience. You start by taking the next step in your journey of obedience to wisdom. After that, take the next step. Then, after that, take the next step. Remember, gaining wisdom requires walking the path of wisdom, one small step at a time, for a very long time. This works no matter where you are in your journey. It does not matter how long you have traveled in the wrong direction; you can always turn around. Now, take that next step in the right direction.

## The Wise Leader's Legacy: Influence, Joy, and Satisfaction

When leaders become wise, they enter an entirely new level of leadership authority. It is an authority that does not flow from the leader's position; it flows from the leader's character. This is the highest level of leadership. This kind of leadership has significant influence. Proverbs 11:30 tells us, "The fruit of the righteous is a tree of life, and whoever captures souls is wise." The last phrase of this passage, "whoever captures souls is wise," is also translated as "wins souls," "gather lives," "wins friends," and "captivates people." The idea is that a wise and righteous leader has a life-giving influence and wins others to wisdom. This is leadership that leaves a legacy of transformed lives.

Wise leaders bring joy and honor to their families and society, "When the righteous are in authority, the people rejoice; but when the wicked rule, the people groan." (Prov 29:2 RSV, see also 10:1; 15:20; 29:2). C.S. Lewis reminded us, "Joy is the serious business of heaven."[12] Wise leadership helps us experience some of that joy here and now. This is a legacy that empowers lives.

Wise leaders gain strength, honor, and reward because of their life (Prov 3:35; 9:12; 21:22; 24:5). As church leaders, we are pressured to measure our success by the numbers, nickels, and noise of our congregations. These things are never ultimately satisfying. People come; people go. Offerings go up; offerings go down. Programs succeed; programs fail. If these are the measures of your success, prepare yourself for disappointment. If you set wisdom as your highest leadership ambition, you will end your days satisfied and full (Prov 9:12; 16:16; 24:13–14). And that, my friend, is a great legacy.

---

12. Lewis, *Malcolm*, 125.

# 4

# The Intoxicating Attraction

Sexual temptation comes up a lot in Proverbs. I mean, a lot.[1] If you read a chapter of Proverbs every day, you will have days where you think, "Why is this guy so obsessed with sexual temptation?" If you look at the Bible as a whole, you will see it, too, devotes a lot of space to sexual integrity and the dangers of illicit sexual behavior. The Bible is filled with these warnings because secret lusts and forbidden passions can destroy in minutes what has taken a lifetime to build. You do not need to look far to see marriages, families, relationships, careers, and reputations destroyed because of sexual sin.

Before we get much further into this discussion, I need to make two observations. First, as mentioned in chapter one, Proverbs was written within a patriarchal culture. Consequently, it addresses sexual temptation from a male perspective. In a patriarchal society, the status of women was much lower than men; they were viewed as easily deceived and their bodies as a source of seductive temptation. This attitude is the result of humankind's fall, and it does not reflect God's attitude, intention, or will for women.

While it reveals divine truth, the Bible also presents an unpolished account of our human condition. The Bible shows us God working within our broken human condition in order to bring us out of our bondage

1. See, for example, Prov 5:1–23; 2:16–22; 6:20–35; 7:1–27; 22:14; 23:26–28; 30:20; 31:3.

and darkness and, ultimately, into his redemptive and eternal purpose in Christ. Sometimes the Bible is showing us the glory and beauty of what God wants, and other times it is showing us the horrible consequences when we as humans do what we want. In other words, just because something is in the Bible doesn't mean it is God's will. It is important that we keep this tension in mind when reading scripture. We live in the "already, but not yet" tension; God has revealed himself and his kingdom in Christ (the "already"), but we do not yet see the fullness of his kingdom revealed "on earth as it is in heaven" (the "but not yet"). While most societies have made progress since the days when women were considered property, women are still too often treated as objects for sexual exploitation or as the sole causes of sexual temptation rather than being treated with dignity as equal image-bearers of God. That said, we can also celebrate that women are finding more and greater freedom, including the freedom to fulfill their God-given calling to serve as leaders in church and society. Consequently, women in leadership will face, in their own way and context, the lure of sexual compromise. The wisdom offered in Proverbs, though written from a male perspective, is equally applicable for women today—if with some modifications.

The second observation about sexual temptation, which is pertinent to our discussion of the matter in Proverbs, has to do with definitions. Adultery is sometimes defined as "sexual intercourse with someone other than your spouse." In this study, I will use a broadened definition, which includes all forms of sexual immorality as well as all the hidden lusts of the heart (Matt 5:28).

Why does Proverbs spend so much time talking about sexual temptations? To answer this question, it helps to keep in mind that Proverbs was written as a training program to develop social, political, and religious leaders so that they would embody character traits of righteousness, justice, and integrity.[2] Part of this regimen includes training for facing sexual temptations. While sexual temptations are common to all people, leaders have an abundance of opportunities to act on these temptations. These opportunities to act come through in at least three situations: confused emotional attachments, misguided affections, and abuse of power.

2. Dunham, "Structure," 361–88.

## Confused Emotional Attachments

Leaders are often involved in helping vulnerable people in crisis. The person in crisis welcomes an understanding and empathetic person who provides strength and help. This level of human interaction can create deep emotional connections. If not guarded against, such emotional depth can cause confused emotional attachments and clouded judgment that result in violating sexual boundaries. Leaders are the ones with the power in these situations, and consequently, they are the ones responsible for keeping the boundaries of protection in place.

## Misguided Affections

As a leader, you may face situations where someone becomes attracted to you because you seem like an ideal person: strong, responsible, caring, secure, and successful. Someone sees you as this "ideal person" and thinks, "I want him" or "I want her." This misguided affection can be experienced by those who only know you from a distance, or it can happen with those who work closely with you, day in and day out. Be very careful of flirtatious comments and behavior. Perhaps you have done nothing to intentionally foster these attractions, but they can happen anyway. Be aware of the dangers of misguided affection. You should also be aware that these misguided affections do not always come from members of the opposite sex.

When I was in my twenties, I attended a pastors' seminar that shocked me. I vividly recall the presenter saying, "Pastors, don't ever forget. There is always at least one person in your church who has the hots for you." I was stunned. I told myself, "That can't be true!" After the shock waned, I accepted this counsel as a word of wisdom. From that point forward, I decided never to drop my guard or to be careless in my interactions. The advice given to Timothy became real to me. Treat older men as you would your father, younger men as your brother, older women as your mother, and younger women as your sister "in all purity" (1 Tim 5:1–2). You need to use wisdom in how you apply this advice. In my younger days, it was drilled into my head, "Never be alone with a woman who is not your wife." I was told to never be alone in a room, a car, or even an elevator with a woman. This advice was intended to protect male pastors from sexual temptation. Unfortunately, the unintended consequence was that the warnings perpetuated the objectification of women by communicating to them, "You are dangerous. Men cannot be around you, not even in an elevator, without being corrupted by you."

I think the advice to Timothy is a good safeguard for all leaders, and the phrasing expresses love and honor: treat people like they are your immediate family. You would not flirt with your sister, so don't flirt with that young lady.

## Abuse of Power

Leaders may also be tempted to use their power and influence to sexually exploit others. News reports of religious leaders who sexually abuse others are far too common. When this abuse of power is exposed, we typically ask questions like, "How did this happen?" "Why didn't anyone see it?" or "Why didn't someone say something?" Some answers can be found by considering that religious leadership, by its very nature, can lay the groundwork for exploitation. Here is what I mean. Abusive leaders generally leverage one or more sources of their power. The basic sources of their power are economic, physical/coercive, and related to trust. Unlike business leaders, religious leaders have little economic power over others. Religious leaders do not hire and fire those who follow them. And unlike political leaders, religious leaders do not use legal force or physical coercion to ensure compliance. Religious leaders rely on a sense of trust, a shared faith, and belief in the divine authority of their office. Perpetrators of sexual abuse within religious settings exploit this trust, faith, and authority to groom victims and keep the abuse secret.[3]

Abusive leaders are masterful manipulators. Their proficiency in the art of lying is remarkable, enabling them to manipulate and control with calculated precision. The ability to lie is the Achilles Heel in communities of trust. The act of lying induces negative emotions, cognitive impairment, and physiological stress. These emotional, mental, and physical consequences of lying are often revealed through nonverbal cues, such as a change in speech patterns, tone of voice, or the direction of the eyes; one's body language tends not to match one's words. Yet, far too often, leaders can lie with a straight face with what seems to be authentic sincerity. How many times have you asked, "How can he lie like that?" The answer, as it ends up, may be quite simple. People with power are

---

3. Raine and Kent, "Grooming," 180–89.

better liars. That was the provocative title of a research paper published at Columbia University.[4] According to the study, the experience of power boosts the same emotional, cognitive, and physiological systems that are depleted by the act of lying. Individuals experiencing power enjoy extra positive emotions, increases in cognitive function, and physiological resilience to stress. In addition, power influences leaders to focus on rewards as opposed to costs, which could shift focus away from a fear of getting caught and toward pleasure in lying successfully. The authors suggest that power acts as a buffer against the stressful impact of lying. Consequently, high-power liars appear emotionally, cognitively, physiologically, and behaviorally as if they are telling the truth.[5]

To make matters more complicated, power is also an aphrodisiac. At a biological level, power and sex are linked as they both cause a surge in testosterone. Testosterone, in turn, ramps up dopamine in the brain's "reward network." Everything you experience as pleasure or reward has its effects through this dopamine-rich system, and power is an exceptionally strong activator of this reward network. Power acts as an aphrodisiac by ramping up the reward system, and this increases the appetite for other reward-rich activities such as sex.[6] This cycle helps explain why some powerful leaders engage in behavior that their self-controlled selves would never contemplate.

We should also remember that we are not only biological ecosystems subject to hormones, instincts, and cultural provocations, but we are also fallen human beings. Sometimes leaders do bad things because they, like all humans, are broken, sinful people. The ancient words of Jeremiah ring true, "The heart is deceitful above all things and desperately wicked: who can know it?" (Jer 17:9 KJV). It is a haunting truth, reminding us of the peril that lies within. For in the depths of our own hearts lies the potential for deception and treachery, even in the noblest of pursuits. The heart has its labyrinthine passages, its shadowy recesses, where desires, ambitions, and power converge to form a heady potion that intoxicates us, blinding us to our own deceitfulness.

4. Carney, et al., "Better Liars," Columbia University.
5. Carney, et al., "Better Liars," 3–4
6. Robertson, "Petraeus," 2012.

## The Anatomy of Seduction (Proverbs 5:1–23; 6:20–35; 7:1–27)

The typical leader does not wake up one day and think, "Today, I will violate my love for God and my commitment to purity because I want to destroy everything I have worked for." At some point, before the seduction of the body takes place, a seduction of the mind has already happened. Seduction is deceitful in part because an internal process of your heart gets projected outward. It then looks as if an external object or person is controlling your desire. When this happens, a loss of self-control seems then to be an ordinary response to an extraordinary temptation. Let's look first at the dynamics and vocabulary of seduction in the context of Proverbs and then at how the heart is ultimately responsible and holds the power of temperance or self-control.

The intoxicating attraction of sexual desire is ever-present and can feel overwhelming. Leaders cannot have a slack, casual attitude about this subtle menace. This is why the warnings against sexual immorality in Proverbs 5–7 begin with the imperative: "Be attentive" (Prov 5:1). The Hebrew word used here (stem: *qšb*; transliteration: *qashab*) means to listen, heed, and pay attention (see Prov 1:24; 2:2; 4:1, 20; 5:1; 7:24). This diligent attention is a requirement for all leaders. Proverbs 4 sets the stage by telling you to diligently guard your heart above all things (Prov 4:23), by guarding where you go (Prov 4:26; 5:8), what you watch (Prov 4:25), and what you want (Prov 6:25–35).

Seduction promises a new and thrilling experience, yet it follows a basic pattern that has remained unchanged for thousands of years. Proverbs 7:1–27 is a vivid story of seduction and the destruction it brings. The writer sees a group of naïve young men, and one young man, in particular, was exceptional in his lack of "common sense" (Prov 7:7 NLT). The Hebrew text literally says that the young man lacked heart.

The word "heart" (Hebrew *lebab*) is the most important anthropological term in the Old Testament. It occurs over 850 times in the Old Testament, with 99 instances in Proverbs. The richness of this word is exhibited by the various ways it is translated into English. The English Standard Version translates this word as heart (Prov 2:2, 10; 4:23), sense (Prov 7:7; 8:5; 9:4, 16), mind (Prov 12:8; 19:21), intelligence (Prov 15:23), opinion (Prov 18:2), "in the midst" (Prov 23:34), to consider (Prov 24:32), and give attention (Prov 27:23). Proverbs refers to the heart controlling facial expressions (Prov 15:13), the tongue (Prov 15:28; 12:23), and the whole body (Prov 4:23–27; 6:18). The heart thinks, reflects, ponders, and plans (Prov 6:14, 18; 16:9; 24:12). It is where decisions are made. As the eyes were meant to see and the ears to hear, the heart is meant to discern and prompt action. When a person lacks insight or judgment, the Hebrew Scriptures speak of a "lack of heart" (Prov 7:7; 10:13).[7] The English language has no equivalent word for heart that combines this complex interplay of intellect, sensibility, and will.

This exceptional absence of heart in Proverbs 7:7 is the theme of the whole chapter. Unfortunately, the passage has often been misunderstood and used to warn young men of the dangers of women, as though just by their very presence a woman will seduce a man. Women have suffered far too long as the scapegoat for men's foolishness. This has been going on since Adam blamed Eve for eating the forbidden fruit.[8] I cannot help but wonder if some of the study notes in our modern Bibles unwittingly perpetuate these stereotypes about women and excuse sexist behavior. Take a few minutes to notice the subject headings inserted into many study Bibles today, and you will see what I mean. The New Living Translation labels Proverbs 7: "Another Warning about Immoral Women." The Common English Bible has the heading: "Avoid Loose Women." Other headlines include: "The Lures of the Prostitute" (NASB) and "Warning Against the Adulteress" (ESV, NIV). However, the point of this passage is not, in fact, "women and their wicked wiles." The absence of heart, not the presence of women, is the cause of the tragedy in Proverbs 7. This passage is about the consequences of lacking heart.

C.S. Lewis referred to this condition as the atrophy of the chest. In *The Abolition of Man*, Lewis argued that the head rules the belly through the chest. He states, "It may even be said that it is by this middle element that man is man: for by his intellect he is mere spirit and by his appetite mere animal." Lewis goes on to say, "In a sort of ghastly simplicity, we remove the organ and demand the function. We make men without chests and expect of them virtue and enterprise. We laugh at honor and are shocked to find traitors in our midst. We castrate and bid the geldings be fruitful."[9] The young man of Proverbs 7 has no heart, no sense, no chest. He is reduced to a blinded intellect led by animal instincts. Consequently, he drops his guard, turns from wisdom, and wanders toward a place he should never go near (Prov 7:8–9).

---

7. Waltke, *Proverbs, 1–15*, 90–92.
8. Gen 3:12
9. Lewis, *Abolition of Man*, 35–37.

The foolish young man takes a walk in the twilight, at the time of night and darkness. He takes the road to pass by the house of the forbidden woman (Prov 7:6–9). This senseless lad has wandered from wisdom, and now his feet are walking toward destruction, straight into a trap he cannot escape. At just the right moment, "the woman meets him, dressed as a prostitute, wily of heart" (Prov 7:10). She is provocatively dressed, physically aggressive, and verbally persuasive. She seizes him and kisses him, and with bold face, she says to him:

> I had to offer sacrifices, and today I have paid my vows; so now I have come out to meet you, to seek you eagerly, and I have found you. I have spread my couch with coverings, colored linens from Egyptian linen; I have perfumed my bed with myrrh, aloes, and cinnamon. Come, let us take our fill of love till morning; let us delight ourselves with love. (Prov 7:13–18)

The seductress tantalizes him with flattery and promises of wonder and hidden delights.

The seduction is subtle, offering justifications to silence any objections (Prov 7:13–14). There is even a spiritual element involved. The woman has offered her sacrifices and paid her vows, and now "I have met you." This seems to imply something like, "I was led here to meet you. God brought us together. It must be OK." (Prov 7:13–15). Her flattery feeds his ego (Prov 7:15). She promises to satisfy his sensual urges and psychological longings (Prov 7:16–17).

"Come, let us take our fill of love till morning; let us delight ourselves with love" (Prov 7:18). She promises him sensual gratification and the thrill of a secret adventure (Prov 7:19–20; 9:13–18). Yet, his eyes are blind, and his heart is hardened to the reality of seduction's deadly end. "With her smooth talk, she compels him" (v. 21), and her victim follows her like an ox going to slaughter, like a deer enticed into a trap, and like a bird lured into a snare; he does not know it will cost him his life (v. 23). Death is the only possible outcome.

This foolish young man is not the innocent victim of a beguiling seducer. He is the victim of his lack of heart: a turning away from wisdom toward destruction. Wisdom says:

> Listen to me and be attentive to the words of my mouth. Let not your heart turn aside to her ways; do not stray into her paths, for many a victim has she laid low, and all her slain are a mighty

throng. Her house is the way to Sheol, going down to the chambers of death. (Prov 7:24–27)

Wisdom promises to protect you from this forbidden woman, this adulteress (Prov 7:5). The Hebrew words used for forbidden woman (*zr*) and adulteress (*nokrî*) are difficult to translate. Bible translators have the difficult task of translating the text without undue or prejudicial interpretation. The English Standard Version translates, "the forbidden woman," and "the adulteress." The Common English Bible translates, "the mysterious woman," and "the foreign woman." The New Revised Standard Version translates, "the loose woman," and "the adulteress." Most English translations follow similar patterns.

The two Hebrew words in question can be translated literally as "strange woman" (*zr*) and "foreign woman" (*nokrî*). A more literal translation may better preserve the original meaning. The seductive appeal of the woman is enhanced because she is different. She is unique, strangely different. She is foreign. She does not look like the local women. Her exotic difference magnifies her appeal. The siren song of Folly, beguiling and deadly, whispers a tantalizing promise, "This woman is different. She is not like the one you have at home." It is a deceitful lure, a treacherous lie that has brought ruin to many, including Solomon.[10]

Temptation begins with a desire, as a longing for something that at first may be mostly subconscious. Keep in mind that God does not want to destroy your sexual desire; he wants to redeem and reorient your desire toward his original intent. The apostle James tells us, "Each person is tempted when he is lured and enticed by his own desire. Then desire when it has conceived gives birth to sin, and sin, when it is fully grown, brings forth death" (Jas 1:14–15). James uses verbs (Gk: *exelkō* and *deleazō*) that refer to a baited field that lures a deer into the hunter's trap or bait that draws the fish to swallow the fisherman's hook. The secret desires of the heart are the bait that lures us into a deadly trap, giving rise to sin. When your heart is lured away by its own desires, your mind is deceived. An arsenal of reasonings and arguments protects and defends the lie that has become a stronghold.[11] The easiest person in the world to deceive is yourself, and you should never underestimate this power of self-deception. When desire and deception collude to justify an action, plans are designed and set in motion to fulfill what has been desired and

10. 1 Kgs 11:1
11. See 2 Cor 10:4–6

rationalized. Desire gives birth to rationalizations; rationalization gives birth to scheming; scheming gives birth to action; action gives birth to death (Jas 1:15).

## The Agony of Adultery

Sexual seduction, alluring and tempting, beckons with promises it cannot fulfill (Prov 5). At first, it appears sweet and enticing, but it ends in bitterness and despair (vv. 1–6). With flattering words, she lures her victims, dripping honey from her lips and speech smoother than oil (Prov 5:3). Yet, when done, she led her prey down the path to Sheol, marked by pain and death (Prov 5:4–6).

Her prey spirals from gain to loss, honor to shame, as wealth is squandered and labor wasted, leaving her victims groaning in regret when their lives are consumed (Prov 5:9–11). Purity gives way to pollution, and freedom to bondage, as the seduced find themselves ensnared, led astray by folly (Prov 5:20, 22–23).

Though momentarily pleasurable, sexual seduction proves to be gradually destructive (Prov 6:20–35). It leaves less of you, not more. Its false allure diminishes and destroys, stripping away the sustaining word of God, the lamp and light that guards against the adulteress's smooth tongue (Prov 6:23–24).

In her magnificent deception, she convinces her paramour he will not be burned by her fire (Prov 6:25–28). Common sense evaporates in the heat of her embrace. In the end, yielding to this seduction leads to self-inflicted wounds and shattered relationships, leaving behind dishonor and disgrace (Prov 6:32–33).

Seduction is an enticing but deadly trap (Prov 7). The dark consequences of its stain and bondage lead to a distortion of the true self, leading to hidden lives and self-destructive behaviors. Bondage may follow, accompanied by addiction, criminality, or abuse.

If you bear the scars of sexual transgressions, hope and healing await. The Bible abounds with stories of broken souls made beautiful, restored, and whole through divine love. No one is beyond God's promise of redemption. Please seek healing and professional help. You have been enslaved long enough. Do not let shame keep you in the darkness. The path of restoration is open for you. God loves broken people because there are no other kind of people.

## The Antidote to Adultery

Sexual integrity is essential for godly leadership. Building this integrity requires intentionality and discipline, especially in this highly sexualized world we live in. The good news is the Bible offers practical advice to help you resist sexual temptation and restore sexual wholeness.

When it comes to dealing with sexual temptation, the Bible offers a clear and simple solution: Run! Run as fast and as far as you can (Prov 5:1–23; 2:16–22; 6:20–35; 7:1–27; 22:14; 23:26–28; 30:20; 31:3). Timothy was instructed to "flee youthful lusts" (2 Tim 2:22). The word "flee" is the Greek word *pheugo*. We derive our English word "fugitive" from this word. It means "to flee, to sprint from danger, to quickly disappear." It is the same word Paul uses in 1 Cor 6:18 when he tells the Corinthians to run away from sexual sin. Sexual wholeness requires both pursuing what is good, godly, pure, and joyful and fleeing the seductive lies and false promises of sexual temptation (Prov 5:1–14).

Sexual temptation is a powerful enemy that should not be underestimated. Samson, the strongest man in the Bible, was not strong enough to defeat the lure of sexual temptation. David, one of the most spiritual men in the Bible, was not spiritual enough to resist sexual temptation. Solomon, the wisest man in the Bible, was not wise enough to overcome sexual temptation. If the strongest, most spiritual, and wisest cannot wrestle with sexual temptation and win, do you think you can wrestle with it and win? You can't! Don't even try. It will beat you down, wear you out, outsmart you, and finally overcome you. Just run. That is how you deal with it.

All the biblical warnings about adultery have led some to believe the Bible presents an overall negative view of sex, that sex is somehow dangerous, dirty, and maybe a necessary evil for reproduction.[12] Nothing could be further from the truth. Sex is God's idea. The Bible celebrates the beauty of passionate sexual love between husband and wife. It even

12. God gives these warnings because of the horrible consequences of sexual immorality, such as curses (Num 5:11–30; Deut 27:20, 22, 23; Job 24:15–18); death (Gen 20:3, 7; 26:11; 38:24; Lev 19:20–22; 20:10–12; 21:9; Deut 22:20–27; 2 Sam 12:14); divine judgments (2 Sam 12:10–12; Jer 29:22, 23; Ezek 16:38–41; Mal 3:5; 1 Cor 10:8; Heb 13:4; 2 Pet 2:9,10,14; Rev 2:20–22; 18:9, 10); exclusion from the kingdom of God (1 Cor 6:9, 10; Gal 5:19, 21; Eph 5:5,6; Jude 7; Rev 21:8; 22:15); and excommunication from the people of God (1 Cor 5:1–13; Eph 5:11,12). The goal of these commandments is not that you become a prude, but rather that you become whole through turning from the way of death to the way of life.

dedicates a whole book to the subject. It is called the Song of Songs. The belief that sex is dirty only exacerbates the struggle men and women face regarding sexual longing, passion, and temptation.

God sanctified sex by setting it apart.[13] Since sex is good and holy, God placed a fence around it, and the fence is there for a reason. G.K. Chesterton wisely advised, "Don't ever take a fence down until you know the reason it was put up."[14] The fence around sex is not there to keep you from having a good time. It is there to protect you.

The fence around sex is the marriage covenant. For those called to marriage, you are invited to drink deeply from the well of sexual delight (Prov 5:15). This is a delight shared deeply between husband and wife (Prov 5:16–17). This "fountain" of sexual love is blessed and a cause of rejoicing (Prov 5:18). Men, rejoice in your wife. "Let her breast fill you with delight at all times," and always be intoxicated with her love (Prov 5:19). Rejoicing in and being intoxicated with your spouse is the antidote to seduction (Prov 5:20). This is a discipline of wisdom (Prov 5:21). Many a man has strayed from home because he failed to delight in his wife (Prov 5:21–23).

For those called to be single, whether that calling is for a season or for a lifetime, God provides other means of grace to bring about a rich and fulfilling life. We only need to look at Jesus, Paul (I Cor 7:7), Anna, (Luke 2:36–38), Jeremiah (Jer 1:1–9), John the Baptist (John 3:22–30), and perhaps Nehemiah and Daniel to see examples of rich, fulfilling lives outside the call to marriage.

Sex is a gift from God and, as such, it is good and holy. But like all of God's gifts, it must be treated with reverence because it is powerful, and it can be dangerous. Sex is like fire. Fire can warm your home and cook your meals. If out of its proper place, fire can also burn down the very home it had once warmed. God's gifts are like this; they are decisive for your healing or your destruction. Wisdom sets the gifts of God in their proper and life-giving place. Sex is so powerful and dangerous that it must be safely confined within the covenant of marriage. Anything less is to miss the mark of what God has designed and what we truly desire and need. Everything else strays from the path of healing and sanctifying grace, which the marriage bed is intended to be.

---

13. To sanctify means to set apart as holy; to consecrate.

14. Chesterton, "The Drift," 157.

The union of body, soul, mind, and strength in marriage, and our longing for that union, is a living icon of our union with God and our longing for God. In the New Testament, marriage is the image of Christ and the church (Eph 5:22–33), and the marriage bed is undefiled (Heb 13:4). Sexual wholeness involves giving yourself in love, and receiving unto yourself in love, whereby you hold fast to each another and become one. This self-giving dethrones selfishness and empowers love, which makes us whole. We then embrace each other without fear or shame.

Redeeming and restoring sexuality begins with turning to God, the fountain of living water (Jer 2:13). Allow God to wash away and cleanse whatever needs to be redeemed and to restore in you whatever needs to be restored. This will include a washing and renewing of your mind to cleanse away the lies you have believed.[15] Lies breed sexual confusion and compromise and truth produces sexual integrity and purity, for the mind is the real sexual organ. Consequently, if you want sexual integrity, you must start with your head, not your hormones. All truth in your actions begins with truth in your mind, which begins, in turn, with a proper understanding of God. Present your mind and your whole body to God to be renewed by his word.

## Reflecting on Chastity

It is easy to misunderstand the Bible's teaching about self-discipline and chastity. Far too often, we regard biblical disciplines as a denial of life and its pleasures and a negation of the goodness of God's creation. After all, we fast, we abstain, we humble ourselves, we embrace discipline, and we speak of dying to ourselves. Unless viewed through the prism of life, these acts of self-denial seem morbid. Unless integrated with the fullness of life before God, these disciplines seem a mockery of the God of joy, life, goodness, and abundance.

We discipline our lives not to negate the joy and goodness of living but rather to prune the fruit-bearing tree so that we can enjoy even more life and goodness. We fast not because food is bad, or our bodies are evil. We fast to prune the life-giving branches. Then, when we give thanks for the meal, we join our voice with the ancient prayer, "Blessed are you, O Lord, who brings forth bread from the earth." Who enjoys food more: the gluttonous man who remains unsatiated, regardless of how often he

---

15. Rom 12:1–2; Eph 4:23; Col 3:9–10

returns to the buffet line, or the disciplined person who has tempered his appetite through fasting and prayer? Which one enjoys a proper and life-giving relationship with his food and drink?

In the New Testament, the word group for "moderation" or "chastity" is, strictly speaking, untranslatable into English. These words derive from *sōsphrēn*,[16] and they express the idea of spiritual health, appropriate reasoning, and moderation that produces inner stability.[17] These words are usually translated: "to be of sound mind, to bring someone to their senses, to be moderate, self-disciplined." The word indicates "moderation," "self-control," "chastity," or "temperance." The word "wholeness" may be the best current translation. This virtue of temperance overcomes the passions. The whole person is brought to completion in Christ.

Ancient philosophers and theologians ranked temperance (chastity), along with prudence, justice, and fortitude, as the four cardinal virtues. In today's usage, chastity has retained a limited definition relative to its original content. It has been reduced to mean a person's sexual habits. While unfortunate, this reduction is understandable. Where else is the broken character of our existence better revealed than in this most intimate of places?

Through chastity we are no longer like animals, satisfying instinctual and biological needs, but rather full human beings, made totally alive, who express the most intimate, tender, beautiful, and life-affirming union between two equals. Here we find the fullest satisfaction. The life of the body is no longer alienated from the control of the spirit. We willingly give ourselves to the other in the beautiful mystery of deepest exchange, the two becoming one, in body as well as soul.

Intimately dangerous, capable of the deepest healing or destruction, the couple—longing, open, and vulnerable—meet in the secret chamber to become one in this most intimate dance of marriage. Chastity is awe's response to this glorious mystery.

---

16. *sōphroneō*, to be moderate, sober–minded, sensible, sane; *sōphronizō*, to instill a sense of moderation, restore someone to his senses, instruct, train; *sōphronismos*, having good judgment, of sound mind; *sōphronōs*, with good sense, with self–control; *sōphrosynē*, prudence, moderation, sound judgment, decency, self–control, mastery of the passions; *sōphrōn*, moderate, sensible

17. Spicq and Ernest, *Theological Lexicon*, vol. 3, 359.

# 5

# Husbands and Wives

IN THE EARLY DAYS of my marriage, I was full of hope and dreams, like any other soul. Yet, as time passed, those hopes faded, giving way to a sense of despair. At my lowest point, I found myself declaring, "Only a bunch of unmarried Catholic priests could dream up the notion of marriage as a sacrament. Marriage is not a sacrament. Marriage is hell!" Our shared aspirations, once vibrant, were now withering away. Those once pure and heartfelt hopes and dreams became tainted by my sinful behavior, personal insecurities, and toxic attitude toward women. Toxic notions about women were sown in my youth at home and then reinforced by the bad theology I learned at church. Though I never spoke it aloud, I harbored a distorted view of women, and shame blankets me now as I admit it. But then, I saw them as sexualized objects, dangerous threats, and, sadly, something a little less than men.

It gets worse. I was also a driven and ambitious young man out to prove myself to the world. Making my mark on the world became my relentless pursuit. Unfortunately, I conflated my role as a leader with my identity as a person. In the absence of an internalized sense of self-worth and identity as a human, I became consumed by my mantle of leadership. Consumed with my pastoral role, the notion of being an ordinary human escaped me entirely. My focus was fixated on the role I held, leaving no room for the soul beneath. Then came the day when my wife confronted me, her words a sharp blade cutting through my delusion, "Leave your pastoral facade outside. I do not need to talk to the pastor right now. I need to talk with my husband." Those simple words became a revelation, a divine intervention that exposed the ugliness of my condition.

I was in deep trouble. Consumed with ambitions to "make my mark," I had missed the mark. I was becoming a thing, not a person. The "thing" I was becoming needed to give way to the human being I was created to be: a human being in relationship with other human beings, bound together by love and trust—not by organizational charts, positional authority, and an unhealthy need to prove myself. Truth be told, I was hiding behind the baggage of leadership. I wanted to be seen as successful, productive, and skillful, but I was terrified to simply be seen.

Too prideful to see a counselor, I hatched a plan to get professional advice without going to a therapist. Dan was a counselor who worked at our church. Under the disguise of "catching up," I would ask his advice about specific situations in relationships "so that I could better serve people as their pastor." It was a classic "asking for a friend" scenario. When I asked him about how marriages break down, he explained that as fallen human beings, we continually seek to exalt our throne above all other thrones, including God's, and this self-exaltation is the substance of all life's struggles, especially in marriage. He explained that the marriage relationship is so intense that the deep-rooted, self-exalting nature of sin will make itself felt here more than in any other relationship. Marriage is "God's house of ambush," he said; It is where God ambushes our pride and self-centeredness. No other relationship seems to get that deep into the soul and place more demands on your heart, choices, and the person you are becoming. Marriage is a strenuous mystery that bids both to "die to self so that the two can become one." My pride was preventing this communion, this oneness with my wife. Whatever offended my pride and exposed my insecurity enraged me, and I would lash out in self-defense, not love.

Once the pressures in my marriage finally broke through my pride, I was ready to listen to Lady Wisdom's voice: "Whoever is simple, let him turn in here!" To him who lacks sense, she says, "Come, eat of my bread and drink of the wine I have mixed. Leave your simple ways, and live, and walk in the way of insight" (Prov 9:4–6). Little did I realize then just how deeply profound a change it would be. It would become a lifelong journey of discovering and rediscovering the power and joy of relationships, of discovering what it means to be a human in a community of humans. I began to learn that relationships are the bedrock of human experience, the context of all human flourishing, and the very currency of the kingdom of God. I would come to learn that God himself exists in and as a relationship—Father, Son, and Holy Spirit. I would come to understand that love, not accomplishment, is what binds us together. These lessons needed to saturate every level of my life, but first, I needed to learn them at home. I needed to unlearn what I had learned in the home of my youth and relearn the way of wisdom in the home of my adulthood. I would also learn it is OK to be seen.

If you are not intentional about it, leadership can become an all-consuming monster. This could be why Proverbs devotes so much attention to husbands, wives, children, friends, foes, and neighbors. These kith and kin relationships transcend your leadership role. And when done well, they keep you grounded in reality and healthy in your soul.

The next three chapters will explore what Proverbs has to say about these relationships. We will start with husbands and wives. But first, I need to clarify a few misconceptions regarding marriage and leadership.

## Five Misconceptions About Marriage and Leadership

While marriage can be awesome, it can also be miserable if laden with endless misconceptions. These misconceptions create tremendous pressure, unrealistic expectations, and false obligations. Here are five misconceptions I see on a regular basis that impact both leadership and marriage.

### Is "Biblical Marriage" Biblical?

The first misconception is to assume that our modern understanding of "biblical marriage" is, well, biblical. Marriages in the Bible, if you look closely at them, look a lot different from what we describe today as "biblical marriages." Abraham, the father of our faith, would not be allowed to teach a marriage class in any church I am aware of today. He was, after all, a polygamist who married his half-sister.[1] Awkward, I know. I point this out for a reason. Many marriage ministries within the broader evangelical Christian community create the image of an "ideal Christian couple" as two "purity pledge" virgins who married in the church with the blessing of both families after a long courtship. They are now packing the pew,

1. Gen 16:1–16; 20:12; 25:1–2

nursery, and youth department with their home-schooled kids. Anything less than this ideal, and the couple would not experience the fullness of God's blessings. Everything else is plan B or C or just downright wrong.

Don't get me wrong. If you are that "ideal Christian couple," that is great. The problem is most of the people I know are not "that couple." Most people I know are more like the people I see in the Bible: messed-up humans who may happen to be married. The "ideal Christian couple" concept is likely to alienate people who do not live in that idealized world. In our attempt to build healthy marriages by holding up the "ideal marriage," we end up pushing away the very people we want to draw close.

Now, that is not to say that the Bible does not present what could be called an ideal marriage. It does. And this model is more inviting and hope-filled than the idealized version popular in some circles, for it invites anyone who wants it to enter a transformative covenant of love, regardless of what life may have thrown at them.

The creation story of Genesis 1 ends with man and woman created together as the image of God and co-commissioned as stewards of God's creation. Then Genesis 2 concludes, "a man shall leave his father and mother and cleave to his wife, and the two shall become one flesh" (2:24). While the ideal marriage presented in Genesis 1–2 was monogamous, we humans tend to live outside of God's ideal.[2] Consequently, in scripture, you find examples of arranged marriages,[3] self-initiated marriages,[4] marriages to close relatives (including half-siblings),[5] mixed marriages,[6]

2. Gen 2:24; Exod 20:17; 21:5; Lev 18:8, 11, 14, 15, 16, 20; 20:10; 21:13; Num 5:12; Deut 5:21; 22:22; Prov 12:4; 18:22; 19:13; 21:9; Eccl 9:9; Job 31:1, 9–12.

3. Hagar selected a wife for her son Ishmael from Egypt (Gen 21:21), Rebekah is chosen for Isaac (Gen 25:20), Pharaoh gave Asenath, daughter of Potipherah priest of On, to Joseph as wife (Gen 37:35–36).

4. David's marriage to Abigail (1 Sam 25), Ahinnoam (2 Sam 2:2), Maacah (2 Sam 3:3), Haggith (2 Sam 3:4), Abital (2 Sam 3:4), Eglah (2 Sam 3:5); or Boaz and Ruth (Ruth 2).

5. Abraham married his half-sister (Gen 20:12), Nahor married his niece Milcah (Gen 11:29). Isaac married his cousin Rebekah (Gen 24:15). Esau married his cousin Malhalath (Gen 28:9). Jacob also married his cousins Rachel and Leah (Gen 29:12).

6. Esau married two Hittites (Gen 26:34) and a Canaanite (Gen 28:6–9). Joseph married an Egyptian (Gen 41:45), Judah a Canaanite (Gen 38:2), Moses a Midianite/ Cushite (Exod 2:21, Num 12:1), Samson a Philistine (Judges 14; 16:4–22), Boaz a Moabitess (Ruth 4:13), David a Calebite and Aramean (2 Sam 3:3), and Ahab a Phoenician (1 Kgs 16:31). Solomon pursued exogamy to the extreme (1 Kgs 3:1; 11:1; 14:21).

second marriages,[7] polygamous marriages,[8] as well as monogamous marriages.[9] It is surprising how few marriages in the Old Testament, if any,
conform to Genesis 2:24. One would have to scour the pages of the Old
Testament to find instances of the man leaving his home, uniting with his
wife, and forming a "one flesh" relationship.[10] What we do have in the Old
Testament are stories about marriages. Some of these stories are pivotal,
others peripheral. Some of these marriages appear to be normal and predictable; others border on the bizarre. Some are marked by righteousness
and integrity, while others are aberrant and profane. Collecting all those
marriage stories, sifting through them, searching for common threads,
and then attempting to form a grand notion of what marriage is all about
is like sitting by the highway, watching the cars roll by, taking note of how
people drive, and then trying to create a driver's manual from all those
observations. In both driving and marriage, what people should do and
what they actually do can be two very different things.[11]

In the wisdom literature of the Hebrew Scriptures,[12] Ecclesiastes and
Proverbs repeatedly affirm the happiness and delight of mutual love in
marriage. Ecclesiastes 9:9 implores the reader to live joyfully with the
wife whom you love. Proverbs reverberates with the same theme.[13] We
have seen already that Proverbs is written from the man's (or husband's)
point of view. The male-centeredness of the book comes obviously clear
when it speaks of marital relationships. Consider, for example, how Proverbs speaks of the husband who must live with a nagging wife who is like

---

7. 1 Sam 25:1–44

8. Abraham with Sarah and his concubines Hagar and Keturah (Gen 16; 25:1–2);
Jacob with Leah and Rachel (Gen 29:15–30); Esau with three wives (Gen 26:34; 36:2;
28:9); Gideon with his "many wives" (Jud 8:30); Elkanah with Hannah and Peninnah
(1 Sam 1:2); David with seven named wives (1 Sam 18:17–30; 25:38–43; 2 Sam 3:2–5)
and additional unnamed ones (2 Sam 5:13); Solomon and his royal harem (1 Kgs 3:1;
11:3; Song of Songs 6:8); and Rehoboam with his eighteen wives (2 Chr 11:21). There is
one law in the Deuteronomic code (Deut 21:15–17) that allows one man to be married
simultaneously to two wives. And the only individual who is admonished in the same
code not to multiply wives is the king (Deut 17:17).

9. Hamilton, "Marriage," 565.

10. Hamilton, "Marriage," 560.

11. Hamilton, "Marriage," 560.

12. The "Wisdom Literature" category is commonly applied to Job, Psalms, Proverbs, Ecclesiastes, and the Song of Songs along with the deuterocanonical books Sirach
and Wisdom of Solomon.

13. See, for example, Prov 5:18–20; 6:29; 12:4; 18:22; 19:14; 30:19; 31:10–31.

a dripping faucet,[14] yet nowhere does it counsel the wife on what she is to do when she must share the home with a brutish and obnoxious husband.

The Song of Songs broadens the scope of our perspective on marriage. Unlike Proverbs, the Song of Songs includes a woman's point of view. This is a passionate love song in which a young bride and groom celebrate their reciprocal erotic love. Especially prominent in this rhapsody is the woman's passion for her lover. She is the one who seeks him not vice versa (Song 3:1–4; 5:6–8), and her recollections of his attractive features are given prominence. The Song extols not fertility, nor the legal aspect of marriage, nor the institution of the family, but rather human love with all its passion and delights.[15]

In the New Testament era, marriage is presented in a monogamous fashion. Jews, Greeks, and Romans were, for the most part, monogamous,[16] though it was common for Greek and Roman males to take mistresses and even young male lovers.[17] Few could afford to be polygamous.

This complex, diverse, and often contradictory presentation of marriage in the Bible may tempt you to throw up your hands and surrender your pursuit of a good marriage. I have presented this information not to confuse but to encourage you: The Bible is not a rule book that neatly lays out what to do in every situation. Instead, the Bible offers illustrative stories about human life in its complexity as lived before God. The richness of the Bible makes it a powerful learning tool that nurtures your spiritual growth. By refraining from easy answers or pat advice, the Bible instead compels and prompts you to acquire wisdom.[18]

## Is "Normal" Normal?

The second misconception is to assume our cultural norms for marriage are normal for everyone. Cultures often shape how we interpret and apply biblical texts and scriptural principles. Consider, for example, that the Bible teaches a wife is to honor her husband (Eph 5:33). How a wife expresses honor to her husband is culturally defined. A couple in a traditional Asian culture may express honor in ways that a modern and

14. Prov 17:1, 14; 19:13; 21:9, 19; 25:24; 27:15–16; 30:23
15. Hamilton, "Marriage," 567.
16. Myers, "Marriage," 694.
17. Johnson, *Sexuality*, 2022.
18. See Enns, *How the Bible Actually Works*, 2020.

egalitarian northern European would find insulting and oppressive to women. The reverse is also very true. A northern European's way of communicating honor could be interpreted as shameful and degrading to those from other cultures. Or consider the biblical mandate, "Husbands, love your wives as Christ loved the church."[19] In some Western cultures, this love for one's wife is given public expression through holding hands, showing affection, or even kissing in public. However, if these same expressions of love were shown in some Middle Eastern countries, you could find yourself in jail for such "shameless and disrespectful behavior."

Take, for another example, the modern American idea of romantic marriage. Our expectations about romantic love in marriage are relatively new innovations, brought about by advances in living standards, technology, and science. While husbands and wives of centuries past no doubt loved one another, it can be seriously doubted they had any concept of a weekly "date night," as necessary as that may be to couples in the twenty-first century. They did, however, have culturally relevant ways of developing their marriages that may seem odd to us today. What we are talking about when we talk about biblical marriages is, at best, a biblically informed and culturally shaped discussion.

## Is Something Wrong with Her?

The third misconception is to assume marriage is for everyone. It's not. Unfortunately, the tendency is to assume if someone is not married, something must be wrong with them, or they just haven't found the right person yet. Perhaps they are called to be single; this too is a gift from God and is equal in calling, value, and worth to marriage.[20] We should celebrate those called to be single just as we celebrate those called into marriage. Both are worthy lifestyles. Paul was clear about this in 1 Corinthians 7:1–40. For those called to be single, whether that calling is for a season or for a lifetime, God provides other means of grace to bring about a rich and fulfilling life. We only need to look at Jesus, Paul,[21]

---

19. Eph 5:25
20. Matt 19:11–12; 1 Cor 7:8–9; Rev 14:1–4
21. I Cor 7:7

Anna,[22] Jeremiah,[23] John the Baptist,[24] and perhaps Nehemiah and Daniel to see examples of rich, fulfilling lives outside the call to marriage.

## Does This Church Focus on My Family?

The fourth misconception happens when the church is reduced to a family ministry center. There are no doubts about it; the church needs to do everything it can to help disciples of Jesus build healthy family relationships. The church does this by keeping the gospel front and center and calling men and women, husbands, wives, young people, and children to faithfully follow Jesus Christ. When men are transformed followers of Jesus they become better men, husbands, fathers, brothers, and neighbors. When women are transformed followers of Jesus they become better women, wives, mothers, sisters, and neighbors. However, when the church is reduced to a family ministry center, it ceases being the church in its fullness. Yes, the church should enrich marriages and families, but sometimes following Jesus will cost you dearly, for he comes before all other relationships.[25] We must keep the main thing the main thing. And the gospel is the main thing.

## Does this Marriage Make Me Look Fit?

Finally, a fifth misconception is to reduce marriage to a kind of "proof" of your fitness for leadership. When this happens, your spouse and family can become objects to use and not subjects to love. While your family is an example of your life, character, and leadership,[26] you must not reduce them to narcissistic extensions of your ego and mere "examples" of your leadership worthiness. If you reduce your marriage to nothing more than a public performance, driven by the sole motive of "we must be examples," you risk turning these relationships into objects of exchange like commodities. You try to validate your leadership by trading on your reputation as a family man or woman. Your loved ones become objects utilized in your self-serving pursuit of position and power. Marriage is

22. Luke 2:36–38
23. Jer 1:1–9
24. John 3:22–30
25. Matt 8:18–22; 10:34–39; Luke 14:25–27; 1 Cor 7:12–16
26. 1 Tim 3:1–13; Titus 1:5–16

not a display case. Marriage is a call to self-emptying and self-sacrificing love that overcomes self-exaltation and enthrones humility as your chief virtue. Your spouse is a person to build up through love, not an object upon which to build your leadership platform.

## Now, Concerning Marriage

Healthy men and women create healthy marriages. Proverbs offers wisdom to help you become healthy and to create a healthy marriage. This wisdom is built around the concept of nobility. Keep in mind that Proverbs is written as King Solomon's guidance to his sons, the heirs to the throne. Consequently, the character, behavior, and responsibilities of kings are highlighted at least thirty-two times in Proverbs.[27] As a training regimen for leaders, Proverbs seeks to build leaders of royal, noble character with the virtuous king and queen as the ideal embodiments of the noble person. Let's look more closely at these passages and what they teach us about noble character.

## Nobility

> He who is noble plans noble things, and on noble things he stands.
>
> —ISAIAH 32:8

*Le Morte D'Arthur*[28] is Sir Thomas Malory's unique version of the legends of King Arthur. First published in 1485, *Le Morte D'Arthur* is a story of love, adventure, chivalry, treachery, and death. Malory's vivid prose style captured the imagination as he recounted Mordred's treason, the knightly exploits of Tristan, Lancelot's fatally divided loyalties, Lancelot's love for Guinevere, and the quest for the Holy Grail. Most of the people who bought the book were members of the classes below the nobility who wanted to read books like Malory's to learn how to think, dress, talk, and act like the nobility.[29] Proverbs functions in a similar way. When it addresses kings and nobles, it is there not just for kings and nobles but also for all to learn to think, talk, and act nobly.

---

27.  Prov 1:1; 8:15; 14:28, 35; 16:10, 12, 13, 14, 15; 19:12; 20:2, 8, 26, 28; 21:1; 22:11, 29; 24:21; 25:1, 2, 3, 5, 6; 29:4, 14; 30:22, 27, 28, 31; 31:3, 4

28.  Malory and Armstrong. *Morte Darthur*, 2009.

29.  Special thanks Dorsey Armstrong, PhD. for this insight.

The Hebrew term *nādîb* appears twenty-seven times in the Old Testament. The English Standard Version translates it as "prince" eleven times.[30] Take Psalms 47:9, for example, where "princes of the peoples gather as the people of the God of Abraham," recognizing God's exalted domain. Proverbs 17:7 warns that fools and false speech do not befit a "prince." Another ten times, *nādîb* is translated as noble, encapsulating the essence of uprightness and just governance. In Proverbs 8:16, the passage extols the guiding role of *nādîb* in the rule of princes, imparting a sense of wisdom and fairness to those in positions of authority. Similarly, Proverbs 17:26 states that punishing the noble for their integrity runs contrary to what is virtuous and right. Moreover, Isaiah 32:5 reveals, "The fool will no more be called noble, nor the scoundrel said to be honorable." emphasizing the intertwined nature of nobility and wisdom. Four times it is translated as "willing,"[31] points to a profound sense of readiness and dedication, such as when Moses collected contributions for the construction of the tabernacle from "all who were of a willing (*nādîb*) heart" (Exod 35:22); or when David, after being confronted for crimes of adultery and murder,[32] cried to the Lord, "Restore to me the joy of your salvation, and uphold me with a willing (*nādîb*) spirit" (Ps 51:12). Finally, the word is translated twice as "generous" (Exod 35:5), "Whoever is of a generous (*nādîb*) heart, let him bring the Lord's contribution: gold, silver, and bronze," and Proverbs 19:6, "Many seek the favor of a generous (*nādîb*) man, and everyone is a friend to a man who gives gifts." Whether used as a noun[33] or an adjective,[34] the word describes one who is generous, willing, noble, and inclined to do what is right.

Throughout scripture, God's intention in salvation is to restore the noble dignity that was stripped from us when Adam and Eve turned from God's way.[35] God's ennobling grace is expressed in Exodus 19:6, where God declares his intent that the whole nation of Israel is to be "a kingdom of priests to me."[36] The word kingdom (*mamlākâ*) includes the idea of royal dignity. In the New Testament, the Gospel restores royal dignity to

---

30. 1 Sam 2:8; Job 12:21; 21:28; Pss 47:9; 107:40; 113:8; 118:9; 146:3; Prov 17:7; Song 6:12

31. Exod 35:22; 1 Chr 28:21; 2 Chr 29:31; Ps 51:12

32. 2 Sam 11–12

33. As when referring to a prince or a noble

34. As when referring to the quality of one's character as willing or generous

35. Gen 3

36. This is mentioned as well in 1 Pet 2:5; Rev 1:6; 5:10; 20:6.

even the most debased and abused among us, crowning us as a kingdom of priests.[37] In Proverbs, this noble quality is the distinguishing feature of men and women.

## A Man of Noble Character

The noble man, according to the Proverbs, is the ideal standard of manhood, a timeless model that transcends societal divisions, calling kings, servants, and friends alike to embody this noble character. Wisdom is the guiding principle of his existence, for by wisdom, "kings reign and rulers decree what is just" (Prov 8:15–16). His words are judicious, for his mouth refrains from sin in matters of judgment (Prov 16:10). His actions are trained by wisdom, leading him on the path of justice and righteousness, for "it is an abomination to kings to do evil, for the throne is established by righteousness" (Prov 16:12) and "By justice a king builds up the land" (Prov 29:4). Walking in wisdom brings him favor and opens doors of opportunity, for even a humble servant finds favor in the eyes of the king when dealing wisely (Prov 14:35), and the one who loves purity of heart, and whose speech is gracious, will have the king as his friend (Prov 22:11).

The man of noble character develops self-awareness, endeavoring to comprehend, harness, and rightly direct his masculine impulses. He recognizes that his wrath, if unbridled, can unleash destruction, yet his favor, when bestowed with wisdom, is akin to the life-giving rains of spring (Prov 16:14–15; also 19:12; 20:2). Displaying a humble demeanor (Prov 15:33; 18:12; 22:4), he embraces genuine meekness, where his strength is under careful control. Instead of seeking to dominate or control others, he exercises control over himself. Consequently, he employs his strength to remove evil and oppression (Prov 20:8, 26). Rooted in righteousness (Prov 24:4–5) and upheld by unwavering love and fidelity (Prov 20:28), he embodies nobility and virtue.

This man of noble walks humbly in the fear of the Lord (Prov 24:21). He carries within himself a sense of humble dignity, fully aware that he is not solely in control of his fate. He is not "his own man." He is God's man. This man does not exploit his power and position for his own gratification. Instead, he dedicates himself to the service of others, seeking to uplift and support them with the gifts he possesses. His heart is attuned

37. 1 Pet 2:5

to the needs of the less fortunate, and he stands as a guardian and protector for the poor and the powerless (Prov 29:14). Through his actions, he exemplifies the true essence of virtue, compassion, and kindness.

This man of noble character is no shallow lightweight, for he cultivates depth of heart and mind, for "It is the glory of God to conceal things, but the glory of kings is to search things out. As the heavens for height, and the earth for depth, so the heart of kings is unsearchable" (Prov 25:2–3). The fortitude of his character is shown in his astute and thoughtful planning, which gives security and stability to those he leads. People trust him because he thinks through his plans and makes provisions to accomplish them. In doing so, he ignites confidence and assurance among his followers, who willingly trust his ability to lead with wisdom and prudence.

> My son, do not lose sight of these—keep sound wisdom and discretion, and they will be life for your soul and adornment for your neck. Then you will walk on your way securely, and your foot will not stumble. If you lie down, you will not be afraid; when you lie down, your sleep will be sweet. Do not be afraid of sudden terror or of the ruin of the wicked, when it comes, for the Lord will be your confidence and will keep your foot from being caught. (Prov 3:21–26)

To a noble man, the value of healthy relationships is paramount. He understands the perils of associating with evil companions (Prov 1:8–19), those dishonest individuals who sow discord and the cunning whisperer who drives a wedge between close friends (Prov 16:28). He steers clear of befriending those with deceitful hearts and dishonest ways for he knows that no good can come from such associations (Prov 16:30; 17:20). Instead, he deliberately surrounds himself with wise and discerning individuals (Prov 14:35; 16:13; 22:11), for he knows that "whoever walks with the wise becomes wise, but the companion of fools will suffer harm" (Prov 13:20). By seeking out the company of the wise, he nurtures his own growth in wisdom and understanding. Shallow friendships and flattery hold no appeal for this noble man, for he delights in the company of those who embody honesty and truthfulness. As the scriptures remind us, "righteous lips are the delight of a king, and he loves him who speaks what is right" (Prov 16:13).

## A Woman of Noble Character

The depiction of a strong, capable woman in Proverbs 31:10–31 arouses varying reactions. A common reaction is that this "woman of excellence" is unrealistic. Consequently, women can feel this is one more place where they are being held to an unattainable standard.

A second objection about this passage is that it reinforces the stereotyped saying that "a woman's place is in the home." This interpretation is built on a cultural assumption rooted in the industrial revolution, which introduced factories as centers for work. Prior to the industrial revolution, homes were a primary center of work. Men generally did not drive to work; they typically walked to their field or shed. The whole family was employed in the family business. The wife played a central role in the economic survival of the family. So, the idea that a woman's place is in the home would not be relevant because both men and women generally worked at home.

Rather than being a sexist passage advocating that women stay at home, Proverbs 31:10–31 is a celebration of strong women, inviting them to fill the world with the benefits of their strength. It begins by asking, "Who can find a strong woman?—her value is far above rubies."[38] While typically translated as "excellent wife" (ESV, NASB), "a woman of excellence" (LEB), "competent wife" (CEB), "capable wife" (NRSV), and "a wife of noble character" (NIV), the literal translation is "strong woman." It is the same phrase used in Proverbs 12:4, "An excellent wife is the crown of her husband," and in Ruth 3:11, when Boaz acknowledges that all the fellow townsmen recognize Ruth as "a worthy woman," "a woman of noble character." (NIV)

The word for wife ( 'iššâ) is the most common word for "woman" and "wife" in the Hebrew Bible.[39] It can be translated as woman, wife, or female, depending on the context. In the context of Proverbs 31:10–31, it is clear the passage is talking about a strong woman who is a good wife. However, it is important to note that she is not a strong woman because she is a good wife; she is a good wife because she is a strong woman.

The word used here for strong (*hayil*) appears approximately 246 times in the Hebrew Bible. It can mean strength, power, might, capability, skill, valor, or wealth. It can mean to show oneself strong, to display

---

38. Goldingay, *Proverbs*, 153.
39. McComiskey, "137 אִשָּׁה, (issa)," 59.

valor.[40] It can also refer to an army, troop, or warrior.[41] It often refers to virtue, uprightness, integrity, and fitness, related to men of capacity,[42] or to virtuous woman.[43] It can even refer to the strength of a tree,[44] or function as a poetic reference to its fruit.[45] This single word opens a window into the world of the noble, strong woman. She is an incredible find, far more valuable than precious jewels.

Proverbs 31:10–31 is the only alphabetical poem in Proverbs. Alphabetical poems are also known as acrostics. they are compositions in which the first letters of successive lines or stanzas follow the alphabet, and they may spell out a word or a motto. Here in Proverbs, the first line begins with the Hebrew equivalent of A (*aleph*), the second with B (*bet*), and so on until it reaches the last of the twenty-two letters of the Hebrew alphabet (*tav*). The Hebrew prophets and poets often used an alphabetical acrostic as a poetic or memory device.[46] You could say the alphabetical poem of Proverbs 31:10–31 covers the subject of the strong woman from A to Z.[47]

A woman of noble character is worth more than any amount of money, and she knows her worth. She is strong and secure (Prov 31:10) and her husband is not intimidated by her strength. Her husband trusts in her (Prov 31:11), praises her, and calls her blessed (Prov 31:28). He recognizes her worth and exalts her above all other women (Prov 31:29). And this man is no slouch either. He is a trusted leader in the land as well (Prov 31:23). The passage drives home the point: strong men are not intimidated by strong women. Rather, they celebrate them. Only weak men are intimidated by strong women. Strong woman, know your worth.

This strong, noble woman is trustworthy (Prov 31:11). She brings good to those around her, especially to her closest relationships. She does them good and not harm (Prov 31:12). She has a strong work ethic. She is not afraid to work. She is a capable businesswoman who excels in leadership and management (Prov 31:13–22). She is a source of strength for her husband, and he trusts her (Prov 31:23). She makes plans and provisions

40. Num 24:18; Pss 60:14; 108:14
41. Mounce, *Expository Dictionary*, 933.
42. Gen 47:6; Exod 18:21, 25
43. Ruth 3:11; Prov 12:4; 31:10
44. Joel 2:22
45. Gesenius and Tregelles, *Lexicon*, 275.
46. See Pss 9; 10; 25; 34; 37; 111; 112; 119; 145; Prov 31:10–31; Lam 1–4; and Nah 1
47. Goldingay, *Proverbs*, 155–56.

for the future. She faces the future with confidence (Prov 31:25). This noble woman is a capable teacher of wisdom (Prov 31:26) and an attentive overseer of her household (Prov 31:27). Her nobility reaches every corner of society, for she is generous and compassionate to the poor (Prov 31:20).

The noble woman is godly, strong, wise, trustworthy, capable, confident, and generous at home and in the marketplace. She remains regal among the powerful and the powerless. Indeed, the woman of noble character is worthy of praise (Prov 31:28–29), she fears the Lord (Prov 31:30), and her life is a testimony to others (Prov 31:31). Her character is her greatest legacy. Is it any wonder that her children arise and call her blessed, and her husband says, "Many women have done excellently, but you surpass them all" (Prov 31:29)?

## Noble Marriages

There is a beautiful tradition in Eastern Orthodox Christian weddings that symbolizes the nobility of marriage. The priest places crowns upon the heads of the bride and groom, asking God to "crown them in glory and in honor." The crowns, joined together by a ribbon, illustrate how the husband and wife have entered a divine mystery of Christ and the church. God crowns them with glory and honor, and Christ now establishes them as king and queen of their home, which they are to rule with wisdom, justice, mercy, and integrity. This ceremony captures the idea that nobility is intrinsic to marriage and that noble marriage requires men and women of noble character.

No other arena of life requires noble character more than marriage. Disagreements and conflicts are common to all human relationships. These are normal and can even be helpful for our growth and for the depth and strength of our relationships. Marriage takes it to a whole other level by digging into the deepest levels of human identity, worth, pride, and self-centeredness. The digging removes the dirt within us and reveals the gold. Sometimes this digging reveals your issues that need to be healed or acknowledged with your partner, and sometimes with the help of a qualified therapist. Conflict is not always harsh or destructive. Conflicts can deepen intimacy if responded to with acts of compassion and reconciliation. However, sometimes people react with destructive behavior, unleashing pain and violence from deep within on those around them. If your relationship becomes violent or destructive, seek legal and professional help immediately.

A friend once told me, "Family has got to be spiritual. Nothing else in this world has so much power for damaging or healing the human soul as family." I could not agree more. Many of the things we call "the ills of society" are the sicknesses contracted in the family. Healthy individuals are best cultivated in healthy families. The key phrase in the previous sentence is "best cultivated," for there are other ways of self-cultivation outside the family. Friends who are closer than family, a local church, or any relationship that allows humans *to be* and *be other*. In a community of love and embrace, each person is invited to offer oneself and so become oneself. In such a community, the first words are always, "Welcome." That has been my experience, having grown up in a very dysfunctional home. I found healing outside my family for the damage done within it. However, I would have preferred a healthy family.

Marriage is also a mystery (Eph 5:22–32). This is not to say that it is a difficult conundrum or impossible to figure out. The word used in this text for mystery refers to a divine secret that has been revealed.[48] Marriage serves as a living icon of Christ and the church. As such, in marriage we satisfy not only the earthly needs of our secular existence, but also the purpose for which we were created. We participate in the ministry of reconciliation between man and woman, husband and wife, parents and children, brother and brother, sister and sister, God and creation. This is a reconciliation of relationships that were torn asunder in the Garden of Eden. Through marriage we have a foretaste of the eternal life God intends for all creation.[49]

Marriage is also a calling.[50] While most people are called to marriage, not everyone is called to walk this path. The fact that Jesus and Paul were both unmarried and celibate was not lost on the early church.

48. μυστήριον, ου n: the content of that which has not been known before but which has been revealed to an in-group or restricted constituency—'secret, mystery.' ὑμῖν δέδοται γνῶναι τὰ μυστήρια τῆς βασιλείας τῶν οὐρανῶν 'the knowledge of the secrets of the kingdom of heaven has been given to you' Matt 13:11. There is a serious problem involved in translating μυστήριον by a word which is equivalent to the English expression 'mystery,' for this term in English refers to a secret which people have tried to uncover but which they have failed to understand. In many instances μυστήριον is translated by a phrase meaning 'that which was not known before,' with the implication of its being revealed at least to some persons. See Louw and Nida, in *Greek–English Lexicon*, 344.

49. Meyendorff. *Marriage*, 2000.

50. I Cor 7:17–40

While Jesus never preached the abolition of marriage, his followers often interpreted his view of the married life as a hindrance to the highest levels of spiritual commitment, as he called on his followers to abandon their families to follow him (Luke 18:29). Paul's advice in 1 Corinthians 7 is difficult to shoehorn into modern evangelicalism approach to marriage as well. Many early Christian writers also adopted the belief that sexual renunciation, in all its forms, was superior to married life. Some of their beliefs and practices we may find quite foreign to our modern sensibilities, yet it was their way of following Jesus. Some are called to marriage, and others are called to other forms of community and living out their faith in Jesus, and this too is deeply rooted in the biblical tradition.

Both marriage and singleness (in all its manifestations) share a greater purpose. Those called to singleness do not deny the existence, importance, appeal, and joy of married life. They do, however, deny that these should rule the heart. Those called to be single remind us to look to God to fulfill our deepest longings, for God is greater than all things, including marriage. Those called to singleness infuse all of creation with the fragrance of devotion to God. Those called to marriage are called to return to the first human relationship, to heal what was broken in Eden, by participating in the mystery of Christ and the church. Marriage says to the man and woman, "If you will reconcile this relationship by God's grace, other relationships that have broken apart in the wake of humanity's original disobedience can also find healing and reconciliation." This too exudes the fragrance of devotion and hope. Those called to singleness point us upward toward God as the source of all joy and fulfillment. Those called to marriage point us outward to our human community and call us to reconciliation. Together, the single and the married call creation to union, reconciliation, healing, and salvation, that Christ may be all in all.

## Choosing Nobility

Good marriages don't just happen. Building a healthy marriage is hard work. Contrary to the fairytales, no one just lives "happily ever after." Nothing magical happens during the wedding ceremony to create "happy ever after." However, something transformative does take place. The man and woman begin a lifetime of choosing "I do." Every day of your marriage, you will be asked, "Do you take this woman to be your wife?" "Do you take this man to be your husband?" Your daily choices are the incremental steps that eventually build a good marriage. Your marriage begins with a choice, "I choose you above all others." Your marriage grows strong because you keep making that same choice every day.

The second choice you must make is equally important, for not only must you choose to take the person you are married to, but you must also choose what kind of person you will be. Here, again, we find wisdom in Proverbs.

## Noble Choices for Husbands

A noble character is for all men and women, regardless of their marital status. There are, however, specific choices married men and women must make that affect their marriage. Here, we will explore the noble choices a husband must make. Later, we will explore the noble choices wives are to make.

Your first noble choice as a husband is to cherish your wife. She is, after all, a gift from God (Prov 19:14) and "He who finds a wife finds a good thing and obtains favor from the Lord" (Prov 18:22). St. Paul tells husbands to love their wives as Christ loves the church, and this love is transformative. When a husband cherishes his wife, this love is healing and transformative, just as Christ's love for his church.

Our English word "husband" comes to us through the Old Norse word *húsbóndi*. The original sense of the verb was "to till" or "to cultivate." Unlike English, the Hebrew language uses one word for husband and man and one word for woman and wife. The context determines how it is translated. In the creation story in Genesis 1–2, man was placed in a garden "to cultivate it and to keep it" (Gen 2:15, LEB). The word translated here as "cultivate" is the Hebrew word *'ābad*. This word has a variety of meanings. In some instances, the verb carries the idea of "to serve" (e.g., Gen 29:15; Exod 1:13; Ps 22:30). In other instances, the term carries the idea of "to worship or honor" (e.g., Gen 2:15; Exod 3:12; 2 Kgs 17:41). But the verb also carries the basic sense of toil or working the ground (e.g., Gen 2:5; Deut 21:4; Zech 13:5).[51] The word translated "keep it" (*šāmar*) means to keep, to watch, or to guard, as one keeps a garden well-served and protected (Gen 2:15; 3:24), or to watch over and protect a flock (Gen 30:31), or to guard and keep secure a house (Eccl 12:3). This is the idea behind the word husbandry, which refers to the cultivation of

---

51. Williams, "Agriculture," 2014.

plants and animals. To be husband to a wife is to cherish, serve, honor, cultivate, watch over, protect, and guard her.

The second noble choice is to be a wise man rather than a foolish child. Most wives will tell you there is still a mischievous little boy lurking beneath the surface of most men. I think all men are afflicted with some level of the Peter Pan Syndrome. We don't want to grow up. But grow up we must. Growing old does not automatically mean growing wise. There are plenty of old fools out there. A man who refuses to listen to wisdom may grow old, but he will not grow wise. This man will become a foolish child hidden within the body of a foolish old man (Prov 9:6). Growing old is inevitable, growing up is a choice.

The third noble choice for husbands is to be responsible. If you do not intentionally choose to be responsible, you will almost by nature run away from or ignore your responsibilities. Since Adam in the Garden of Eden, we men have avoided personal responsibility and cast blame on women, God, and everyone else for our problems.[52] Wisdom teaches us the liberating power of taking responsibility for ourselves, our marriages, our families, and everything else God has entrusted to us (Prov 27:8). It's your life and your marriage. You need to own it.

The fourth noble choice for husbands is self-control over controlling others (Prov 25:28; 29:8, 11). Too often, biblical teaching about authority and submission is misunderstood and twisted to become a tool for weak men to be domineering and controlling. Folly teaches the fool to serve himself and to control others, while wisdom teaches the wise to control himself and to serve others. Domineering, demeaning, controlling, and abusive behavior is for ignoble and insecure men. This behavior is unworthy of a noble man.

## Noble Choices for Wives

In the same manner, wives, too, must make wise and noble choices. First, a noble wife chooses to be the crown of glory in her marriage (Prov 12:4). She is acutely aware of the power of her influence. She knows she can be a crown upon the head or cancer in the bones of her husband (Prov 12:4). The wise noble woman learns to use her influence to give wisdom, counsel, understanding, and insight to her husband. This is why he who

---

52. Gen 3

finds a noble wife "finds a good thing and obtains favor from the Lord" (Prov 18:22).

Second, a noble wife chooses to build up her husband (Prov 14:1). Wives, never underestimate your power to build up or tear down your spouse. This ability is not because he is weak but because you have such strength and influence. Your influence on your husband is unmatched in any other relationship. You are one with him; your bond with him is deep. His ego may be strong and tough to outsiders, but to you, it is delicate and vulnerable. A single glance from you can say more than a thousand words. A look of admiration and a kind word of affirmation carries such power that your husband can face any challenge when he is strengthened by you, his wife. You also have the power to use cutting words and contemptuous looks to eviscerate him. You are Eve-kind, life-giver of all. Your words have the power of life and death (Prov 18:21). You can build up or tear down your husband. A wise, noble wife chooses to build him up.

Third, a noble wife chooses to embrace her beauty. I am not talking about being pretty or looking good or giving in to the cheap imitation of beauty that is vanity (Prov 6:25; 11:22; 31:30). Beauty is not a character-istic of a woman's appearance; it is a fundamental attribute of her nature. It is a grace upon her life as the image-bearer of He Who is Beauty Itself. This beauty flows from the noble woman, beautifying and ennobling all around her.

Women seem to be graced by God to be stewards of the gift of beauty; they beautify everything they touch. Most men I know could live in a cave for thirty years and never do much to beautify it. They may build shelves and boxes for storage or furniture for comfort and a place to eat. But your typical man hasn't improved much when it comes to beautifying his cave since the time when of our ancestors painted stick figures on the walls.

However, put a woman in that musty cave and in a week, it will have the imprint of beauty all over it. Ladies, you beautify life by your existence. You beautify your home with your touch. You beautify rela-tionships by pressing for authenticity and transparency. You beautify society and the workplace with dignity, nobility, and compassion. We are all better because of you. It is a powerful and life-changing gift you have. Steward it carefully. When the power of your beauty is tainted by broken ways, beauty becomes vanity, which is ugly and destructive. When your beauty is used to bring dignity to others, you give life. You can be Beauty, or you can be the Beast. Choose Beauty.

This beauty exhibits God's eternal design.[53] He told Moses to make the priestly garment "for glory and for beauty."[54] We are attracted to the beauty of the Lord; it entices us to worship him.[55] The Royal Wedding Psalm (Ps 45) declares, "All glorious is the princess in her chamber, with her robes interwoven with gold" (v. 13) and "the king will desire your beauty" (v.11). In God's promise of redemption, he says, "I will give you beauty for ashes."[56] Beauty is integral to God's character and his work of creation and redemption. I think Fyodor Dostoyevsky was onto something profound when he wrote, "Beauty will save the world."

Finally, a noble wife chooses to be content. Proverbs 21:9 states, "It is better to live on a corner of a roof than in a house shared with a contentious woman" (NASB). You can be content, or you can be contentious, but you cannot be both.[57] Contentment is not complacency. Contentment is an emotional state of satisfaction and a mental state of ease in your life situation. It does not mean that you settle for bad things because "it is your lot in life." Contentment is about being free from avarice, that insatiable desire to have more and more. Contentment destroys the uncontrollable longing to accumulate more attention, more power, or more things. Contentment silences the condemning voice in your head that says, "You are not enough! Look at you! Your nose. Your weight. Your hair. Your skin. Your teeth. You are not as pretty or as perfect as others. You are not enough! You do not have enough! You need more attention! You need more things! More house! More shopping! More shoes!" Contentment slays this tormenting voice. It frees you from the competition of keeping up with your neighbors. It frees you from peer pressure and feeling like a victim. Contentment empowers you to help others. Contentment restores praise and gratitude to your heart. No wonder the scriptures says, "Godliness with contentment is great gain."[58] The wise, noble woman chooses contentment, and she is empowered because of it.

53. Pss 24:4; 96:6

54. Exod 28:2, 40

55. Ps 27:4; 50:2; 96:6

56. Isa 61:3, KJV

57. Prov 19:13; 21:9, 19; 25:24; 27:15–16

58. 1 Tim 6:6

## Five Propositions on Marriage and Leadership

More than thirty-five years of marriage coupled with a daily reading of Proverbs has stripped away from me the five misunderstandings about marriage and leadership discussed above. I propose we exchange those misconceptions with the following five propositions on marriage and leadership.

### The Depth of Heart-change Caused in Marriage Helps Root Out Self-exaltation in Leadership

> Pride goes before destruction, and a haughty spirit before a fall.
>
> —Proverbs 16:18

The temptation of pride and self-exaltation is real for everyone, regardless of their stage or station in life. It is especially dangerous for leaders. When pride becomes a stronghold in a leader, it becomes hubristic or narcissistic, destructive not only for the leader as an individual but also for the whole organization. Marriage should play a critical role in rooting out the temptation of self-exaltation.

Hubris is a grandiose sense of self, characterized by disrespectful attitudes toward others and a misperception of one's place in the world. Although hubris people share grandiosity with narcissists, hubris is more than a manifestation of pathological narcissism; it is an acquired condition caused when an individual attains a position of significant power and then overestimates their abilities and significance. Hubris is a reactive disorder that grows to fruition when an unhealthy leader obtains power in an unhealthy organizational system that lacks constraints on how a leader exercises power.[59] Narcissism, on the other hand, is a personality disorder.

Narcissistic Personality Disorder (NPD) is one of 10 personality disorders recognized in the American Psychiatric Association's Diagnostic and Statistical Manual of Mental Disorders.[60] The hallmark signs of NPD read like a laundry list of what not to look for in a significant other: an inflated sense of self-importance, grandiosity, self-absorption, vanity,

59. Asad and Sadler-Smith. "Differentiating Leader Hubris," in Leadership 16, no. 1 (February 2020): 39–61.

60. Lu, *Mental Disorders*, 2022.

a lack of empathy for others, and a deep, incessant need for constant attention, adulation, and power.

Research presented to the American Association of Christian Counselors in 2015 found that pastors are 500–3000 percent more likely to be narcissistic than the general population.[61] You read that correctly, 500–3000 percent. According to the research, the ministerial profession attracts individuals with narcissistic personality disorder as a way to supply their psychological needs. The authors assert, "Ministry attracts narcissists for the same reasons that elementary schools and playgrounds attract pedophiles: these institutions provide access to victims."[62] Clinical psychologist and neuro-theologian James Wilder states, "Virtually all Christians will experience a narcissistic pastor during their lifetime."[63] The research of Ball and Puls found that 30–90 percent of churches in the Western world are run by narcissists. Wilder concluded that because of the pervasiveness of narcissistic leaders in pastoral ministry, Christian churches are to a significant extent "unable to recognize personality disorders and may even find these disorders desirable in leaders."[64]

In *The Pandora Problem: Facing Narcissism in Leaders and Ourselves*, James Wilder asserts that narcissists "seem to lack something needed to be fully human. Scripture says that what is missing is *hesed*."[65] *Hesed* is a Hebrew word often translated as steadfast love, kindness, faithfulness, and loyalty. The core idea of this term relates to loyalty within a relationship, specifically the covenant between God and God's people. It denotes God's faithfulness to his people.[66] Wilder describes *hesed* as attachment love. "Attachment love is the kind of force that can form and transform character."[67] Wilder argues throughout the book that attachment love lived out in community is the solution to overcoming narcissism.

In the absence of community, Wilder argues, professional counseling has limited or no success in treating narcissists. Transformation cannot be done alone. It depends on a community rooted in *hesed*. The fundamental human community is the family. The foundational relationship in a family is the husband and wife.

61. Ball and Puls, "Narcissistic Personality Disorder in Pastors," 2015.

62. Ball and Puls, "Narcissistic Personality Disorder in Pastors," 2015.

63. Wilder, *Pandora Problem*, 17.

64. Ibid.

65. Wilder, *Pandora Problem*, 16.

66. Nettelhorst, "Love," 2014.

67. Wilder, *Pandora Problem*, 20.

In the New Testament, love is characterized as *agape*. *Agape* signi-fies the true and pure love of the Father for his Son (John 17:26), for his people (Gal 6:10), and for all humanity (John 3:16; Rom 5:8). The Bible declares the very nature of God is love (1 John 4:8, 16). Love is the law of the New Covenant (Rom 13:8–13). When we walk in love, we are walking in the light (1 John 2:10). When you betray the law of love, you enter into the darkness of self-deception.[68] Your view of reality becomes distorted. You begin to see the world in a way that justifies yourself and condemns others. This is what John is talking about in 1 John 2:9–11:

> Whoever says he is in the light and hates his brother is still in darkness. Whoever loves his brother abides in the light, and in him there is no cause for stumbling. But whoever hates his brother is in the darkness and walks in the darkness, and does not know where he is going, because the darkness has blinded his eyes.

The depth of heart-change by *agape* love in marriage helps root out self-exaltation, hubris, and narcissistic tendencies. This positively impacts one's character and leadership. For the marriage relationship to become a healing bond, both spouses must be committed to health and wholeness as individuals and as a couple. It is for this reason, I believe, that Proverbs celebrates both the man and the woman of noble character. Both the noble husband and the noble wife are equally committed to the path of wisdom; they feast at wisdom's banquet and listen to wisdom's voice. The way of wisdom in marriage heals the wounds of sin and the craving for self-exaltation.

## Married Leaders are to Model the Transformative Grace of Marriage

Marriage involves two individuals joining together in love to become one flesh. The grace of the Holy Spirit empowers this love and creates the union. This transformative love does not suppress the character of the individuals or the complexity of emotions, actions, joys, or struggles. It does, however, transform the bonds from mere human affection and pas-sion to something of grace, something from God. Marriage becomes a mystery from God (Eph 5:32).

---

68. 1 John 1:5—2:11

As "mystery," marriage is elevated above a merely pragmatic or legal institution. The contract made on earth between two people before the civil authorities has been transformed; it reflects and points to the kingdom of God. This is why, for the Christian believer, marriage is more than a civil or a moral agreement. As a mystery of the kingdom, marriage introduces humankind to the eternal love and joy of the Savior. As a mystery, it transcends and uplifts the two humans who are bound together. Marriage is to be an experience where partners do not struggle alone but rather strive together in communion with God, who has made the relationship holy and set apart for a divine purpose. In marriage, then, people are called to participate in the reality of the Holy Spirit, making all things new and granting the new covenant promise: Hearts of stone are replaced with hearts of flesh.[69] Marriage, like all the mysteries of God, is aimed at creating a new heart, a new life, a new humanity. And like all the mysteries of God, marriage is a calling to true life, true healing, and true humanity.

Leaders are called to be first in obedience in order to lead others to obedience. For leaders who are married, this means if you want to see marriages and families healed, you must go first as partakers of the transformation brought about by the mystery of marriage.

## The Marriage of a Leader Reflects the Heart and Character of the Leader

> He who finds a wife finds a good thing and obtains favor from the Lord.
>
> —Proverbs 18:22

The word "thing" is not in the Hebrew text of Proverbs 18:22. It is provided by the translators. The literal translation is better reflected in the Lexham English Bible, "He who finds a wife finds good." The wife is not called a thing; she is called good. The second part of the verse, "obtains favor from the Lord," repeats the words of Lady Wisdom in Proverbs 8:35: "Whoever finds me finds life and obtains favor from the Lord." Did you catch it? Finding a wife is on par with finding wisdom. After wisdom itself, the best of God's blessings is a wife, for in both finding a wife and in finding wisdom one "obtains favor from the Lord." The value of both wisdom and a wife is far above that of precious jewels (Prov 8:11; 31:10).

69. Ezek 36:22–28

If I could summarize the father's advice to his son in Proverbs in a single sentence, I would say, "Son, if you want to be wise, fear God and marry a strong woman."

Ancient Israel reached its political and economic apex under the leadership of King Solomon (c. 970–931 BCE). The tumultuous history of Israel that followed Solomon's reign started with the divided kingdoms of Israel and Judah (1 Kgs 12) and culminated in Judah's exile into Babylon (2 Kgs 25). Subsequently, Babylon fell and the Persian empire rose (c. 550–330 BCE). These political dynamics produced within the exiled Hebrew community a social crisis that could not be accommodated by old ways. The response in Proverbs was to emphasize the family as the vehicle for preserving the community's values.[70] Proverbs elevates the status of marriage and family, when guided by the wisdom of God, as the place where humanity becomes the best version of itself. This understanding of family carried over into the New Testament and the Christian tradition. The early church understood the family to be an incubator of godly love and the primary conduit for Christian formation.

Marriage, hemmed together by love, faithfulness, patience, kindness, persistence, and forgiveness, is a pathway of discipleship par excellence. It is here, in the covenant of marriage, that one discovers the joys and potential dangers of intimacy, tenderness, and vulnerability. Marriage is to be a place of learning, or relearning, to love and to trust through sharing life, experiencing conflict and misunderstanding, and yet reaching beyond the conflict to remain faithful, connected, and committed to the other. It is a calling to become one: To have one heart, one mind, one hope, one desire, one life, to be undivided in flesh and spirit.[71] This life, this mystery, can only happen through the life of the Holy Spirit living in each covenant partner.

Consequently, marriage is not a platform to prove your leadership worthiness. Rather, marriage is a gymnasium for disciples of Christ, an arena "in which the skills and arts of apprenticeship to Christ can be learned, practiced, and demonstrated through the power of the Holy Spirit."[72] This is why the marriage of a leader is so important. It is the best reflection and indicator of the leader's heart condition, and it is out of the heart that all the forces of life flow (Prov 4:23).

---

70. Belcher, *Finding Favour*, 11.

71. To paraphrase Tertullian when writing to his wife, see Hall, *Living Wisely*, 156.

72. Hall, *Living Wisely*, 158.

## Married Leaders Need the Wisdom of God to Navigate the Demands of Marriage and Leadership

Building a healthy marriage while in a leadership role is difficult work because you are experiencing not only the pressure and demands of marriage but also the pressures and demands of leadership. And these are happening at the same time. So yes, it is normal to feel overwhelmed if you are married and in leadership. And no, you are not a failure if you feel overwhelmed; you are just human. By placing such a high premium on marriage and family, the book of Proverbs helps you learn to deal wisely with the pressures and demands of leading while married.

A wise older pastor once told me, "Jeff, one day, everyone in your church will leave you. Those relationships are not permanent. Your wife and children will always be your wife and your children. They are your permanent relationships. Live in such a way that when all those people are gone from your life, your wife and kids still love you and want to be around you." This advice saved my marriage, my family, and my ministry. It reoriented my thinking and behavior and helped me deal with the demands of leadership, which might otherwise cause conflicts within me and in my most significant relationships.

Your position as a leader will end someday, but you, the person, will still be there. If you have confused your position with your person, the day after your position has ended will be a sad day indeed, for you will no longer know who you are. Sad not only for that day but for all the days preceding it, for they were poorly lived.

## When Both Spouses are Called to Leadership, They Should Seek to Outdo One Another in Showing Honor

While Proverbs is primarily written from a male perspective, its conclusion highlights a woman as the embodiment of a life of wisdom (Prov 31:10–31). This is a fitting conclusion to the whole book. Recall that Proverbs begins with wisdom personified *as* a woman (Prov 1:20–33; 8:4–36; 9:1–6). Now, here in the closing chapter, wisdom is personified *in* a woman, a woman of strength (Prov 31:10). The wisdom presented throughout Proverbs is gathered up and presented in a beautiful and practical presentation of wisdom embodied in this "excellent wife." The excellent wife is now canonized as a role model. Wise daughters aspire to be like her, wise sons seek to marry her, and all wise people aim to embody her virtues.[73]

If, as I have proposed in this chapter, marriage is the central human relationship, it is no wonder Proverbs culminates in a home focused on a wise woman with glimpses of her equally wise husband and their shared life. This poem of enthusiastic praise of the strong woman not only exalts the woman's astounding virtues; it also illustrates the life-giving relationship she shares with her husband. The poem contains three stanzas.

The first stanza declares her worth (Prov 31:10–12). The second stanza declares her works (Prov 31:13–27). The third stanza declares her praise (Prov 31:28–31). Each stanza progresses from her husband's trust *in* her (v. 11) to his political empowerment *by* her (v. 23) to his praise *of* her (v. 28). Though the division of labor and the precise tasks mentioned in 31:10–31 are not what are required in many parts of the world today, the character traits that are praised are still valuable. The specific tasks are not essential, but rather the excellent virtues of this woman and her husband are. Each makes significant contributions to their relationship, to their family, and to society. They are not in competition nor are they in conflict with one another. They are neither intimidated nor threatened by the strengths and abilities of the other. Rather, they seek to magnify one another. They are bound together in mutual love that strengthens and releases greater potential in one another. Who they are together is greater than the sum of who they are as individuals. They have become one.

## Conclusion

Marriage is not only an excellent place to raise kids; it is an excellent place to raise adults. At your wedding, you had no idea what you were getting into. Perhaps you have had some rough spots along the way. Maybe you are in a rough spot now. Maybe you have made some foolish decisions that have damaged your marriage. Do not lose heart. Hope is not lost. You still have the power to make wise choices. Take the next step in the right direction, just one step. It may be a phone call to a therapist. It may be an apology to a wounded spouse. Whatever the next right step is, take it. Then, after that, take the next right step. Then, after that, take the next right step.

---

73. Waltke and De Silva, *Shorter Commentary,* 432.

I have changed a lot since that dark night many years ago. I am learning to embrace it when God ambushes my selfishness and reveals my brokenness. I am learning to clamor for the way of humility rather than assert my rights, defend my position, or justify myself. I have come to see marriage differently. The change has been subtle, gradual, and imperceptible.

I did not realize it until a few weeks ago when I was asked to review notes for a global training program within our denomination addressing marriage and family. As I read the material, I had a sudden flash of memories. It was like microfilm from the archives department playing through my mind about all the things I have read over the years about marriage—all from within my Protestant background. I began to realize that because traditional Protestant theology does not include marriage as a sacrament, we run the risk of reducing marriage to a transactional agreement between two parties. No mystery to it. No "otherness" about it. Just two people making a mutually beneficial agreement.

Marriage is more than a transactional agreement. It is a divine mystery, a living icon of Christ and his church. The love, passion, and longing I have for union with my wife—union of spirit, soul, and body—is an echo of my soul's longing for union with Christ. When my soul's longing is fulfilled at the resurrection of the dead, marriage as an icon will cease to exist, not because it will be outdated but because it will be fulfilled. Creation will be fully healed and restored to its God; the two joined together in the song of the redeemed.[74] The icon fades into what was signified. Longing gives way to fulfillment. Promise and hope burst forth in all things becoming new. The shadow of marriage becomes the substance of what was longed for.

Marriage is about more than two people being joined together; it is about the human community becoming whole and holy unto the Lord. It is about healing the wound of death and destruction we inherited from our first parents. It is about love reaching into the deepest, darkest, and most fiercely protected citadels of the human heart and healing it with love, grace, and a persistent presence. It is here, in this house of ambush, that we see the healing and restorative power of grace incarnate in human flesh for the life of the world.

Perhaps my Protestant mind cannot utter the words, "Marriage is a sacrament," but my transformed heart, healed and being healed by the

---

74. Rev 4:1–11; 5:9–14; 14:1–5

grace-infused love of that woman—the one who captured my imagination more than thirty-five years ago—gladly confesses that marriage is sacramental. And like all means of grace, it is for the healing of the nations. I wish I had known this when I started. I am glad I know it now.

# 6

# Parents and Children

As a young, bi-vocational church planter, I aimed to leave a lasting impact on the world, all the while striving to be a devoted husband and father. I had aspirations of ministry greatness and visions of domestic bliss. Yet, the ideals and fantasies I clung to soon met the harsh reality of juggling multiple roles—husband, father, church planter, and employee. The gulf between my dreams and the unyielding truths of reality became all too apparent, and now reality was teaching me some hard lessons. It did not take long to discover that I was way over my head. I found myself ill-prepared for the roles of husband and father, wrestling to provide for my family on meager earnings, and wrestling further with the challenges of being a pastor. I was in a tight spot. The mounting pressure led to restless nights; my teeth clenched so tightly that my jaws ached for hours.

Self-doubt gnawed at me, questioning every aspect of my identity and the choices I had made. The weight of stress and anxiety bore down on me, exacting an emotional, mental, and physical toll. I began to lash out in anger at the slightest irritation. I was so volatile that I toyed with the idea of creating a T-shirt to warned others, "Danger: Contents Under Pressure!" as a fair and honest warning that I might explode at any moment.

The financial and ministry pressures were bad enough, but I had a larger issue I was dealing with: I was married with children. I felt slightly more confident about my marriage than I did about my parenting skills because, frankly, I had absolutely no parenting skills. I knew Debbie and

I loved each other enough that we could make it through about anything, but when it came to parenting, forget it. I was clueless. This only added to the pressure because I knew the biblical standards of marriage and parenting for ministers. So, if I failed as a parent, not only would I damage my kids for life, but I would also be out of a job. As they say, I was in a world of hurt. C.S. Lewis wisely observed, "God whispers to us in our pleasures, speaks in our conscience, but shouts in our pains: it is His megaphone to rouse a deaf world."[1] It is safe to say that God was shouting at me with his megaphone turned all the way up. He had to. I would not listen to anything else.

Parenting is hard work, and parenting while leading is even harder work. I cried out to God for wisdom to know how to parent while leading and to lead while parenting. I began reading books, attending seminars, and listening to anyone who promised to teach me how to focus on my family and to grow kids God's way. I read books with titles like the *Handbook for Biblical Parenting*, the *Christian Parenting Handbook*, and *What the Bible Says About Parenting* (this one promised me biblical principles for raising godly children). I wanted to learn "the Bible way to raise kids." I needed help. Every time I would look at one of my kids, I'd think, "I have no idea what I am doing here. I sure hope I don't mess up your entire life." I desperately wanted someone to tell me, "If you follow these rules, your kids will be perfect humans."

As I would eventually learn, most of these well-intentioned books taught parenting tactics, which may or may not be biblical, even though Bible verses were used to support their claims. I learned a lot of helpful rules and tools, but I needed more than rules and tools. I needed wisdom. You see, parenting is far more relational than some of these books tended to assume. I do not blame those books. I might read them differently today. But back then, I translated their parenting message into a set of static and transactional behaviors. For example, every time one of my children argued with me, I assumed it was their sinful nature in rebellion against God and his ordained authority in the home (that would be me). So, every time such arguments happened, I was to enact a certain type of discipline, and most often, it was supposed to be something called the "rod of correction"–but in our case, it was more like a wooden spoon. This discipline (or what my kids liked to call "punishment") was intended to ween those little sinners off their twisted behavior and teach them

1. Lewis, *Pain*, 92.

to submit to God's delegated authority in the home—which was me. I probably should not have read parenting books written by over-zealous Calvinists. But that's another story.

Parenting as a relationship is different from tactical and transactional advice. A relationship requires wisdom, not just rules, to thrive. Wisdom, not rules, will teach you the finely tuned but emotionally crucial distinctions. Is my child's behavior motivated by fear, anxiety, or misunderstanding? Or, in fact, by overt rebellion? Yet, though I should have been fine-tuning my awareness, I was too task driven and tone-deaf. I was trying to do parenting as someone does chores. The task needed to be done so I could check it off my to-do list. I have always loved checklists. I have been known to make checklists, even *after* I have done things, just so I can feel the excitement of checking items off that list. Well, parenting is not a checklist to be completed. Parenting is a relationship that is never done. My mental framework had to change. The idea that children are a gift[2] and parenting a relationship needed to take deep root.

Not only was I task-oriented, I was also time-oriented. I had a huge day planner for scheduling my every hour. Parenting as a relationship threw out my calendar, because the first thing children eat is time.

Parenting feels all-consuming because it is all consuming. There are seasons when you are stretched beyond your limits. You feel emotionally drained, mentally taxed, physically exhausted, and relationally strained. You have times when you feel like you are a failure, and you cannot go on. You cry out for just one quiet morning or one peaceful afternoon, or one full night of sleep. You have entered an alternate state of reality called parenthood: that joyous, painful, demanding, agonizing, fulfilling, and heart-wrenching condition where the days are long and the years are short.

Reality was also teaching me that leadership is demanding work. Like parenting, leadership also has its seasons when you are stretched beyond your limits. Unfortunately, for most leaders, the demanding seasons of parenting and the demanding seasons of leadership typically happen at the same time. The obligations are on a collision course. You are entrusted with the care, provision, protection, and love of a family. Yet, the demands of leadership do not take a vacation during school events or family crises. Nor do your children care that much about your work project, your incredible ministry opportunity, or your boss's phone call. If only you could clone yourself or create a few more hours in a day, you

2. Ps 127:3

could meet all the needs and obligations. However, cloning yourself or creating 29-hour days is not a reality—nor a strategy. You do not need more hours in your day; you need more wisdom in your life.

This is where Proverbs comes in to teach you how to gain a heart of wisdom and become skillful in life. Wisdom does not provide you a one-size-fits-all approach to the struggle for work-life balance. Instead, wisdom gives insight into your unique situation at this season of your life. You may never have work-life balance. What is that balance, anyway, and is it even possible? The goal is not work-life balance. The goal is to be skillful in both roles, as parent and leader. Let's face it, if you are not a skillful parent, more time with your kids may not necessarily help. However, skill as a parent, in the limited amounts of time you have, can pay huge dividends. Sometimes there is no difference between the abundance of time and the quality of time. Other times, there is a vast difference. Wisdom helps you see the difference and to recognize which is which.

## The Power of Family

> Grandchildren are the crown of the elderly, and
> the glory of children is their parents.
>
> —Proverbs 17:6 CEB

The Hebrew word for glory (*tip̄'ārâ*) used in Proverbs 17:6 appears fifty-one times in the Hebrew Scriptures. Its significance extends across a spectrum of meanings, encompassing glory, beauty, splendor, honor, respect, ornament, distinction, and pride.[3] At times, this word can refer to outer beauty and adornment, like the delicately crafted jewelry or precious stones that adorned Solomon's temple with an exquisite touch (2 Chr 3:6). In other instances, the term evokes notions of honor or dignity associated with specific objects. For instance, Exodus 28:2 attests that the priestly garments, intended for Aaron and his sons, bestow upon them "glory" (*kābôd*) and "beauty" (*tip̄'eret*). We also find this word used when the Lord declares Israel as his treasured possession, promising Israel "he will set you in praise and in fame and in honor (*tip̄'eret*) high above all nations that he has made," and "you shall be a people holy to the LORD your God, as he promised" (Deut 26:18–19).

---

3. Swanson, "9514 תִּפְאָרֶת (tip̄·'ĕ·rĕṯ)," 1997.

In Proverbs 17:6, the word captures the power of parents to impart glory, beauty, splendor, distinction, and honor upon their children. The significance of this legacy cannot be overstated, for when the splendor and glory of parenting are ignored, or this beauty neglected or distorted, or the distinction dishonored, left to wither or warp, it is children who suffer. Stripped of the rightful inheritance owed to them—the glory, beauty, splendor, distinction, and honor that should have been theirs, bestowed within the nurturing embrace of home—these young souls find themselves seeking it elsewhere. The inner longing for this glory will seek fulfillment in relationships, possessions, accomplishments, or status, but their inner thirst for true glory can never be quenched by such fleeting substitutes.

As discussed earlier, Judah's exile into Babylon, the subsequent fall of Babylon, and the rise of the Persian empire produced a crisis for the exiled Hebrew community. Older modes of coping no longer worked. The Hebrew nation had disappeared. Gone were its temple and political structures which upheld the community's values. Israel had transitioned from a nation state to a people scattered among the nations. During this period of social disruption, Israel's wisdom literature reached its maturity.[4] In response to this turmoil, Proverbs put the emphasis upon the family as the way to preserve the community.[5] Judaism would survive not because of its temple or its powerful kings. Judaism would survive because of the family.

Proverbs elevates the status of marriage and family, when guided by the wisdom of God, as the ideal place for human flourishing. It is a wonderful ideal. Unfortunately, many of us did not grow up in the ideal family setting, so we have to learn in other ways. What can we do then if we want a place of strength in family, but the reality is, it's just not there? Spiritually, we do have resources, and hopefully, the church and other communities of faith can be a source of hope and healing. Thankfully, God is our Father above all fathers, and he is the redeemer of all situations, including our family of origin. He heals by placing us in his family, as the Psalmist proclaims, "Father of the fatherless and protector of widows is God in his holy habitation. God settles the solitary in a home" (Ps 68:5–6a).

In the New Testament, the apostle Paul tells us,

---

4. Brown, *Wisdom's Wonder*, 136–83.
5. Belcher, *Finding Favour*, 11.

> For this reason, I bow my knees before the Father, from whom every family in heaven and on earth is named, that according to the riches of his glory he may grant you to be strengthened with power through his Spirit in your inner being. (Eph 3:14–16)

God the Father is the source of every family in heaven and earth. He is the *paterfamilias* of all families. He is the root, source, and model for all families. The Spirit we have received from him cries out, "Abba! Father!" (Rom 8:15; Gal 4:6). Jesus taught us to pray, "Our Father" (Matt 6:9–13). The Triune God is continually bringing us back to the house of the Father. It is in the house of the Father that the wayward and the callused are healed and restored (Luke 15:11–32).

As a leader, you will have many pressures placed upon you, but please do not let these crowd out your family, the central location of your life and calling—and the family rooted in God. Relationship, not work, is the centerpiece of God's essence and his kingdom. Life and ministry happen through relationships.

## The Promise of Children

Untold numbers of parents have claimed the promise, "Train up a child in the way he should go; even when he is old he will not depart from it" (Prov 22:6), only to see their children choose to walk away from God and the good path. The confidence expressed in Proverbs can be disarming and yet unattainable. It can seem that Proverbs promises peace, prosperity, success, and every blessing in life if you only follow the rules.

Does Proverbs make promises to us that are guarantees of security and good outcomes? To answer this question, we must first place Proverbs within its proper context, along with Job, Psalms, Ecclesiastes, and the Song of Songs—all in the genre of Old Testament wisdom literature. These books wrestle with some universal concerns since the dawn of creation, such as love, suffering, devotion to God, and the meaning of life. The Psalms, with their mixture of hymns, laments, and thanksgivings, have been central to the prayers and worship of both Jews and Christians. The Song of Songs does not speak of wisdom, the Law, or the God of Israel. Instead, it is a poem celebrating sexual love. Here two lovers are yearning and inviting one another to come to enjoy love. Sex was, after all, God's idea. That's why he has so much to say about it in the Bible. Proverbs focuses on the general rule for life, while Ecclesiastes and Job concentrate on the exceptions to the general rule. Life has meaning and purpose; this is the general rule. But life can still seem meaningless, so Ecclesiastes deals with the exception. Living a righteous life is rewarded; this is the general rule. But sometimes the righteous suffer, and Job speaks profoundly to this exception.

Do we hold to the pronouncements of Proverbs and trust that God will indeed bless us and our families? Absolutely. Yet, what do you do when you follow the rules and things still go bad? This is the conundrum Job faced. Job was blameless, upright, and God-fearing, and he turned away from evil (Job 1:1), yet unimaginable pain and suffering were visited upon him, his children, and all that he had. The book then unfolds into a series of long speeches full of unanswered questions. His friends are no comfort. Accusations and self-accusations are made, along with self-justifications. Religious and ethical arguments attempt to explain what is not explained in the story. The book leaves us to wrestle with questions about justice, forgiveness, righteousness, suffering, and the sovereignty of God. In the end, Job does not find answers to all his questions, but he does encounter God, and that seems to be the point: in spite of tremendous suffering, God can and will reveal himself. God's revelation is substantive and sustaining—and goes beyond mere answers to questions (Job 40–42).

Proverbs deals with probabilities. If you fear the Lord and walk in his wisdom, then things generally go well for you. If, on the other hand, you do not fear the Lord and you walk in foolishness, things generally go bad for you. We have all seen exceptions to these rules, but we know that, in general, they are true. Life is far too complex for simplistic formulas; we need all the wisdom literature, including the stories of exceptions, to give us a broader and more precise understanding and to live skillfully.

Proverbs offers more than promises *for* children; it offers us wisdom for the promise *of* children. Throughout scripture, God is focused on the legacies of generations.[6] The prophet Malachi declared,

> Did he not make them one, with a portion of the Spirit in their union? And what was the one God seeking? Godly offspring. So guard yourselves in your spirit, and let none of you be faithless to the wife of your youth. (Mal 2:15)

Consider God's word through Isaiah,

6. Gen 9:12; 17:7; 50:23; Exod 3:15; 12:14; Lev 23:43; Josh 22:28; 2 Kgs 10:30; Esth 9:28; Pss 22:30; 49:11; 78:4; Joel 1:3; Eph 3:21.

> I will pour my Spirit upon your offspring, and my blessing on
> your descendants. They shall spring up among the grass like
> willows by flowing streams. This one will say, 'I am the Lord's,'
> another will call on the name of Jacob, and another will write on
> his hand, 'The Lord's,' and name himself by the name of Israel.
> (Isa 44:3–5)

A few chapters later we read, "All your children shall be taught by the
Lord, and great shall be the peace of your children." (Isa 54:13; See also
Isa 59:21; 61:8–9; 65:23).

The Psalms declare,

> The children of your servants shall dwell secure; their offspring
> shall be established before you. (Ps 102:28)

> Blessed is the man who fears the Lord, who greatly delights in
> his commandments! His offspring will be mighty in the land;
> the generation of the upright will be blessed. (Ps 112:1–2)

Proverbs affirms these promises, stating,

> In the fear of the Lord one has strong confidence, and his chil-
> dren will have a refuge. (Prov 14:26)

And,

> The righteous who walks in his integrity—blessed are his chil-
> dren after him! (Prov 20:7)

The wisdom of God, in these and similar passages, teaches us to build on
the power of family from generation to generation.

Consider these verses from Proverbs regarding a legacy for your
children: "You can be sure that evil people will be punished, but the children of the godly will go free" (Prov 11:21, NLT); "The wicked die and
disappear, but the family of the godly stands firm" (Prov 12:7, NLT); "In
the fear of the Lord one has strong confidence, and his children will have
a refuge" (Prov 14:26); "Grandchildren are the crown of the aged, and the
glory of children is their fathers" (Prov 17:6); "The righteous who walks
in his integrity—blessed are his children after him!" (Prov 20:7); "Train
up a child in the way he should go; even when he is old he will not depart
from it" (Prov 22:6); and "Discipline your child, and it will bring you
peace of mind and give you delight" (Prov 29:17, CSB).

A godly legacy, to pass from one generation to the next, is a central
concern for the wise leader. You may obsess over the fledgling church

plant you are leading or the mega-church you have been entrusted with, but your greatest legacy is probably not in your ministry, but rather in your family. Proverbs 13:22 tells us, "A good man leaves an inheritance to his children's children." I have applied this verse to my life regarding my legacy. This requires a long-term perspective, unfolded through a multi-generational process.

Jonathan Edwards (1703–1758) was an American revivalist preacher, pastor, theologian, philosopher, and former president of Princeton University. He is considered the central figure to ignite the Great Awakening in the eighteenth century. His accomplishments as a minister, educator, and philosopher are staggering.[7] Perhaps even more significant than his accomplishments in life is the disproportionate impact on American culture of his descendants with his wife Sarah. According to a study by A.E. Winship in 1900, this single marriage produced thirteen college presidents, sixty-five professors, one hundred lawyers, a dean of an outstanding law school, thirty judges, sixty-six physicians, a dean of a medical school, eighty elected officials that included mayors of three large cities, three governors, a controller of the United States Treasury, and a Vice-President of the United States.[8]

Early in our marriage, Debbie and I decided we would not pass on to our children the unhealthy family dynamics of our families of origin. We chose instead to create a new family legacy, resulting in a new family heritage and new generational wealth. Not financial wealth but family wealth. According to the wisdom of Proverbs, this is the true source of our leadership legacy. I am glad for our priorities, which help me find balance in ministry. Perhaps a hundred and fifty years from now, someone will decide to check on ancestry.com to discover a long line of our descendants who, like the descendants of Jonathan and Sarah Edwards, have carried the blessings of God from generation to generation. That is the promise of children. And the fulfillment of that promise to you and your children is yet to be told. So, take heart. But I do need to warn you. You should not only take heart, but you should also take heed, for not only does Proverbs declare the promise of children, it also tells us about the problem with children.

7. Marsden, *Jonathan Edwards*, 2004.
8. Winship, *Jukes-Edwards*, 1900.

## The Problem with Children

Not every child is a "problem child," but every child has a problem. It is congenital. They cannot help it; they were born that way. No child can escape it. No parent can prevent it, not even the overly protective "helicopter parent" hovering over every aspect of their child's life. The sooner you accept it as a parent, the sooner you can get down to the serious business of teaching your child to overcome this affliction. What is the problem? The problem is that "folly is bound up in the heart of a child" (Prov 22:15). That's right. That precious little bundle of joy has an intruder lodged in the core of his being that is conspiring to make a fool out of your little boy. This malignant intruder is laying plans to cloud his mind and deceive his heart in order to take him down a path of folly and destruction.[9]

Please notice this critical fact. Though folly is locked within the heart of a child, the Bible never calls children fools. The Bible does, however, warn you as a parent about the conspiracy that is afoot in the heart of your child, and it is your job to equip your children to overcome this destructive trap. Your job as a parent is to train your children to resist the "call of folly" (Prov 9:13–18) and to follow the call of wisdom (Prov 4:1–27; 9:1–12). You train them as children to overcome folly so they will be equipped as adults to walk the path of wisdom (Prov 22:6). Folly is an ever-present seducer. No one outgrows the temptations of folly. The difference between the childhood struggle against folly and the adult struggle against folly has to do with the responsible party: the one who serves as the primary agent of discipline.

You are not raising children; you are raising adults. The values, disciplines, and habits you cultivate in your children will continue to guide them long after they have become adults. Proverbs 22:6 tells us, "Train children in the way they should go; when they grow old, they won't depart from it" (CEB). Children should learn to overcome folly through the

9. The Hebrew word "bound" (qāšar) is used to refer to binding instruction to your life, as in Proverbs 3:3, "Let not love and faithfulness forsake you; bind them around your neck," Proverbs 6:20–21, "My son, keep your father's commandment, and forsake not your mother's teaching. Bind (qāšar) them on your heart always; tie them around your neck," and Proverbs 7:3, where the son is to bind his father's instructions on his fingers. These verses are reminiscent of Deuteronomy 6:8, where God instructs Israel to bind his laws to their hands and foreheads. The word is also used of human relationships, as when people are bound together in love (Gen 44:30; 1 Sam 18:1), or when they are bound together in conspiracy (1 Sam 22:8, 13; 2 Sam 15:31; 1 Kgs 15:27; 2 Chr 33:24).

wise guidance and mentoring of their parents so that, as adults, they are equipped to discipline themselves away from folly and towards wisdom. Though folly is bound up in the heart of a child, "the rod of discipline drives it far away" (Prov 22:5b).

Unfortunately, "the rod" has been understood by many as if limited to an instrument of corporal punishment, or even violently beating, not only directed at children, but also slaves, servants, employees, students, and even wives. The rod (šēbeṭ) in Proverbs was a key piece of shepherding equipment. In the Hebrew Scriptures the word refers to a shepherd's staff (Lev 27:32), a rod for striking someone as punishment (Prov 23:13), or a scepter as a symbol of kingship (Gen 49:10). Biblical writers refer to God as a shepherd (Ps 23:1; Mic 7:14) and his rod (šēbeṭ) as an instrument of comfort (Ps 23:4), discipline (Isa 30:31), and righteous kingship (Ps 45:6). God, as paterfamilias of all creation and the great Shepherd, is the model exemplar for all parenting; the parental rod of discipline should not be a terror to their children, but rather a sign of compassion, protection, and godly leadership in the home.

Discipline is about training. Yelling at your children to stop doing something is not training. Spanking your children is not training. "Yelling and telling" is not training. Training involves modeling, demonstrating, involving, and passing on knowledge and behaviors. You are teaching them to replace destructive thoughts and behaviors with good thoughts and behaviors. In other words, you teach them to "overcome evil with good" (Rom 12:21).

Training your children is a process by which you model and impart knowledge and skill for living. It involves at least four stages. The first stage can be called "I do, you watch." It begins on day one of parenting. Just as a child learns to speak her mother tongue because she is immersed in the language from birth, so too does she learn the language of her family through immersion into the daily rhythms, habits, and attitudes of her parents. As parents, you create the culture that shapes the values, ambitions, and behaviors of your children. They may not remember your words, but they always remember your example.

The second stage is "I do, you help." Involve your child in household chores and family events while they are still eager to participate. I observed the power of early involvement with my son. He watched me mow the lawn every week. When he was small, we bought him a toy lawn mower so he could pretend to mow the lawn with me. He thought it was a great thing to help Dad mow the lawn. This act of pretending to mow the lawn made it far easier to enter the next stage of discipline, the stage where he started doing more of the work. The third stage is, "You do, and I help." As my son grew older, he took over the real mower. He learned how to mow the lawn and maintain the equipment. He was doing the work, and I was helping him as a mentor.

As my son grew in skill and confidence, he moved into the fourth stage: "You do." It was now his job to mow the lawn, and he was able to do it with little, if any, mentoring from me. He soon realized he could make money mowing our neighbors' lawns. As a young teenager, he started his own business. That little business making real money started years before with a toy lawn mower. Someday, if my son has children, he will have the skills to pass on this same ability.

You can use this four-stage process to teach your kids to clean their room, do their chores, or carry out a whole host of other practical disciplines that will eventually help them succeed as adults.

In chapter two, we did an extensive study into wisdom and folly in Proverbs. This may be a good place for you to go back and review that discussion so that you have a clearer picture of folly (which has bound itself to the heart of your children) and wisdom (which is the aim and target of your parenting). Recall that folly is loud, undisciplined, and without knowledge—it does not like to be corrected (Prov 9:13). As a parent, you want to cultivate in your children a love for peaceableness, discipline, and knowledge (Jas 3:17). Cultivate within them from an early age the love of learning, self-discipline, teachability, and personal growth. These qualities are best cultivated in your children by your own example. You, as parent and leader, are the model teaching them to love learning, practice self-discipline, be teachable, and have a growth mindset.

Recall how folly is destructive, and it cannot be compromised with (Prov 16:22). The folly bound in your child's heart lures your little one into throwing rocks at windows, pulling hair, and breaking things. As a parent, you will want to discipline them away from destructive behaviors and train them in constructive behaviors. How can you model this to your children and then use the four-stage discipleship process to dethrone folly and enthrone wisdom in the heart of your child? Training your children to take good care of their toys, clean up after themselves, and show respect for the rights and property of others are components of your parenting strategy for driving out folly.

Remember from chapter two that folly continues to grow and expand wherever it takes root (Prov 14:24). Folly is like a malignant invasive weed that will take over the whole garden of your life. It must be rooted out, or it will take over. Small, foolish behaviors in children can become foolish strongholds in adults. If a parent placates a child's temper, for example, this immature folly can grow in adulthood into a foolish, destructive stronghold of anger and rage (Prov 14:16,29; 29:11). As a parent, teach your children to think about the consequences of their actions. Find creative ways to demonstrate how small actions can become big problems, just like small eggs can hatch big snakes. It is easier to crush the egg than to kill the serpent.

Folly speaks without knowledge, and it cannot be quiet (Prov 18:13). Folly thinks it knows everything, and in its grip, your child will be inclined to suppose that she knows everything. This know-it-all attitude will train your child to be a fool when she grows up. When your children speak without knowledge, you might want to yell at them. But yelling at them to be quiet because they do not know what they are talking about is not a good discipline that pulls your child away from folly. You have not trained them yet. Instead, walk with them through the learning experience. Let the learning experience show them that there are things they do not know, and through this, they will discover for themselves both the enjoyment of learning and the folly of speaking without knowledge.

Children thrive in an atmosphere of orderliness and security, yet when left to themselves, they love unruliness. This is folly seeking to build a stronghold in their lives, for folly is unruly, and it cannot be controlled (Prov 9:13). As a parent, your job is to help them overcome unruliness and to learn the value of a well-ordered life. Teaching your child self-control around his impulse to push buttons and create chaos is, for the child, a pathway toward wisdom.

One summer, I was working in my garage when my five-year-old grandson came in, went straight to the freezer, and pulled out an Otter Pop, one of those frozen fruit-flavored treats kids love so much. I asked him, "Grandson, what are you doing?" He said, "Grammy said I could have an Otter Pop." I said, "Oh, OK." And away he went, Otter Pop in hand. I walked into the kitchen just in time to hear the conversation on the back deck. Grammy asked, "Where did you get that Otter Pop?" To which our grandson promptly replied, "Grampy said I could have it." No one taught him to be a sly, cunning conniver. No one taught him to use deception and wordplays to abscond with his beloved Otter Pop. Nope, no one needed to do this because folly was already at work, seeking to establish patterns of deception (Prov 14:8, Jer 17:9). The key is to help train your child away from deception and cultivate in them a love for truth and transparency.

Folly is hard at work, conspiring to entrench into your child's character an avoidance of responsibility by blaming others, for folly is a blamer. Folly refuses to be responsible for itself (Prov 19:3). Here's how blame works. If they make a mistake in a game, the sun was in their eyes. If they did not do their homework, the dog ate it. If they are grumpy, it's not their fault, for they say, "I'm having a bad day." Parents, you have the incredible ability and opportunity to train a child in the ways of personal responsibility. Teach them to own their thoughts, actions, and emotions. When your child wants to pass the blame, this is your teaching opportunity to show them a better way of life by accepting responsibility for themselves and their actions.

If, through your words and actions, you train your children away from folly and toward the ways of wisdom, you will set them up for success in life. Hold tight to the promise that when you train up a child in the way they will go when they are old, they will not depart from it (Prov 22:6).

## Priorities of Wise Parents and Wise Leaders

Proverbs utilizes multiple voices to communicate to its readers. These voices include a father and mother (Prov 1:9—7:27), Lady Wisdom (Prov 1:20–33; 8:1–36; 9:1–18), Solomon (Prov 10:1—22:16), a group called "The Wise" (Prov 22:17—24:34), the authority of King Hezekiah, who made a collection of Solomon's proverbs 250 years after Solomon (Prov 25:1—29:27), and two mystery figures named Agur (Prov 30:1–33) and King Limuel (Prov 31:1–31). The centrality of the mother's and father's instructions in Proverbs highlights the family's role in maintaining the values of the children of Israel (Prov 1:8; 6:20). The family became even more important after the Babylonian exile when, as people, they were without a temple, centralized religious authorities, or even a nation (2 Kgs 24–25). As shown by the books of Samuel, Kings, and Chronicles, Israel and Judah had witnessed the corruption of their religious world with its temple, priests, and prophets, the collapse of its political systems, and the inability of kings to remain faithful or to produce a faithful nation. Now, in exile, the community of God's people were finding a new way forward by anchoring their survival as a people to the health of their families.[10]

---

10. Belcher, *Finding Favour*, 11.

We who live as exiles in a strange land can take comfort in this wisdom.[11] We have neither a centralized religious system nor a powerful political state to enforce our values or achieve our mission. Nor would we want either of these since scripture attests to the utter bankruptcy of such an agenda. But we do, however, have the power of family. And that is saying a lot.

If Proverbs was indeed a training regimen for socio-political leaders, why does it speak so extensively about parents and children? I think there are at least three reasons. The first, as mentioned above, is that the family is the bedrock and stabilizer of society. Even at a personal level, family helps stabilize and anchor the leader to what is essential. I discovered this myself when going through a church split. It was a painful season of betrayal, accusations, and fearful anxiety about the future. I would come home at the end of the day and go to the playroom with my kids. We would play together until I could feel the stabilizing effects of my family as I disconnected from the church drama and reconnected with the haven of home. It was the bedrock of security for my leader-weary soul.

Second, parenting is a proving ground for leadership. Family is the central place we demonstrate our ability to accept responsibility and to lead others. If we broaden our scope of scripture to include the Pastoral letters of 1 Timothy and Titus, we gain additional biblical evidence that the family is the proving ground for ministry leadership (1 Tim 3:1–13; Titus 1:5–9). For example, Titus is left on the island of Crete to set things in order within the churches and to "appoint elders in every town" (Titus 1:5). This recalls a very early moment in the Christian movement, probably sometime in the mid-sixties CE.[12] The Gospel was expanding rapidly throughout the Roman world and leaders were needed everywhere. Where was Titus to look to find qualified leaders? He was to look at the home. Whoever had a healthy marriage and children showed evidence of leadership ability. Pick those people for leaders, for they have shown they can do the job.

A third reason is that your priorities as a parent are pretty much the same as your priorities as a leader. In other words, not only is parenting the proving ground for leaders, it is also a template for leadership. Consider, for example, how the apostle Paul uses both father and mother as metaphors for his ministry. He does not hesitate to refer to himself as a

11. 1 Pet 1:1; 2:11
12. Knight, *Pastoral Epistles*, 54.

father in Christ (1 Cor 4:15). In his letter to Philemon, Paul refers to the runaway slave, Onesimus, as his son whom he had "begotten" while in prison (Phlm 10, KJV). Timothy is "my true son in the faith" (1 Tim 1:2, NIV). It is not difficult for us to imagine Paul as a father, or as a farmer (1 Cor 3:6) or a skilled master builder (1 Cor 3:10). What some may find odd is that he also uses maternal metaphors to describe his ministry leadership.[13] He told the Galatians, "My little children, for whom I am again in the anguish of childbirth until Christ is formed in you!" (Gal 4:19).

Paul uses the image of a father in begetting children and the image of a mother in birthing children. Not only does he use the imagery of giving birth, but he also describes his ministry as being like a nursing mother. He told the Corinthians, described as infants in Christ, "I fed you with milk" (1 Cor 3:2). The implication is that he nursed them like a mother feeding her babies. The imagery of Paul as a nursing mother is explicitly stated in 1 Thessalonians 2:7, "We were gentle among you, like a nursing mother taking care of her own children." Paul, unafraid to compound and mix metaphors, rounds out his description of his ministry among the Thessalonians by stating in one place, "we were gentle among you, like a nursing mother taking care of her own children" (1 Thess 2:7) and then a few verses later saying, "For you know how, like a father with his children, we exhorted each one of you and encouraged you and charged you to walk in a manner worthy of God, who calls you into his own kingdom and glory" (1 Thess 2:11–12).

For Paul, both father and mother were worthy templates for effective ministry leadership. Mother and father as ministry templates are appropriate because the church is a family, and not in a metaphorical sense, but as an ontological reality. In Mark 3:34–35, Jesus looked at those who sat around him and said, "Here are my mother and my brothers! For whoever does the will of God, he is my brother and sister and mother" (Mark 3:34–35). In Matthew 23:8, he instructed his disciples to call one another "brother." In Hebrews, we read, "For it was fitting that he, for whom and by whom all things exist, in bringing many sons to glory, should make the founder of their salvation perfect through suffering. For he who sanctifies and those who are sanctified all have one source. That is why he is not ashamed to call them brothers" (Heb 2:10–11). The apostles thought of the church as a family and frequently spoke and wrote in familial terms (Acts 9:30; 15:13; Rom 12:1; 1 Cor 7:29; Gal 4:12; Heb 3:12; Jas 2:1; 2

13. Gaventa, *Our Mother*, 2007.

Pet 1:10; 1 John 3:13). As it says in Ephesians 2:19, "So then you are no longer strangers and aliens, but you are fellow citizens with the saints and members of the household of God."

Since we are the family of God, our templates for ministry leadership include mothers and fathers because parents and ministry leaders share at least eight common priorities. These priorities are pursuing *shalom*, protecting from danger, providing security, nurturing life, equipping for wise living, creating culture, knowing your limits, and persevering. Let's explore these.

## Wise Parents and Wise Leaders Pursue Shalom

> Her ways are ways of pleasantness, and all her paths are peace *(shalom)*.
>
> —PROVERBS 3:17

*Shalom*[14] and its related words *šālēm, šelem* are among the most important theological concepts in the Hebrew Scriptures.[15] These words coalesce around a central theme of peace, well-being, and completeness, whether on a personal level or within the context of a community. They embody a profound longing for well-being and harmony in the lives of individuals and communities alike.[16] *Shalom* is a comprehensive Hebrew word that speaks of wholeness of life and well-being.[17] It appears at least 237 times across 209 verses. Translated by the English Standard Version as peace, peaceful, peacefully, or peaceable in 165 instances, it assumes varied forms, each adding a distinctive nuance to its richness. Other translations of shalom include wellness, welfare, safety, and prosperity, each revealing the multifaceted dimensions of its essence in the sacred

---

14. I have generally followed the Society of Biblical Literature academic system but here I transliterate the Hebrew word by the familiar *shalom* rather than the more scholarly preferred *šālôm*.

15. Carr, "2401 שָׁלֵם (šālēm)," 931.

16. *Shalom* (שָׁלוֹם)—This is a well-known Hebrew word that translates to peace in English. It conveys a sense of harmony, well-being, and tranquility. *Shalom* is often used as a greeting and a blessing, wishing for peace and wholeness upon others. Šālēm (שָׁלֵם)—This word also translates to peace in English and is closely related to *shalom*. It carries similar connotations of completeness, safety, and harmony. Šelem (שֶׁלֶם)—This word is related to *shalom* and *šelem* and also translates to peace or completeness in English. It can refer to the act of making restitution or fulfilling an obligation, leading to the restoration of peace and wholeness.

17. Chris Byrley, "Healing," 2014.

texts (Gen 29:6; Jer 29:7, 11; Deut 29:19; Jer 33:6). These words bear witness to the enduring yearning for well-being and harmony, for peace and completeness, within the human heart and the human community.

In Judaism, *shalom* is an underlying principle of the Torah. It plays a central role in the covenant and also in the message of the Hebrew prophets, such as Isaiah,

> For the mountains may depart and the hills be removed, but my steadfast love shall not depart from you, and my covenant of peace shall not be removed, says the Lord, who has compassion on you. (Isa 54:10)

In Psalm 34:14, the psalmist charges, "Turn away from evil and do good; seek peace (*shalom*) and pursue it." Here *shalom* does not simply happen; it is a content-laden object that one can lay hold of. *Shalom* is not a mere byproduct but an end in itself.[18] In Proverbs, this fullness of life, *shalom* (Prov 3:17) is shaped by devotion (Prov 2:1–4; 4:7; 8:33–35), character (Prov 2:7; 4:23), skill (Prov 1:4; 8:5,12), general well-being (Prov 5:1–23; 6:1–35), blessings (Prov 3:6; 4:10; 9:11), and the knowledge of God (Prov 2:5; 9:10).[19] *Shalom* is the result of God's activity in covenant (Num 25:12; Isa 54:10; Ezek 34:25; Mal 2:5) and the fruit of righteousness (Isa 32:17). In nearly two-thirds of its occurrences, *shalom* describes the state of fulfillment which is the result of God's presence.[20]

This is clearly seen in the Aaronic blessing recorded in Numbers 6:23–26,

> Thus you shall bless the people of Israel: you shall say to them, The Lord bless you and keep you; the Lord make his face to shine upon you and be gracious to you; the Lord lift up his countenance upon you and give you peace (*shalom*).

Here, *shalom* has a comprehensive meaning that describes the experience of the person who fully enjoys the presence of God, as one blessed, guarded, and treated graciously by him. In the Old Testament, the term often indicates a comprehensive kind of fulfilment, completion, and perfection in life and spirit, which transcends any success that humans alone, even under the best of circumstances, can attain.[21]

---

18. Healey, "Peace," 5:206.

19. Estes, *Hear, My Son*, 19–85.

20. Carr, "2401 שָׁלֵם (šālēm)," 931.

21. Silva, *Dictionary*, 113.

Previously, we discussed how after the Babylonian exile, the Hebrew language fell into disuse.[22] Then, with the rise of Alexander the Great and the Greek empires, the Jews in the diaspora were Hellenized, and for some Jews, especially those living in Ptolemaic Egypt, Greek became the primary language. Thus, it became necessary for the scriptures to be translated into Greek. The first five books of the Hebrew Bible were translated in the mid-third century BCE; the rest of the Hebrew Bible was translated over the next century or so. This translation is known as the Septuagint (abbreviated LXX).[23]

The influence of the Septuagint on the New Testament cannot be overstated. It was the primary theological and literary context within which the writers of the New Testament and most early Christians worked. For example, there are approximately 300 Old Testament passages quoted or alluded to in the New Testament, and over 75 percent of these quotations, some scholars claim it reaches 90 percent, are taken from the Septuagint.

The relevance of the Septuagint becomes obvious when you consider how the vocabulary of the New Testament is shaped by the language of the Septuagint. For example, the Septuagint mostly translates *shalom* with *eirēnē*, the Greek word for peace.[24] Peace (*eirēnē*) in the New Testament corresponds to *shalom* in the Old Testament. *Eirēnē* occurs over ninety times in the New Testament and in every book except 1 John.[25]

Peace (*eirēnē*) is what God wills, not merely for the soul or for the human race, but for his whole creation. In Luke 1:79 *eirēnē* is the awaited eschatological salvation. In Luke 2:14 peace is the salvation that has now come to the earth. Melchizedek as a type of Christ is the king of peace (Heb 7:2), the gospel is the gospel of peace (Eph 6:15), and Christ leaves peace with his disciples (John 14:27). When the disciples go out in Christ's name, they offer peace (Luke 10:5–6; Matt 10:13). We are to seek this peace (Heb 12:14). It is a power which protects us (Phil 4:7) and which rules in the heart (Col 3:15).

---

22. Neh 13.24

23. Reeves and Hill, *Know How*, 2018.

24. The LXX sometimes uses other terms for *shālôm*, mostly in greetings or when external welfare is plainly at issue, e.g., Gen 26:31; 28:21; 29:6; Josh 10:21; Exod 18:7. The aim in such cases is to keep more closely to common Greek usage. See Kittel, et al., *Abridged*, 208.

25. Silva, *Dictionary*, 114.

Occasionally *eirēnē* denotes peace with God. This is the point in Ephesians 2:14–22. As the law has both divided Jews and Gentiles and separated humanity from God, so Christ our peace has healed both relationships, for he has broken down the wall of hostility by reconciling us all to God. Peace with God is solely at issue in Romans 5:1. It is the relationship in which God places believers by his reconciling work in Christ.

This *eirēnē* is also to exist between one another. When Paul in Romans 14:17 says that God's kingdom is peace, he is stating that the rule of God is one in which there is no evil or discord; he can thus exhort us to pursue what makes for peace (v. 19). In Romans 15:13 *eirēnē* also includes peace of soul.[26]

In Matthew 5:9, Christ says those who make *shalom* are blessed and called children of God. *Shalom* is the central characteristic of the relationship between God and his sons and daughters; it is the essential quality of his presence among his people. Our aspiration as followers of Christ, as parents, and as leaders is to become *"shalom-makers"*—both to experience and to make available this wholeness of life and well-being in the presence of God.

The most important thing for raising healthy kids is to live in *shalom* as a spiritually, emotionally, mentally, relationally, and physically healthy person yourself. If you are healthy, chances are your children will be healthy. Proverbs teaches us that it is not only what we do for children that matters but also what we *do in* children. What we *do in* children has to do with the quality of health present in us as parents. Healthy parents raise healthy children who become healthy adults.

The same is true for leaders. The lasting impact of your leadership is not what you do *for* people; it is what you do *in* people. You are in the people formation business. Poor leadership uses people to get things done. Wise leadership uses things to get people done. I once had a young man who volunteered to serve in our church. He was very zealous. He felt called to great things. He went for far as to tell me that he had a great calling and he would not waste his time cleaning the church bathroom. I told him, "I clean the bathrooms in our church. If you are too good to clean the bathroom, you are 'to good' to do anything in our church." I was not interested in clean toilets; I was interested in a clean heart. A few months later, his attitude had changed so much that while at our men's prayer gathering some of the guys asked him, "Your attitude has really changed.

---

26. Kittel, et al., *Abridged*, 209–10.

What happened?" He told them about our conversation and how God had used a discussion about cleaning toilets to clean out the pride in his heart. He became a faithful and teachable young man. Help your people grow and excel in *shalom* and you will find hearts transformed by God's grace.

*Shalom* as a parent and leader means you embody virtues such as humility, teachability, justice, and a well-ordered life. When your character, competence, and words as a parent or leader are consistent with one another, you are a leader/parent of influence. Becoming this type of parent or leader is a life-long process. You do not achieve this in a day, a week, or a few years. It is a lifetime of personal development. Developing yourself is not selfish. It is responsible parenting and responsible leadership. Timothy was instructed to "Practice these things, immerse yourself in them, so that all may see your progress. Keep a close watch on yourself and on the teaching. Persist in this, for by so doing you will save both yourself and your hearers" (1 Tim 4:15–16). This is important because while you teach what you know, you reproduce what you are.

## Wise Parents and Wise Leaders Protect from Dangers

Through his speeches, the father in Proverbs wants to save his son from the things that will destroy him. In the first speech (Prov 1:8–33), the father doesn't pull any punches when warning his sons: if people tempt you with claims of an easy, deceitful life of "ill-gotten gains," do not follow them. It will only bring ruin. Then, in his eighth speech (Prov 5:1–23), the father warns that the house of the adulteress is a place of destruction, but the home of your bride is the fruit of life. Then, in his ninth speech (Prov 6:1–35), he warns that there are four hunters out there looking to ambush your soul and rob you of the good life: These are debt (Prov 6:1–5), laziness (Prov 6:6–11), corrupt characters (Prov 6:12–19), and lust (Prov 6:20–35).

Like a wise parent, a wise leader will also warn those they lead of these same dangers. There are dangers of cutting corners and economic corruption, sexual exploitation and seduction, financial mismanagement, debt, laziness, corrupting influences, and all manner of greed and lust war against leaders and the organizations they lead. Just as a wise parent will set parameters around the home to help safeguard against these dangers, such as parental controls on media devices and limitations on the influence of bad characters, so too the wise leader will institute safeguards of economic stewardship and accountability, diligence and honesty in the workplace, and precautions against lust and greed.

## Wise Parents and Wise Leaders Provide Security

Provisions for your children extend beyond the basics of food and shelter. Parents provide discipline (Prov 3:11–12; 13:24). This discipline includes correcting bad habits in a child while there is still time—before they become character flaws (Prov 22:15). The hard way to wisdom and life is better than the easy way to folly and death (Prov 23:24; 19:18). Discipline is to be firm, but not harsh, because (1) folly is locked within the heart of a child and it will take more than mere words to dislodge it (Prov 22:15), and (2) character is a plant that grows sturdier with pruning (Prov 15:32, 33; 5:11,12; Heb 12:11).

Consider how the fourth father speech (Prov 3:21–35) focuses on wisdom as the way of peace. If you want to sleep well, live without fear, and avoid traps that other people easily fall into, then give people what they are owed, don't think of ways to harm people, don't accuse people without evidence, and don't envy people who get things through violence. The father's fifth speech (Prov 4:1–9) calls the son to cherish Lady Wisdom, for she will lead him on the good path and crown him with honor if he embraces her. In his sixth speech (Prov 4:10–19), the father makes clear that there are only two ways of life: wickedness or righteousness. There is no third option. Choose light or dark, life or death; it's up to you. This training in the ways of wisdom provides security for those you lead, be they your children, congregation, or staff.

## Wise Parents and Wise Leaders Nurture Life

Parents provide a loving, secure, and predictable atmosphere. This atmosphere provides security and protection so the child can flourish. The innocence of children is to be celebrated; it can infuse the child with a strong optimism and a sense of wonder. Basic family stability, along with family rituals and traditions, cultivate the heart and mind over time. These act like support structures for young saplings, allowing them to take root while being protected from damaging winds that would threaten the young tree.

Notice how the ten father speeches combine tones of warning and amazement. The father provides guidance and protection for his children by giving real-life warnings about the dangers in this world; he also instills a feeling of amazement and joy at the vast and dazzling universe. If these positive feelings are denied during childhood, they will most likely be lost for a lifetime. As parents, we can either cultivate or numb their sense of wonder.

When my kids were young, every summer we would head to a nearby creek to witness the salmon run. It's an annual migration, where salmon journey from the ocean to their birth rivers for spawning. It is a wonder of nature. The salmon's journey commences when mature adults, after years at sea, feel the pull to return to their freshwater birthplaces. They brave rivers, facing waterfalls, rapids, and predators, all in pursuit of reaching their spawning grounds. Some runs cover vast distances, even thousands of miles, while others are shorter but no less remarkable.

Standing beside that small creek, we bore witness to the indomitable spirit of these creatures, marveling at their tenacity and resolute will. Their relentless determination to reach their spawning grounds left us mesmerized, caught in a state of awe and wonder. Time has marched on, and my children, now grown, continue to visit that little creek when possible, drawn back to experience again the wonder of God's creation. The tradition is now being passed on to their kids.

It is in the home and from the family that people learn security in who and what they are. You, as a parent, can help nurture in your children self-acceptance, the willingness to dream, and the desire and drive to develop themselves to reach their fullest potential. Secure relationships, stable environments, open communication, family traditions, and safe spaces create atmospheres to revive the weary and tumultuous soul of a child. Fear and insecurity can flood a child's heart. Life and neighbors can press emotions to a breaking point. Parents do well to see their home as a place to revive the heart.[27] Nurture your children like a new garden. Tender affection, words of blessing, and large quantities of quality time nurture their soul, just as sunlight, water, and fertilizers do the soil.

The wise leader will, in like manner, nurture life in the hearts of those they serve and inspire within them a sense of awe, celebration, and joy. Teach those you lead to embrace all of life and the full human experience, from the joys of birth to the agonies of death.

27. Lev 10:11; Deut 4:9–10; 6:6–9; 11:18–21; Eph 6:4

## Wise Parents and Wise Leaders Equip for Wise Living

Parents instill in their children vital social, relational, and professional skills by living these values daily within the home. Wise parents understand the significance of preparing their children for life, both within the family and out in the public sphere. This skillful wisdom best flourishes at home, where invaluable lessons on work ethics, relationships, and the art of resolving disagreements are taught and absorbed.

Proverbs offers practical advice throughout its verses, providing a blueprint for navigating life. Key lessons include the importance of attentive listening to others (Prov 1:8; 4:10, 20; 5:1; 23:19, 22: 19:27), the value of embracing wisdom and not neglecting it (Prov 1:8; 3:1, 21; 6:20), and the significance of choosing friends wisely (Prov 1:10, 15; 24:21; 28:7; 29:3). It underscores the necessity of heeding wise words (Prov 2:1; 4:4), treasuring instructions (Prov 2:1; 3:1; 7:1) and embracing discipline (Prov 3:11–12). The book imparts the importance of wise planning (Prov 3:21), avoiding sexual immorality (Prov 5:20), and cultivating sound financial management (Prov 6:1–3). The book emphasizes the significance of listening to instructions (Prov 13:1; 15:5; 19:27; 23:26), honoring one's parents (Prov 15:20; 19:26; 20:20; 28:24; 30:17), and spreading joy to others (Prov 17:21, 25; 19:13, 26; 23:15, 24, 25; 27:11; 28:7; 29:3; 30:11). In this wealth of wisdom, parents play a pivotal role as guides, nurturing the development of their children's character and skills, laying a strong foundation for their future journey in the world.

Consider how in the second speech (Prov 2:1–22), the father advises that if you seek wisdom, you will find it, but you've got to look hard, for wisdom requires work. Notice how in his third speech (Prov 3:1–20), he encourages his son to actively develop his character. Then consider how in his seventh speech (Prov 4:20–27), the father makes his son ready for the path of wisdom by stressing that it will require the full devotion of his heart, eyes, ears, mouth, and feet because the pursuit of wisdom requires your whole being.

The wise parent and the wise leader will seek to equip those they lead to live life to its fullest potential as God intended it. This means that both the parent and the leader understand that the dynamic impulses to think, desire, dream, strive, build, create, and thrive are placed in the heart by God. They are good impulses, but they have been distorted by sin and death. They need to be healed, not killed; purified, not purged;

educated, not eradicated, so that the person can thrive in the wisdom of God and live a skillful life.

## Wise Parents and Wise Leaders Create Culture

The book of Proverbs is set in a specific cultural context, yet it also seeks to create a different culture. In the same way, both parents and leaders exist in a particular culture but are also called to create culture. More often than not, the culture created by wise parents and leaders is counter to the dominant culture of their surroundings. Consider these two examples. First, as we saw in chapter five, polygamous marriage was far more common in the Old Testament than monogamous marriage. Anyone familiar with the stories of Solomon is quick to realize that the life of Solomon is very different from the wisdom in Proverbs—even though they are "the proverbs of Solomon" (Prov 1:1; 10:1). For example, while Proverbs celebrates monogamous marriage relationships[28] (Prov 5:18; 12:4; 18:22; 19:14; 31:10), Solomon is notorious for his 700 wives and 300 concubines (1 Kgs 11:3). Solomon embodied the cultural norms of the nations around him while ignoring the biblical warning that kings are not to accumulate wives, horses, or gold (Deut 17:16–17). Solomon ran headlong in the opposite direction, amassing not only hundreds of wives but thousands of horses (1 Kgs 4:26; 10:26) and 666 talents of gold each year (1 Kgs 10:14). Yet, here is Proverbs consistently warning against the dangers of greed and lust. Proverbs works like yeast in dough to create a new, alternative culture that is subversive to its dominant cultural context. It accomplishes this not only by its explicit statements but also by its implicit contrast between the life of Solomon and the wisdom of Solomon.

A second example of the cultural context of Proverbs is the subservient role of women in society. Yet, Proverbs contains seeds to develop a new cultural norm for women. Consider, for example, the paired references to both the father and mother in Proverbs 1:8 and 6:20. This pairing is unique to Hebrew Wisdom Literature in comparison with the wisdom literature of Egypt, Babylon, and Mesopotamia during the same era.[29] Also consider how the virtuous woman of Proverbs 31:10–31 fulfills the challenge set forth in Proverbs 1:7.

---

28. Note: it is "wife" and not "wives."

29. Estes, *Hear, My Son*, 32, 45.

In its cultural setting, Proverbs acts as a subversive text that deconstructs these oppressive systems from the inside out by aiming to create a different, alternative culture. This new culture builds a worldview where God is the creator of the universe (Prov 3:19–20) and actively involved in the affairs of life (Prov 19:21; 21:30). His creation is both knowable and yet awe-inspiring (Prov 8:22–31), and the proper attitude of all humanity is to fear of the Lord (Prov 1:7; 2:5; 8:13; 9:10; 10:27; 14:26–26; 15:16, 33; 16:6; 19:23; 22:4; 23:17; 29:25). This worldview produces wisdom (Prov 4:5–7; 7:4), teachability (Prov 1:33; 5:7; 7:24; 8:34, 36; 9:9; 25:12), righteousness (Prov 1:3; 2:9, 20; 3:33; 4:18; 8:20; 10:26), and a life of *shalom* (Prov 3:1–2).

So, while Proverbs was set within a particular cultural setting, it sought to create a new culture for those who followed the way of wisdom, which subversively overthrows the powers and authorities that would subjugate humanity to the ways of folly. In the same way, wise parents and leaders are also creators of cultures that serve human flourishing.

As parents and leaders, we establish the norms of behavior and shared values among a group of people, and that's what it means to be a culture creator. Parents create the culture of the home, and leaders create the culture of their organization. It is the culture you create that creates the collective experiences, beliefs, values, traditions, customs, and behaviors that define your family, ministry, or organization. This culture becomes the lens through which they see the world, and it shapes their thoughts, attitudes, and interactions with others. It is the invisible bond that binds people together, fostering a sense of belonging and identity.

The culture you create is more powerful and more determinative than any strategy or event you plan. You cannot create a culture of family conflict and then hope a three-day trip to a Disney Resort will restore peace and harmony. Nor can you, as a leader, create a culture of suspicion and control and then hope a weekend retreat will restore trust and transparency. It will not. Culture wins every day. "Culture eats strategy for breakfast" is a popular aphorism mistakenly attributed to Peter Drucker. Granted, the aphorism seems to carry more authority when attributed to Drucker than when proper credit is given to an obscure article in *PIMA North American Papermaker: The Official Publication of the Paper Industry Management Association*, written by two paper recycling consultants named Bill Moore and Jerry Rose. The truth of the statement remains regardless of its source.

Culture encompasses the social behavior, norms, institutions, knowledge, beliefs, arts, customs, laws, capabilities, and habits found in human societies that form the individuals in these groups. Humans acquire culture through the learning processes of socialization and enculturation. Here is an example of what I mean. My mother raised us to value hard work. I do not recall her giving any "mother speeches;" my siblings and I all learned the importance of hard work from the culture she created in our family. We would never dream of taking a sick day when not bedridden, arriving late for work, or slacking off. The cultural value of hard work she created in our home codified for us acceptable conduct in society; it guided our behavior, dress, language, and demeanor. It also served as a template for our expectations of others. We expect people to work hard, carry their own weight, and get things done. Wise parents and leaders will be very intentional about the types of cultures they are creating, for these cultures will not only create your future but also create your present.

## Wise Parents and Wise Leaders Know Their Limits

Air traffic controllers have one of the most stressful jobs in the world. They are responsible for the safety of planes, pilots, and passengers. They must keep up to date with weather conditions, make sure the runway is cleared, give take-off and landing instructions, schedule landings, approve flight plans, transfer flights to other controllers, accept new flights into their zone, and communicate with pilots and alert them of flight updates—all at the same time while working long hours. Doing one of these tasks on its own can be difficult, let alone all of them at once. Air traffic controllers need to be able to bounce around from task to task without letting any responsibilities fall through the cracks. One small mistake can be fatal.

Parenting and ministry leadership feel a lot like the job of an air traffic controller. Not only are parents and leaders responsible for those under their charge, all while multitasking for long hours, but they share another similarity. Like air traffic controllers, parents and leaders are responsible for something they do not actually control. That is the real stress point. Consider that while the air traffic controller is responsible for all the movements of the airplane, she is not in the pilot's seat. For the controller to be successful, she needs the cooperation of the pilot. As a parent, you need the cooperation of your children, and as a leader, you need the cooperation of those whom you lead. This forces you, as a parent and leader, to know your limits.

I would love to tell you that if you do everything right, your children will turn out OK. But I cannot. Consider our forefather, Adam (Gen 1–3). Luke refers to him as "Adam, the son of God." God provided a perfect home and a loving environment, yet Adam still went astray. Risk is always present in love. The problem in dealing with children is that they are not neat little machines you can program; they are human beings endowed by God with mind, will, and emotion. These are fallen human beings with free will. A good home may produce an idler (Prov 10:5) or a profligate (Prov 29:3): he may rebel enough to despise (Prov 15:20), mock (Prov 30:17) or curse (Prov 30:11; 20:20) his parents; he may be heartless enough to run through their money (Prov 28:24), and even to turn a widowed mother out of doors (Prov 19:26). While there are parents who have only themselves to thank for their shame (Prov 29:15), we must also acknowledge that individuals are responsible for choosing wisdom (Prov 29:3a; 2:2ff), and they make decisions for themselves (Prov 1:10).

Parents should do everything within their power to impart glory, beauty, splendor, distinction, and honor to their children *while at the same time* remembering that parenting involves both parents and children. Children have a role to play as well. Proverbs tells us a son may be too opinionated to learn (Prov 13:1; 17:21). Children may end up as lazy (Prov 10:5), as gluttons (Prov 28:7), promiscuous (Prov 29:3), or as rebels (Prov 19:26; 20:20; 30:11–12, 17) and robbers (Prov 28:24). However, these bad outcomes should be despite parental training and not because of it.

At best, parents give their children the opportunity to encounter God. Children, after all, are made in the image of God, not the image of their parents. They are the "sheep of his pasture," not ours. Before you were a parent, God was Father. He is the original parent to whom we parents present our children. God is God and we are not. As parents, we can point the way, show the way, and walk the way, but we cannot be the way. That role is reserved for God and God alone. Our role as parents is to present opportunities to encounter the living God. Their role as children is to walk in obedience to him, the one to whom we must all give an account.[30]

Karl Barth was right when he said that parents, in the end, cannot make their children healthy in body and soul, let alone happy or successful. Nor can they make their child into one who seeks and hears and

---

30. Heb 4:13

pleases God. As parents, we can hold before our children the promise of life in God, but we cannot endow them with it. We can only do our best within the scope of our responsibilities and then humbly commit them to the hand of the God from whom we have received them.[31]

## Wise Parents and Wise Leaders Persevere

Good sense makes one slow to anger.

—PROVERBS 19:11

Patience may be the most undervalued virtue of parents and leaders, yet it may also be the most transformative. Consider how "with patience a ruler may be persuaded" (Prov 25:15), or how "whoever is slow to anger is better than the mighty, and he who rules his spirit than he who takes a city" (Prov 16:32), and "whoever is slow to anger has great understanding, but he who has a hasty temper exalts folly" (Prov 14:29). Forbearance, longsuffering, and being slow to anger are various ways to translate this idea of patience. Biblically speaking, patience is the ability to take a great deal of punishment from people or circumstances without losing one's temper, without becoming irritated and angry, and without taking vengeance. It includes the capacity to bear pain or trials without complaint, the ability to forbear under severe provocation, and the self-control to keep from acting rashly even while suffering opposition or adversity.[32]

The great biblical illustration of patience in operation is God himself. Several passages speak of him, in conjunction with other gracious attributes, as "slow to anger." In a context which stresses Israel's rebellion and provocation of God, he is contrasted as a God who is forgiving, gracious, compassionate, slow to anger, and abounding in loving-kindness (Neh 9:17). The psalmist declares, "But you, O Lord, are a God merciful and gracious, slow to anger and abounding in steadfast love and faithfulness" (Ps 86:15; see also Exod 34:6; Num 14:18; Ps 103:8; Joel 2:13; Jonah 4:2).[33]

This idea of the Lord's unfailing goodness—dependability, grace, and patience—is surprising in the world of ancient Near Eastern religions, where the gods were thoroughly inconsistent. If they were good on some occasions, they were bad on others. If they were dependable in some

31. Barth, *Dogmatics*, III.4. 284–85.
32. Elwell and Beitzel, "Patience," 1619.
33. Elwell and Beitzel, "Patience," 1619.

instances, they were quite fickle in others. But YHWH, "the Holy One of Israel" was not so.[34] His character was the same in all circumstances.[35]

This slowness to anger is not an absence of standards. As the apostle Paul tells us, "Do you presume on the riches of his kindness and forbearance and patience, not knowing that God's kindness is meant to lead you to repentance?" (Rom 2:4). God's ultimate goal is that we love the Lord our God with all our heart, soul, mind, and strength, and love our neighbor as our self.[36] The problem is that we humans are slow to yield to the ways of God. It is good for us that God is patient toward us, not wanting that any should perish but that all should reach repentance.[37] His patience is not about slack standards. Rather, it expresses a greatness of love that demands of itself longsuffering patience. It is a love that is not measured by some standard of compliance but rather by how it is poured out upon people, and people take time. Sometimes a lot of time.

We do not serve God like slaves who fear the lash of his whip. He does not want to enslave anyone. He wants sons and daughters filled with love because they have been transformed by his love, goodness, beauty, and grace. We are not human chattel who comply out of fear of his wrath. We are sons and daughters transformed by his love and patience. Now, we love him because he first loved us. This is the power of patience. Patience makes room for the long process of transformation. God shows us by his example that we too should be patient. This is what we are called to as followers of Jesus Christ, and it is what we are called to as parents and leaders. This virtue of patience is extolled in Proverbs.[38] Through patience we make room for imperfect humans to encounter a perfect God and to be transformed by him.

Our children may never conform to all we hope and dream for them. We love our children more than we love our desires for them. This love calls us to suffer long while they are on their journey to encounter God, the one who has fashioned them and called them to himself. They may never fulfill your ideal plan. So what? Love them anyway. Suffer long with them anyway, for they too are being transformed from glory to glory and from faith to faith, and that is a very long journey.

---

34. Pss 71:22; 78:41; 89:18
35. Oswalt, "God," 247–49.
36. Matt 22:36–40
37. 2 Pet 3:8–10
38. Prov 14:29; 15:18; 16:32; 25:15

Parenting is hard work. Keep at it. Do the right thing no matter what. Entrust your children to God. Be patient with them. Take to heart Paul's words, "And let us not grow weary of doing good, for in due season we will reap, if we do not give up" (Gal 6:9). You may feel overwhelmed, but keep showing up, keep putting one foot in front of the other. Persevere, dear parent, persevere, and remember, "It was by perseverance that the snail entered the ark."[39]

I am embarrassed to admit that this lesson in patient love was hard for me to learn. As a parent, I found it easier to get mad than to be patient. As a leader, I was equally impatient and sometimes angry when the church I was leading did not look like the church in my vision. I lament this now, and I pray for grace and forgiveness. I did finally discover that it is easy to love the church you want, and it can be hard to love the church you have. But that is the calling, to love the people, regardless of their conformity to my vision. Love will prevent your angry outbursts when those you lead are not measuring up to your vision. Love takes your focus away from your glorious vision and refocuses your eyes on that broken, stubborn, slow-to-repent, hope-filled, glorious image-bearer of God who stands before you and walks beside you and sometimes stabs you in the back.

Timothy was told:

> The Lord's servant must not be quarrelsome but kind to everyone, able to teach, patiently enduring evil, correcting his opponents with gentleness. God may perhaps grant them repentance leading to a knowledge of the truth. (2 Tim 2:24–25)

The family, church, ministry, or organization you lead may never fulfill your great vision. So what? Love them anyway. Suffer long with them anyway. For they, too, are on a long journey toward the one to whom they must give an account.

The children you have and the people you lead are not yours; they are his. Love them as his. Be patient with them and slow to anger, for he is working in them. Sometimes it is slow, and you see no movement. Sometimes it is dark, and you cannot see your way forward. Sometimes it is lonely, and you feel no presence. Yet, he is there, slowly working the night shift to bring them to the light, to bring them to himself. Your job is to help them in that journey, to give them the opportunity to encounter the Living God.

---

39. Attributed to Charles Spurgeon

## Leaders and Their Family of Origin

There is one final issue to discuss with you about parents and children. You have parents; you are someone's child. To be a wise and healthy leader, you must face your own family of origin issues. If you are unaware of how your family of origin impacts the way you think and behave, you will never understand why you think what you think and do what you do.

Your family of origin—the family you grew up in—is the place where you typically learn to become who you are and where you first learn your values and beliefs. It is here that you learn to communicate, get your needs met, and process thoughts, beliefs, and emotions. You can spend a fortune developing your leadership skills, yet if you are not aware of how your family of origin impacts your life at a fundamental level, you have wasted your time and money. For example, you can take a course on delegation, but if you are not aware of how your family of origin shaped your bias toward being a control freak, you will never actually delegate anything.

You typically develop a sense of self in the context of your family of origin. Here are some conditions to consider: poverty and abandonment; sexual, emotional, or physical abuse; alcohol or drug addiction; domineering, hyper-critical parents; nurture deficient families; an emotionally distant, non-communicative upbringing; childhood traumas; the divorce or death of a parent or sibling; and being adopted. These all have profound impacts on your development. Your family of origin was the first place that shaped your sense of self, your understanding of the world, and your relationships. William Wordsworth was right; the child is the father of the man. Your family of origin may explain much about your condition, but this is never a justification for you to remain in your condition, for wisdom also cries out to you (Prov 8).

For some, the biblical mandate to honor your parents[40] is a challenging and painful prospect. For others, it can often feel like a betrayal to examine the influence of your family of origin. However, through God's grace and perhaps professional therapy, you can learn to honor what is honorable and be free from whatever has been debilitating and dehumanizing. If you have the slightest hint that you may be dealing with issues surrounding your family of origin, please seek out a qualified professional. You will be glad you did. So will those who follow you.

---

40. Prov 15:20; 19:26; 20:20; 28:24; 30:17

# 7

# Friends, Foes, and Neighbors

What is desired in a man is steadfast love, and a poor man is better than a liar.

—PROVERBS 19:22

YOU CAN EXCEL IN casting a vision, managing details, and motivating the masses, but if you are not growing in your love for God and people, you are falling short of God's call on you as a leader. You are called first to love. You are called to be holy and to show forth God's presence in the world through loving your neighbor, enemy, and stranger. You are called to participate in the priestly ministry of democratizing holiness.[1] A holiness that moves from the sanctuary to society, from your private world to your neighborhood, and from a generic love of humanity to a specific love for the human next to you—even when that person hates you or you feel threatened because he or she is different than you.

This command to love informs Proverbs. "Let not steadfast love and faithfulness forsake you; bind them around your neck; write them on the tablet of your heart" (Prov 3:3) for "what is desired in a man is steadfast love" (Prov 19:22).[2] This is instruction given to leaders. Foolish leaders rally people to themselves by fanning flames of hatred and division,

---

1. Rom 15:16
2. See also Prov 10:12; 14:22; 16:6; 17:9; 19:22; 20:28; 25:21; 24:17

tearing apart the fabric of society, and polarizing groups into *us against them*. Wise leaders appeal to something more demanding, something higher. Wise leaders rally people to love one another, serve one another, and care for one another. This makes sense when you consider the central message of the Bible that begins in the Torah and reaches its crescendo in Christ is love.

It seems strange to me that one of the two "greatest commandments" is buried in Leviticus 19. This chapter in Leviticus brings together a hodge-podge of random and seemingly unrelated laws, ranging from moral precepts (e.g., don't gossip, don't hate, don't take revenge, don't bear a grudge) to social justice mandates (e.g., leave parts of the harvest for the poor; don't pervert justice; don't withhold wages; don't use false weights and measures). Then there are the odds and ends, from agricultural advice (don't crossbreed livestock; don't plant a field with mixed seeds) to ritual and religious prescriptions (don't wear a garment of mixed wool and linen; don't make your daughter a prostitute; don't eat blood; don't practice divination; don't cut yourself; and avoid certain haircuts). Buried right in the middle of this eclectic array of commandments is one of the two greatest commandments, "You shall love your neighbor as yourself" (Lev 19:18).

I admit it. Leviticus is a challenge. The whole book seems devoted to blood, guts, and fire, mixed with those prohibitions against what this gentile considers very tasty foods, such as pulled pork and bacon double cheeseburgers. The book is so forbidding that it almost thwarts my well-laid plans and New Year's resolutions. I have the habit of reading through the Bible every year. I start the new year with Genesis, a book with fantastic stories and interesting characters. Then comes Exodus. This one is also exciting at first. God delivers his people from Egyptian slavery. Then things get messy. But I keep reading. After Exodus comes Leviticus, the graveyard of Bible reading plans. Well-meaning Bible readers have walked into Leviticus, never to be seen again, lost somewhere between burning bulls, tossing blood, and fat-covered entrails. Leviticus is usually the last book Christians read. It is, however, traditionally the first book Jewish children learn in the Rabbinic system of education.[3] And I think they have the better of it.

The English name Leviticus comes from the Latin *Leviticus*, referring to the tribe of Levi (the priests). This is the Latin equivalent of

---

3. Sacks, *Leviticus*, 3.

*Leuitikon*, the title for the book in the Septuagint.[4] The Jews, however, used the opening word, *Vayikra*, "And he called," as the title for Leviticus.[5] Jewish rabbis explain that "He called" is a term of endearment. Many of God's messages in the Torah are prefaced by the words, "he said," "he spoke," or "he commanded," but *Vayikra*, "And he called," is the language of invitation, friendship, and love. It was because of his love that God called Abraham to follow him. It was because of his love that God led the children of Israel through the wilderness with a pillar of cloud by day and fire by night. It was because of his love that God called the people of Israel to come close to him, to be regular visitors at his house, to share in his "holiness, difference, apartness: to become, as it were, mediators of his presence to the world."[6] This tender description warms me to Leviticus. Through it, God calls us to share holiness and to mediate the divine presence.

Leviticus focuses on the newly consecrated priests, Aaron and his sons, and functions as a manual of priestly regulations and procedures. The Israelite priests were given detailed instructions about the care of God's sanctuary to ensure God's continuing presence with his people.[7] The book is a call to be holy because God is holy, for not only are we created in God's image, but we are also called to live in God's ways. While it seems Leviticus is about as far removed from our world as a book could possibly be, it is a key text, if not the key text, in Judaism, and consequently, it played a primary role in the early education of Jesus and other Jews in the New Testament, including Paul, the twelve apostles, and Mary of Nazareth.

This command to love goes beyond what is often called the Golden Rule. Don't get me wrong, the golden rule is wonderful. Jesus tells us, "So whatever you wish that others would do to you, do also to them" (Matt 7:12). The idea of the golden rule is not unique to Judaism or Christianity. Similar moral counsel is found in Hinduism, "This is the sum of duty: do not do to others what would cause pain for you" (*Mahababharata* 5.1517); Confucianism, "Do not do to others what you would not have them do for you" (*Analects of Confucius* 15:23); Buddhist writings, "Hurt not others in ways you yourself would find hurtful" (*Udana-Varga* 5.18); and ancient Greek philosophy, "May I do to others as I would they should

4. The Greek translation of the Old Testament.

5. Harrison, *Leviticus*, 13.

6. Sacks, *Leviticus*, 5.

7. Harrison, *Leviticus*, 26.

do unto me" (Plato, *Laws* II).[8] The concept appears as well in Islam, Taoism, Zoroastrianism, and most of the world's major religions.[9]

Notice, however, that the golden rule, as stated by Jesus, is not actually a direct quotation of the commandment recorded in Leviticus 19:18, 33–34. Jesus will give a direct quotation later. The golden rule, as generally communicated, is not about love, but rather about justice and ethics, or perhaps what psychologists call "reciprocal altruism." The Leviticus passages do not tell us, "Be nice to your neighbor, because you would want him to be nice to you," but instead, "*Love* your neighbor." This rule is different and far stronger—a sense that Jesus captures in stating the greatest commandments. When asked, "Teacher, which is the great commandment in the Law?" Jesus replied:

> You shall love the Lord your God with all your heart and with all your soul and with all your mind. This is the great and first commandment. And a second is like it: You shall love your neighbor as yourself. On these two commandments depend all the Law and the Prophets. (Matt 22:34–40)

Notice how Jesus takes us beyond a universal decree to be nice and toward a specific call to love. It is possible to do righteous works, to be kind, to do justice, and yet still not love. St. Paul alludes to this in 1 Corinthians 13:3, "If I give away all I have, and if I deliver up my body to be burned, but have not love, I gain nothing." In other words, it is possible to do the most virtuous acts of self-sacrifice for reasons other than love. This will not suffice. Yet, that does not mean that you should only do good deeds when you feel your heart strangely warmed by love. Sometimes you need to do righteous acts to mold your heart toward love. In Luke 6:27–36, Jesus so intermingles acts of justice and mercy with the command to love that it can be hard to distinguish one from the other.

> Love your enemies, do good to those who hate you, bless those who curse you, pray for those who abuse you. To one who strikes you on the cheek, offer the other also, and from one who takes away your cloak do not withhold your tunic either. Give to everyone who begs from you, and from one who takes away your goods do not demand them back. And as you wish that others would do to you, do so to them. If you love those who love you, what benefit is that to you? For even sinners love those

8. Westmoreland-White, "Golden," 331–32.
9. Collins, "Golden Rule," 2:1070.

who love them. And if you do good to those who do good to you, what benefit is that to you? For even sinners do the same. And if you lend to those from whom you expect to receive, what credit is that to you? Even sinners lend to sinners, to get back the same amount. But love your enemies, and do good, and lend, expecting nothing in return, and your reward will be great, and you will be sons of the Most High, for he is kind to the ungrateful and the evil. Be merciful, even as your Father is merciful.

The call to love reorients our affections (Love your enemy), behavior (Do good to those who hate you), attitude (Bless those who curse you), and spirituality (Pray for those who abuse you). The call to love presses us out of the comforts of our affectionate relations with family and friends and into the disorienting world that is no longer divided into "us and them." The golden rule has been radicalized into an extraordinarily demanding ethic of love that comes not from our hearts but from heaven. We are to do far more than treat people the way we want to be treated. We are to love, do good, bless, and pray for those who hate us and seek to do us harm.

I think Jesus places these acts of obedience and the command to love side by side for a sound psychological reason. Deeds of justice and mercy nourish feelings of love for neighbor and enemy, and the process also works in reverse, where feelings can motivate deeds. Sometimes I must do acts of kindness to plant seeds of love in my heart. Other times, I may feel love for a person, which I express with acts of justice and mercy. Most of the time, though, my heart is hard and loveless, filled with judgment and prejudice against those who are not like me. It is here that I must learn again the power of deeds: doing justice, loving mercy, and walking humbly with my God (Mic 6:8). Loving deeds hammer away at my heart of stone, cracking it open, so that love for my neighbor and my enemy may find lodging where once there was enmity. The act of obedience becomes an organ of spiritual knowledge and the pathway to transformation. I learn to love when I learn to be kind and merciful. It is this love of the other, both neighbor and enemy, that helps ensure the continual presence of God in my life, and in this world. When read through the lens of Christ's gospel, Leviticus starts to make sense to me.

In *Love: A History*, Philosopher Simon May writes, "If love in the Western world has a founding text, that text is Hebrew."[10] Unfortunately, Christian history has generally been neither fair nor balanced in

10. May, *Love*, 14.

distinguishing between the Old and New Testaments. For centuries many Christians have believed, either implicitly or explicitly, that God in the Old Testament is full of laws, wrath, retribution, and judgement and God in the New Testament is nice, loving and forgiving. This false dichotomy can make it sound as though Jesus saves us from God, or as though God had a conversion experience between Malachi and Matthew. Sadly, May was right:

> The widespread belief that the Hebrew Bible is all about vengeance and an eye for an eye, while the Gospels supposedly invent love as an unconditional and universal value, must therefore count as one of the most extraordinary misunderstandings in all of Western history. For the Hebrew Bible is the source of not just the two love commandments but of a larger moral vision inspired by wonder for love's power.[11]

Throughout scripture the relationship between neighbors involves moral and social obligations. The ninth and tenth commandments prohibited bearing false witness, defaming, or slandering a neighbor and condemned envy of a neighbor's wife, servant, livestock, or possessions (Exod 20:16–17; Deut 5:20–21; Prov 25:18). We are not to deal falsely with our neighbors, defraud them, frame malicious devices, or harbor evil thoughts against them (Exod 20:17; Lev 6:2; 19:13; Deut 23:24f; Ps 15:3; 101:5; Prov 24:28; Jer 22:13; Zech 8:17). Nor may we lead them into shameful conduct (Hab 2:15) or wrong our neighbor by having a sexual relationship with their spouse (Lev 18:20). All of these actions destroy human community.

Now, back to Leviticus 19. This chapter contains two of the most powerful of all God's commandments: to love your neighbor and to love the stranger. "You shall love your neighbor as yourself: I am the Lord" (Lev 19:18). In Leviticus 19:33–34, the command to love your neighbor is taken to unheard-of heights, for God commands that we also love the stranger, the alien, the one who is unknown and unlike us.

> When a stranger sojourns with you in your land, you shall not do him wrong. You shall treat the stranger who sojourns with you as the native among you, and you shall love him as yourself, for you were strangers in the land of Egypt: I am the Lord your God.

---

11. May, *Love*, 19

The command to love—not just God—but humanity, all of humanity, including strangers, is extraordinary and a world-changing idea. Most people in most societies in most ages have feared, hated, and often harmed the stranger, the alien, the one who is different. People don't usually love strangers. Yet, this is exactly what God commands us to do. It is this love that helps ensure the abiding presence of God among his people. This love sanctifies and makes holy, setting apart humans as the temple of God. This love opens your eyes to see God in his image-bearers, as broken and as hostile as they may be. And this love marks you as a disciple of Jesus (John 13:35).

Simon May describes love as the rapture we feel for people and things that inspire in us hope, the hope that is an abiding grounding for our life.[12] Love sets us on and sustains us through the long search for a secure relationship with others. Love builds the connections we need to feel at home in the world, to root our life in the present, to give substance and meaning, and to create the indescribable joy that comes from loving and being loved. Love is a universal human need.

The call to love as a leader is not about loving those who follow you. It is more demanding than that; it is love for people outside your arena of leadership. Because leadership can feel all consuming, it is easy to reduce your world to the boundaries of your leadership. If your world only fits within those boundaries, you cut yourself off from God's much larger world and sever yourself from your fullest humanity. For if it truly is love that sustains you, then to live without obedience to the two great commandments entails a great loss; it means to live without groundedness, without rootedness, without at-homeness—to live as vagabonds cut off from the life source and from what makes you human. This alienation is ultimately debilitating to both your personhood and your position as leader.

I saw this breakdown happened in real time as I watched a man of God unravel at the seams. At one time, he led a fruitful ministry, impacting thousands of lives. Yet, he began to reduce his world to the boundaries of his leadership. Soon, his ministry became his everything. Everyone and everything was evaluated according to how they supported his ministry. Then he began to disintegrate. Fruitful ministry gave way to erratic and abusive behavior. People became tools to be used. The ministry, like an all-consuming monster, required increasingly more money, more growth, and more impressive stories—whether these stories were

12. May, *Love*, 6.

stretched far beyond the truth, or fabricated, or recycled from the good old days—all to feed this monster which had once been a work of God's grace. Love, joy, and a sound mind degenerated into abusive demands, unhinged tirades, and bizarre conspiracy theories. When I asked those closest to him how this had happened, the common refrain was, "He is alone. He has no friends."

This leader was not physically isolated. He was surrounded by people. Unfortunately, these people were employees, subordinates, and adoring followers; not friends, not colleagues, not equals, and certainly not ones to whom he was accountable. Those who spoke out were driven away. He cut himself off from the earnest council of his friends (Prov 27:9). Those who remained were voiceless; some because of loyalty, others because of a misguided belief in the leader's God-given authority, and still others cowered in fear with all sense of agency having been beaten out of them. The leader was alone even though surrounded by people. His isolation from true community exacted a devastating toll. It was not good.

In the Torah, the words "not good" (*lo tov*) appear twice, both in connection to being alone. In the creation account in Genesis 2, God says, "It is not good for man to be alone" (Gen 2:18), and when Jethro, Moses' father-in-law, sees Moses leading alone, he says, "What you are doing is not good" (Exod 18:17). It is not good to live alone or to lead alone.

Loneliness is what you experience when your social needs, whether at work, with family, or through friend groups, go unmet. It is a mental state—when the mind perceives isolation, loneliness settles in. We can be totally alone and not feel lonely, and we can be surrounded by people and still feel alone. Loneliness and isolation have driven untold multitudes of gifted and called leaders away from ministries where they once thrived.

You may never experience a catastrophic implosion due to loneliness. However, you will, by the very nature of your leadership role, experience prolonged seasons of feeling alone, feeling that no one understands what you are going through or that you cannot share life with those you lead. While it is easy to hide behind the clichés—like "it's lonely at the top"—and to fantasize about being a lone leader who swoops in to save the day, the book of Proverbs gives no quarter to such destructive myths. Instead, Proverbs calls for the leader to be a fully integrated human being, living as part of a larger community of friends, foes, and neighbors.

Leadership gives the public appearance of recognition; you are seen, heard, and known. But this is only an illusion. Speaking to the crowds may feed your ego, but it does not feed your soul. In fact, the soul may be depleted. We see this even in Jesus. After a full day of teaching the multitudes and then performing the miracle of feeding five thousand men, plus the women and the children (Matt 14:13–21), Jesus dismissed the crowds and then he "went up on the mountain by himself to pray" (Matt 14:23). Jesus sought to teach this practice to his disciples in Mark 6:7–13, where he sends his twelve apostles on their first solo ministry trip. During this intensive and fruitful ministry, "they cast out many demons and anointed with oil many who were sick and healed them" (v. 13). When the apostles returned to Jesus and "told him all that they had done and taught," Jesus said to them, "Come away by yourselves to a desolate place and rest a while" (Mark 6:3–31). The King James Version translates verse 31, "Come ye yourselves apart into a desert place, and rest a while." The lesson is simple: Come apart for a little while, or you will come apart for good.

While solitude can do wonders for soul care and mental health, isolation and loneliness are deadly because your soul craves deep human connection. There is a longing to be seen, heard, and known, and this is more likely to happen around the table with friends than on the platform of ministry. This is why you must be intentional about building community.

The desire for human connection can play havoc, given the unique demands of leadership. This typically results in two very flawed responses: Either the lines are blurred, or walls are built. The lines can get blurry because we love and care for those we serve, and they, in turn, love and care for us. When these feelings of love and care are translated to mean, "We are friends," expectations of friendship are attached to a relationship between the leader and the led. Then, when the expectations of friendship are not met, people are hurt.

It gets even more complicated if such people are on your payroll. Consider what happens when the organization you lead must make cuts in staff due to an economic downturn, a new direction, or new cost-saving technology. The organization's financial responsibilities then appear to conflict with the organization's family feel. When this happens, once happy employees who believed they were part of a family now feel betrayed, deceived, and thrown away.

The pain of having a friend become a fierce critic is bitter and then numbing. You begin to relate with the psalmist, "Even my close friend in whom I trusted, who ate my bread, has lifted up his heel against me" (Ps 41:9). There are times when this break in the relationship happens for clear reasons, such as a disagreement about aims or beliefs. Then there are times when you cannot identify what went wrong, and you never see any reconciliation, and that makes the break even more painful.

You may become so weary and wounded by betrayal or criticism that you decide to build walls of self-protection as an act of survival. The walls that were intended to protect you from those who would do you harm eventually become walls that isolate you from those who can do you good. The walls isolate you from the human community you desperately need. You cease being protected and secure, and you become isolated as if banished from your own humanity.

One Sunday after church, I stood looking out my dining room window, staring at nothing, with a mixture of anxiety, stress, depression, hopelessness, and irritability. My wife asked, "Honey, what is wrong?" Fighting back my emotions, I told her, "I feel like I built a prison and locked myself inside, and I don't know how to get out." Little did I know then that I was experiencing the consequences of my misguided worldview regarding what it meant to be a leader, a Christian, and even a person. I had built walls of protection and strategies for success, but I had not built a community where I could be vulnerable. Now I felt like a prisoner in solitary confinement.

"There are many ways to destroy a person, but one of the simplest and most devastating is through prolonged solitary confinement."[13] These are the opening words of Lisa Guenther's profound and challenging book, *Solitary Confinement: Social Death and Its Afterlives*. Guenther examined the experience of solitary confinement in America from the early nineteenth century to today's supermax prisons. Solitary confinement undermines a prisoner's sense of identity and ability to understand the world. They are more likely to develop anxiety, depression, suicidal thoughts, and psychosis. The confinement also adversely impacts physical health, increasing a person's risk for a range of conditions, including fractures, vision loss, chronic pain, hypersensitivity to sounds and smells, and problems with attention, concentration, and memory. There may be hallucinations, paranoia, poor impulse control, social withdrawal, outbursts of violence, and psychosis. Yes, solitary confinement, whether in prison or in life, is very destructive. It is, as Guenther argues, a violent attack on the structure of being itself.

It is not only prisoners in solitary confinement that suffer the consequences of isolation. We live on a planet with more than eight billion

13. Guenther, *Solitary Confinement*, 2013.

people, and yet loneliness is a pervasive source of human suffering in the world today. Loneliness is so acute that the British government took the drastic action of appointing Tracey Crouch as the nation's first Minister of Loneliness in 2018. According to research, loneliness damages your health by raising the levels of stress hormones and inflammation, which in turn increase your risk of heart disease, arthritis, Type 2 diabetes, dementia, and even suicide. Whether in a maximum-security prison cell or in the crowded intersection of London's Piccadilly Circus, isolation and alienation are ruling powers of this present darkness, a spiritual host of wickedness.[14] Leaders are called to lead the way in overthrowing the dominion of loneliness by acts of welcome and embrace, and this is why Proverbs seeks to make you wise when it comes to friends, foes, and neighbors.

## Friends: People Who Like You

The fact that Dale Carnegie's *How to Win Friends and Influence People* was published in 1936 and has remained to this day a perennial best seller illustrates our longing for friends. We humans are, above all things, social beings. Unfortunately, we have become proficient at categorizing and commoditizing our social networks and are poor at building relationships.

The Hebrew word *rēᵃ ʿ* can mean friend, neighbor, companion, or associate. When used this way, it refers to any person you associate with and for whom you have affection and personal regard (2 Sam 16:17). It can also refer to a fellow citizen (Exod 2:13; 22:6), or acquaintance.[15]

In this chapter, I am using the word "friend" in the modern sense of the word. People who are bound together by affection, trust, and the shared joy of being together, regardless of family or professional relations. It is critical that you as a leader know how to distinguish between your friends and the friendly relations that exist because of your leadership role.

When you become a leader, the landscape of your relationships changes. Your world becomes larger and smaller at the same time; larger because you have more responsibilities, more access to "the levers of power," and a bigger perspective on the work of your organization. You may even gain a greater understanding of the world around you. But your

---

14. Eph 6:12
15. Langford, "Friendship," 2014.

world also becomes smaller. You have more responsibilities but less free-dom. More social influence, but fewer social relationships. You are no longer part of the crowd; you are leading the crowd, and that makes your world smaller. You cannot bring your old way of thinking about your social networks into your new role as leader. Your relationship context has changed. You cannot be everyone's buddy as a leader. But this does not mean you must be alone. You will need to find new ways to develop community and connection with others.

As a ministry leader, you do not get to choose who you lead. You do not get to choose only the positive, uplifting, financially generous people; you must also love, serve, and lead the demanding, the emotionally needy, and the ones who always open their mouths in opposition but never their wallets in support. This is the flock you are called to love, serve, and lead. You must follow the Chief Shepherd and care for all the Lord entrusts to you. It does not matter if they are demanding and unrealistic; they are to be loved and led as those for whom Christ died.

However, when it comes to friends, it is a different story. When it comes to choosing friends, you can be picky. Proverbs tells us, "The righteous choose their friends carefully, but the way of the wicked leads them astray" (Prov 12:26, NIV). Choosing your friends is a life-altering decision because it plays a critical role in developing who you are, who you will become, and what your world will look like.

It is easy to think this demanding ethic of love means that you are to ignore destructive behavior or become a doormat. Here is where Proverbs can help, for it is clear about the kinds of people you are to avoid in your relationships. People with a wicked heart (Prov 4:14–17) or who do not control their tongue (Prov 11:9; 16:28; 20:19) bring only death and de-struction. Stay away from short-tempered and angry people; it is a snare to your soul (Prov 22:24–25). Sadly, some want to be close to you because of your position or your resources, and they only want to use you; they are your "friends" if you have something to give them (Prov 14:20; 19:4, 6–7). You can love these people without becoming their victims.

It is hard to overstate just how important your friends are. Their in-fluence on your thinking and behavior shapes your character. Your friends can build you up or tear you down. They make you, or they break you. If you walk with the wise, you will become wise (Prov 13:20), and if you walk with fools and the wicked, you will follow the path of destruction (Prov 12:26). The quality of your friends makes you better or worse. One of the most powerful ways to change your life is to upgrade your friendships.

You may only be a few friends away from the breakthroughs you need. These enriching, transforming, and refreshing friendships are built on faith, hope, and love.

## Friends Are Faithful

Many a man proclaims his own steadfast love, but a faithful man who can find?

—PROVERBS 20:6

Friends are bound by faithfulness (Prov 17:17; 27:10). When you are going through hard times, "a friend sticks closer than a brother" (Prov 18:24). J.R.R. Tolkien captures the beauty and strength of friendship in *The Lord of the Rings*. Every time Frodo tries to go alone in his quest to destroy the ring of power, his friends refuse to let him. At the beginning of his quest, he tries to slip out of the Shire unnoticed, only to discover that Merry and Pippin have conspired with Sam to go with him, and not only that, but they have also known about his secret ring for some time. Frodo did not know if he felt angry, amused, relieved, or merely foolish at this discovery. Sam reminded Frodo of Gandalf's words that he was not to go alone; he was to take with him someone he could trust. Frodo replied, "But it does not seem I can trust anyone." Merry responded,

> It all depends on what you want. You can trust us to stick with you through thick and thin—to the bitter end. And you can trust us to keep any secret of yours—closer than you keep it yourself. But you cannot trust us to let you face trouble alone and go off without a word. We are your friends, Frodo.[16]

Faithful friendship is an underlying theme within Tolkien's saga, whether it was when Frodo attempted to leave the Shire or when he broke away from the fellowship of the ring and Sam followed after him, refusing to break his promise of companionship, or when Éomer marshals the cavalry of Rohan with his stirring speech:

> Now is the hour come, Riders of the Mark, sons of Eorl! Foes and fire are before you, and your homes far behind. Yet, though you fight upon an alien field, the glory that you reap shall be

---

16. Tolkien, *Lord*, 105

your own forever. Oaths ye have taken: now fulfill them all, to lord and land and league of friendship![17]

When Frodo and Sam are finally at the Mount of Doom, and Frodo is too spent to continue, Sam tells Frodo, "I can't carry it for you, but I can carry you." It is friendship that makes Samwise Gamgee the greatest hero among all the heroes in *The Lord of the Rings*.

Another word for faithful is trustworthy. Friends are people you can trust. You can trust them to tell you the truth and give you good advice. "Oil and perfume make the heart glad, and the sweetness of a friend comes from his earnest counsel" (Prov 27:9). While professional counseling has its place, sometimes you just need a good friend and a good conversation to make it through a tough spot. You do not need friends who merely flatter you and tell you things you want to hear. You need friends who are willing to tell you hard truth when it will help you, for "faithful are the wounds of a friend" (Prov 27:6). After all, "In the end, people appreciate frankness more than flattery" (Prov 28:23, TLB). You can trust these friends to protect you, even when they need to protect you from yourself.

You can trust friends to listen to you. Good friends will not minimize your struggles. I was recently sharing with a small group of people about my lifelong struggle with sleep. Just as I was sharing that if I could get five or six hours of sleep, that was a victory, one of the participants interrupted and said, "God bless you, Jeff, five or six hours, that's nothing. I sometimes get four hours of sleep." That ended the conversation. I knew then that this was not a place to have that level of conversation. Friends do not minimize nor seek to one-up you, nor do they gloss over your struggles with shallow answers. Sometimes you need a friend to listen, not a meaningless platitude or religious jargon like, "Don't worry. Be happy," "Trust God," or "Just pray about it." As Proverbs says, "Whoever sings songs to a heavy heart is like one who takes off a garment on a cold day, and like vinegar on soda" (Prov 25:20).

You can trust friends to control their tongue and keep a confidence (Prov 25:9–10; 11:12, 13; 20:19; 16:28; 17:9; 11:9; 11:12; 24:28–29; 25:18; 26:18–19). Good friends do not slander by revealing another's secret (Prov 25:9–10; 11:13) or belittle their friends and neighbors (Prov 11:12), nor do they go about whispering to others, separating close friends (Prov 16:28; 17:9). Rather, good friends can be trusted with your secrets (Prov

---

17. Tolkien, *Lord*, 836

11:12, 13). This is why Proverbs warns you, "Do not associate with a simple babbler" (Prov 20:19). I once heard a pastor at a leadership conference jokingly state, "If I am going to confess my sins and temptations to anyone, it is going to be to a rabbit in the woods, and then I will shoot the rabbit." We all laughed because we understood the dangers of confiding our struggles to others. One ill-advised acknowledgment of weakness could destroy your ministry. While I do not suggest you confess to rabbits and then shoot them, I do suggest you develop a few trusted friends who can be as confidential as a dead rabbit.

You can trust friends to respect healthy boundaries. A friend demonstrates respect, sensitivity, and common sense (Prov 18:19; 15:17; 27:14; 25:20). This includes respect for your family, time, privacy, needs, and what you are going through. A good dose of common sense goes a long way in friendship. "Whoever blesses his neighbor with a loud voice, rising early in the morning, will be counted as cursing" (Prov 27:14).

Remember, when you are a leader, some people will press into you to be your friend because they want to be close to "the leader." They are not seeking friendship with you as a person. They are seeking a relationship with your position. Keith was a faithful member of his church and a nice guy who was delightful to be around. But he wanted more of a friendship than his pastor could deliver. He would show up at the pastor's house unannounced. He would insert himself into situations, trying to position himself into the "trusted friend" category. While responding courteously, both temperament and prudence demanded that his pastor proceed with caution and keep things cordial and professional. Keith was well-liked by the congregation. He was even elected by the congregation to serve on the church board. This only increased Keith's expectations and demands for friendship. Keith's unmet expectations festered until things eventually exploded during a board meeting. He vented this full anger at his pastor, pounding his finger into the pastor's chest while screaming, "You have not made yourself emotionally available to me."[18] It went downhill from there. Keith became a fierce critic and caused dissension within the church. Long-term relationships were poisoned and destroyed. He eventually left the church, but he continued stirring up strife with others and trolling his former pastor online. The pastor eventually had to block Keith from all forms of contact, including social media. It was a sad end that did not need to happen that way, but it always seems to end this way

---

18. While the phrase has an awkwardness that may suggest some type of sexual attraction, it was not meant that way.

when someone demands friendship to satisfy some internal unmet need or unhealed wound rather than simply walking with love and respect, rejoicing in whatever form the relationship takes.

## Friends Inspire Hope

> A man of many companions may come to ruin, but there
> is a friend who sticks closer than a brother.
>
> —PROVERBS 18:24

I ran my first marathon when I was 49 years old. I had taken up running because I needed some form of exercise that I could do consistently while also keeping a demanding travel schedule. After running for a few years, I thought, "I want to run a marathon." Debbie and I lived in Athens, Greece at the time so I enrolled in the local marathon, "The Authentic." The course is inspired by the Ancient Greek legend of Pheidippides, a messenger who is said to have run from Marathon to Athens to bring news of the Greek victory over the Persians at the Battle of Marathon. It starts in the city of Marathon (yes, that's where the name comes from) and continues for 26.2 miles (42.2 km), ending in the old Olympic Stadium in Athens. The Athens Marathon is considered one of the most difficult major marathons. The course is uphill from the 6-mile mark (10 km) to the 19-mile mark (31 km). Yes, that's 13 miles (21 km) running up a hill. It is the toughest uphill climb of any major marathon.[19] I had made it up the hill, but I was hurting, exhausted, and barely moving.

Then I saw my friend Stelios yelling and cheering me on. At first, I thought, "Stelios, what are you doing here? Your wife is about to go into labor at any moment. Why are you here?" Yet, there he was, wading through more than 16,000 runners, looking for me, just so that he could run into the street and give me a high-five and tell me I could do this, I could make it, keep going. Stelios cared enough about me to come alongside me and give me the courage to finish the race. His love and encouragement inspired hope in my aching body and weary mind. I finished the marathon, in part because of Stelios. He pulled something out of me that I did not know I had.

19. Butcher, "Athens Marathon Record Broken by Nearly Two Minutes: News: World Athletics." worldathletics.org. https://www.worldathletics.org/news/news/athens–marathon–record–broken–by–nearly–two–m.

In *The Four Loves,* C.S. Lewis notes, "In each of my friends, there is something that only some other friend can fully bring out. By myself, I am not large enough to call the whole man to activity; I want other lights than my own to show all his facets." He goes on, "Now that Charles is dead, I shall never again see Ronald's [J.R.R. Tolkien] reaction to a specifically Caroline joke. Far from having more of Ronald, having him 'to myself' now that Charles is away, I have less of Ronald."[20] Such is the power of friends. They illuminate facets of our lives that no one else can shine upon, and they make us better people because of it. This inspires hope that we are more than we can see in ourselves and that we are capable of change with a little help from our friends.

That's what friends do. They inspire us; they cause us to dig deep, to keep going, to hold on to hope. True friends make you a better version of yourself, for "As iron sharpens iron, so one man sharpens another" (Prov 27:17).

Ecclesiastes tells us:

> Two are better than one, because they have a good reward for their toil. For if they fall, one will lift up his fellow. But woe to him who is alone when he falls and has not another to lift him up! Again, if two lie together, they keep warm, but how can one keep warm alone? And though a man might prevail against one who is alone, two will withstand him—a threefold cord is not quickly broken" (Eccl 4:9–12).

## Friends Love You at All Times

> A friend loves at all times, and a brother is born for adversity.
>
> —PROVERBS 17:17

It is easy to love someone who is on top of the world, "and everyone is a friend to a man who gives gifts" (Prov 19:6), but real friends can handle the real you. They can handle it when you are going through difficulty, for "a man of many companions may come to ruin, but there is a friend who sticks closer than a brother" (Prov 18:24). While everyone needs, expects, even demands, something from you as a leader, friends replenish you. Friends are a safe house when threatened, a shelter during a storm,

---

20. Lewis, *Four Loves,* 58–59.

and a house of healing when you are not well. Friends love you when you are winning and when you are losing because "a friend loves at all times."

Martin, an acquaintance of mine, once led a global organization. Days filled with interactions with people from every corner of the globe placed him at the center of all the action. His work relationships were rich, diverse, and friendly. Then his role changed. He was no longer the leader of the organization. His phone went silent. His "friends" were no longer calling him every day. He felt discarded like a broken toy. He had confused his friendly work relationships with friends. Once he was no longer in the leadership role, his relationships changed. It was not that the people had changed or that their relationships were not real. The people did not change; the context of the relationships changed. My friend did not understand that these were friendly work relationships; they were work colleagues but not friends. Friends are different from those connected to you by reason of your position. Friends are bound to you not as a leader but as a person.

## Foes: People Who Do Not Like You

> God commands us to love both our enemies and our
> neighbors because usually they are the same people.
>
> —G.K. Chesterton

Leadership will give you fake friends and real enemies. Yes, even you will have foes. As much as we all want to be liked, leadership means you will upset people. Some of these people will move from being upset with you to being at enmity with you. They will not be satisfied to disagree with you; they will want to be at war with you. They will "muster the troops" against you, enlisting others in their quest to stop you. A root of bitterness springs up and causes trouble, and by it, many become defiled (Heb 12:15).

This is what happened with Keith, mentioned above. He was disappointed that his pastor could not give him the friendship he demanded. The offense was deep, and it turned his heart against his pastor. Love was replaced with hate, and the hatred with which he hated his pastor was greater than the love with which he had once loved him. And since "hatred stirs up strife" (Prov 10:12), he stirred up strife within the congregation, and a battle began. People who were once friends were now divided by animosity. As is the case so many times, the conflict took on a life of its own and soon people were hurt for reasons they did not even know. It is painful when friends become foes.

It is not only disgruntled congregants who fall into this trap. Leaders fall into it as well when a follower does not meet their expectations. Kenneth was a newly appointed pastor in a mid-sized church. He was filled with a vision of what he wanted the church to become. He had expectations of all the key leaders and influential members. When they did not live up to his expectations, he began to see them as people who needed to leave the church because they were getting in his way. Their every action was judged on how they did or did not fulfill Kenneth's expectations of how they should serve the church he envisioned.

From time to time, Kenneth would meet with Rick to talk about how things were going. Rick, as an older, more experienced pastor, was an occasional mentor for Kenneth. In one conversation, Kenneth complained to Rick about how a particular lady in the church was not as active as he thought she should be, and she was not supporting the church. Rick pointed out that this woman had recently lost her husband after a long battle with cancer; rather than complain that she was not doing enough for the church, he ought to be more concerned about how the church ministered to this widow in her time of grief. The advice fell on deaf ears. The mentoring relationship ended shortly after that. A couple of years later, Rick heard Kenneth say, "I finally ran off all those people who were getting in the way and causing me problems." Rick happened to know many of those people. They were good people. The problem was that they were also strong people, and Kenneth felt threatened by them. If these people questioned his decisions, behavior, or the direction he wanted to take the church, Kenneth interpreted it as rebellion against his leadership. He soon could not speak of them without an acrid taste in his mouth.

Both Keith and Kenneth allowed love to give way to hatred. In both cases, people went from wonderful friends to horrible enemies. Maximus the Confessor—a seventh-century Christian leader who had his tongue pulled out and his right hand cut off to prevent him from proclaiming the truth of the Gospel—warned:

> Do not, because of the hate which has arisen in you today from the evil of one's abuse, judge as bad and vicious the brother who yesterday was spiritual and virtuous. Instead, through the patience that love gives, cast out today's hate by thinking of yesterday's goodness. Do not, because you changed from love to hate, disparage today as bad and vicious the one whom yesterday

you praised as good and honored as virtuous, and blame your brother for the evil hate within you. Rather, continue in those same praises even though you are still full of hurt, and you will easily return to the same saving love.[21]

Let's go back to Leviticus for a moment. Leviticus 4 prescribes different sin offerings depending on who sins. There are four categories specified: an ordinary individual (v. 2), the anointed priest (v. 3), the whole congregation (v. 13), and a leader. In three of the four cases, the regulation is introduced by the word "if"—if such a person commits a sin then do thus and so (Lev 4:2, 3, 13). In the case of the leader, however, the regulation is prefaced by the word "when"—"when a leader sins" (Lev 4:22). The Hebrew word *nasi* is the generic word for leader and refers to one who governs or rules a group.[22] Leviticus is warning that, when it comes to leaders, it is not a matter of "if they sin," it is a matter of "when they sin." In leading it is easy to get it wrong; it is hard to get it right. A good dose of humility is needed to be a wise leader—a humility that is quick to acknowledge, "I have sinned." Unfortunately, the power that comes with the leadership role tends to magnify the human impulse toward self-justification.

When your actions as a leader cause others, whether rightly or wrongly, to feel they have been sinned against, it is all too natural to fight back, justify yourself, and rally people to your cause against those who are opposing you. Weak and foolish leaders need an enemy to rally against. It is the easiest thing in the world to become a leader by mobilizing the forces of hate to rally one group against another. This is the unmistakable mark of all toxic leadership. Wisdom calls for a greater response, a response of love.

> Do not say, "I will do to him as he has done to me; I will pay the man back for what he has done." Proverbs 24:29

Leadership at its highest level transforms both leaders and followers. Great leaders make people better, kinder, and more noble than they would otherwise be. This is our goal as leaders, even with our enemies.

It is a fact of life for leaders: someone is always angry at you. Leadership requires decision making and taking stands that may be unpopular. And let's face it, some people just do not like anyone in leadership. How

---

21. Maximus, *Selected Writings*, 78.

22. See Aitken, "נָשִׂיא (nāśî᾽ I), chief, king (#5954); < נָשָׂא (nāśā᾽), lift up," 171–72.

you handle your foes reveals much about your character. So, if you are going to be a leader, you will have foes, and you need to know how to deal with them according to the wisdom of God. Here are five instructions from Proverbs.

First, recognize that the fear of man is a trap. Proverbs 29:25 tells us: "The fear of man lays a snare, but whoever trusts in the Lord is safe." It is emotionally devastating when someone you love and trust rises up against you. It will cause you untold pain and self-doubt. Due to the fear of man, you may crave affirmation, become a people pleaser, compromise your values, and give in to peer pressure. When the fear of man influences your decisions, you avoid doing the right but difficult thing; you sidestep what's unpleasant or unpopular. Guard yourself from an unhealthy need for approval. This is another trap set by fear.

Second, do not rejoice when bad things happen to your foes. Proverbs 24:17 warns us, "Do not rejoice when your enemy fall, and let not your heart be glad when he stumbles." Do not secretly wish for another's misfortune. Remember: You are called to love your enemy. Do not allow the bitter experiences of betrayal and criticism to make your heart rancid. Bitterness is a cancer that eats you from the inside out. Choose to love your enemy, to pray for those who have spoken ill against you.

Third, be kind to your foes. Proverbs 25:21–22 instructs us,

> If your enemy is hungry, give him bread to eat, and if he is thirsty, give him water to drink, for you will heap burning coals on his head, and the Lord will reward you.

Here, "your enemy" can be translated as "your hater." The American colloquialism, "Haters gonna hate," recently became a catchy song; it's a phrase meaning no matter what you do, some people will never like you—because haters are going to hate you. Wisdom's response to hatred is shocking: Feed the hater! Instead of seeking revenge, give your foe the means to live. In Exodus, we find the commandment,

> If you see the donkey of one who hates you lying down under its burden, you shall refrain from leaving him with it; you shall rescue it with him. (Exod 23:5)

The Aramaic translation takes the phrase "You shall rescue it with him" to mean not just the physical burden but also the psychological burden of enmity, translating the phrase, "You shall surely let go of the hate you have in your heart towards him."[23] Doing kindness to your enemy helps break the power of hatred that seeks to take root in your heart.

Paul made use of Proverbs 25:21–22 in Romans 12:17–21, and it bears quoting here for the wise counsel it offers you as a leader:

> Repay no one evil for evil, but give thought to do what is honorable in the sight of all. If possible, so far as it depends on you, live peaceably with all. Beloved, never avenge yourselves, but leave it to the wrath of God, for it is written, "Vengeance is mine, I will repay, says the Lord." To the contrary, "if your enemy is hungry, feed him; if he is thirsty, give him something to drink; for by so doing you will heap burning coals on his head." Do not be overcome by evil, but overcome evil with good.

Fourth, do not be naïve about your foes. You are to love them, feed them, give them water if they are thirsty, pray for them, and work for reconciliation. But be wary of trusting them. Do not give in to the temptation to win them over by acting as though they are trustworthy. Far too many trusting leaders have been taken in by flattery, sympathy, empathy, or a desire to appease, only to discover it was a foe's tactic for gaining access to do damage. Proverbs 25:19 warns, "Like a broken tooth or a lame foot is reliance on the unfaithful in a time of trouble" (NIV).

As a young pastor, Jerod always enjoyed time with older believers. He valued their wisdom and stability. Randy and Margaret seemed to be that kind of couple. Randy and Margaret would often invite Jarod and his wife, Deja, over for lunch. During relaxed conversations, Margaret would coyly ask what appeared to be innocent questions about situations and people, interjecting signs of empathy along with the occasional compliment and word of affirmation. The relationship seemed friendly and harmless until Deja caught on to what was happening. Deja warned Jarod, "You need to be careful about what you say around Margaret. She is fishing for gossip, and she is using our conversations to stir up strife. You cannot trust her." Sadly, it did not take much more time for the truth to come out, but by then, the damage was done.

Relationships years in the making were damaged and broken. Margaret used flattery, sympathy, and empathy as distractions while she dug for information she could use as gossip; some people are not happy unless they are causing misery. "For they cannot sleep unless they have done wrong; they are robbed of sleep unless they have made someone stumble"

---

23. *Targum Onqelos*, and more explicitly, *Targum Jonathan*

(Prov 4:16). Jarod and Deja learned the painful lesson contained in Proverbs 20:19, "Whoever goes about slandering reveals secrets; therefore do not associate with a simple babbler." You need to be wise as serpents and harmless as a dove because "Faithful are the wounds of a friend, profuse are the kisses of an enemy" (Prov 27:6).

Finally, always work for peace and reconciliation, "Deceit is in the heart of those who devise evil, but those who plan peace have joy" (Prov 12:20). The Pastoral letter to Timothy included these instructions:

> The Lord's servant must not be quarrelsome but must be kind to everyone, able to teach, not resentful. Opponents must be gently instructed, in the hope that God will grant them repentance leading them to a knowledge of the truth, and that they will come to their senses and escape from the trap of the devil, who has taken them captive to do his will. (2 Tim 2:24–26, NIV)

Love your enemies, pray for those who speak ill of you. This is the way of wisdom. This pleases the Lord, and "When a man's ways please the LORD, he makes even his enemies to be at peace with him" (Prov 16:7).

## Neighbors: People Who Live Near You

In addition to friends and foes, you also have neighbors, people who live near you. Loving your neighbor is placed side by side with loving God as the essence and sum of human duty (Matt 22:35–40; Mark 12:28–31). This love for neighbor should be like God's love, impartial and for all people (Matt 5:43 ff). The apostle James calls loving your neighbor as yourself "the royal law," that is, the supreme, governing law (Jas 2:8). Paul, too, tells us this is the supreme commandment (Rom 13:9–10; Gal 5:14).

To be a neighbor—to be part of the larger human community— roots us to our humanity and helps us see ourselves not as leaders but as fellow companions as we share in the life of the community outside of our responsibilities. The social and civic responsibilities of living within a larger human community help to protect our mental and emotional health and tie us to other people who are not related to us as leaders.

As mentioned above, the Hebrew word *rēᵃ ʻ* can mean a friend, neighbor, companion, associate, or fellow citizen. Perhaps it was this diverse spectrum of possible meanings that fueled the lawyer's response to Jesus in Luke 10:25–37. The lawyer stood up to put Jesus to the test, saying, "Teacher, what shall I do to inherit eternal life?" Jesus said to him, "What is written in the Law? How do you read it?" And the lawyer answered, "You shall love the Lord your God with all your heart and with all your soul and with all your strength and with all your mind, and your neighbor as yourself." And he said to him, "You have answered correctly; do this, and you will live. But the lawyer, desiring to justify himself, said to Jesus, 'And who is my neighbor?'" (Luke 10:25–29). It seems he was saying, "And who is my neighbor? Is it my fellow countrymen, the Jews? Is it my close-knit group of friends that believe and think like me? Is it the people who live near me, even those disgusting Samaritans and vile Romans?"

Jesus did not fall for it. Instead, he turned the tables on the lawyer with the story of the Good Samaritan, with its powerful punchline, "Who proved to be a neighbor to the man who fell among robbers?" "The one who showed mercy," replied the lawyer. "You go and do likewise." (Luke 10:36–37). Rather than defining who our neighbor is, Jesus reorients our perspective and calls us to be the neighbor. Jesus shows that the neighbor relationship is moral, not physical. It is based on the opportunity and capacity to help, to do good for others. In other words, to be a neighbor means those who are near you are safe because of you. In Proverbs, you will discover ways to love your neighbor in thought, word, and deed.

## Loving Your Neighbor in Thought

Social norms of how to behave in public and laws that prohibit discrimination are wonderful, but they are limited to outward behaviors. It may be illegal or sociably unacceptable to show hatred, but that doesn't keep you from having hatred in your heart. To love your neighbor in thought can be exceptionally difficult. Yes, I can be courteous to my neighbor, but when she puts a political sign in her yard supporting a political candidate or social issue that I abhor, it is all too easy for me to belittle her within my heart. "What an idiot! How can she support that person? She must really be a bigot." Or a communist, a fascist, or whichever faction is most repugnant to me at the moment. And then, I can hear that faint voice of prayer issuing forth from my darkened heart, my innermost heart of hearts, "Lord, I thank you that I am not like that person." How easy it is to secretly belittle and despise my neighbor. Yet, Proverbs tells me, "Whoever belittles his neighbor lacks sense, but a man of understanding remains silent" (Prov 11:12), and "Whoever despises his neighbor is a sinner" (Prov 14:21).

The Hebrew word for belittle and despise (*bwz*) means to trample under foot, to hold as insignificant, to scorn, to disrespect, to hold in contempt, or to look down upon. To belittle or despise your neighbors means that you have issued a judgment against them, and you have demeaned them—stripped them of their dignity as fellow image-bearers of God. You have determined they have not met your standards or expectations, that they are beneath you and less than you, maybe even worthless. Your contempt may express itself through a highly visceral emotion such as disgust, or it may show itself through a cold disregard.

Rwanda was, and remains, one of the most Christianized nations in Africa, with 93 percent of its population identifying as Christian. Yet how did this "most Christian of African nations" give way to hatred and genocide, killing hundreds of thousands of Tutsis, as well as moderate Hutu and Twa, between April 7 and July 15, 1994?

The process was quite simple. Hutu leaders, inflamed with a lust for power, unleashed the power of their contempt for the Tutsi minority and mobilized soldiers, police, and militias to commit genocide. It is the same process that led to the Nazi Holocaust, Stalin's intentional starvation of millions of Ukrainians, and every other act of violence perpetrated by one group against another. The violence begins inwardly by categorizing a group of people according to perceived differences, such as nationality, ethnicity, skin color, class, religion, gender, sexual orientation, or geography, and then identifying that group as inferior and using an "us vs. them" mentality to alienate the group.

This process is called "othering." Othering involves zeroing in on differences and using those differences to dismantle a sense of connectedness. This sets the stage for discrimination or persecution by reducing empathy and preventing genuine dialogue. Taken to an extreme, othering can result in one group of people denying that another group is even human, as did the Hutus, the Nazis, the Soviets, and a whole host of demagogues who have risen to power, channeling collective aggressions, by labeling entire groups of people as rats, human vermin, flees, enemies of the people, or a bunch of murderers and rapists. Once people are demeaned and dehumanized, any act of violence against them is easy to justify and seen as virtuous and deserved.[24]

It is easy to illustrate the dangers of contempt on a mass scale. But you will probably never lead a mass murder campaign. You will, however,

---

24. Fiske and Rai, *Virtuous Violence*, 2015.

have to face the hatred that tries to lodge in your heart when you belittle your neighbor in your thoughts. It could be that group of people
who leave your church for the church down the road, or it could be that
group of people whom your in-group loves to demonize and dehumanize. Guard your heart above all things (Prov 4:23), and "Do not plan evil
against your neighbor, who dwells trustingly beside you" (Prov 3:29).

While the commandment not to despise your brother in your heart
(Lev 19:17) is for everyone, it is especially important that you, as a leader,
deal with it within your own heart because you have influence over others.
Othering is evil and it is foolish, and leaders who are fools use it to inflame
entire populations; it is what they live for and thrive upon (Prov 29:8).

Unlike the bonds that unite families, or the affection that bonds
friends, or even the pragmatic necessities of good professional relationships, we are called to love our neighbor for no other reason than that
they exist and that they, too, are image-bearers of God. C.S. Lewis reminded us,

> There are no ordinary people. You have never talked to a mere
> mortal. Nations, cultures, arts, civilizations—these are mortal, and
> their life is to ours as the life of a gnat. But it is immortals whom
> we joke with, work with, marry, snub, and exploit—immortal
> horrors or everlasting splendors. This does not mean that we are
> to be perpetually solemn. We must play. But our merriment must
> be of that kind (and it is, in fact, the merriest kind) which exists
> between people who have, from the outset, taken each other seri-
> ously—no flippancy, no superiority, no presumption.[25]

Your ability to love others is transformed when you see others not as
mere mortals, but as immortal image-bearers of God. You love them at a
deeper and more profound level. The light of the resurrection is already
glistening upon their souls, and they, like you, long to be clothed in the
glory that shall be revealed in them, freed from their debilitating passions
and weaknesses. They, like you, ache for the restoration of all that was
lost in them. They, like you, are called by God and deeply loved by him.
And they, like you, are offered the promise of new life recreated in Christ.
These are the ones we are called to love as ourselves. This requires that I
love them even in my secret thoughts.

---

25. Lewis, *Weight of Glory*, 47.

## Loving Your Neighbor in Word

When contempt for your neighbor comes out in your words, you are bearing a type of false witness, and Proverbs tells us this is as destructive as a war club, a sword, and an arrow (Prov 25:18). Your contempt may compel you to pummel them as with a war club, or fight with them up close and personal, as with a sword, or shoot your words from a safe distance like an archer with an arrow.

The ninth commandment states, "You shall not bear false witness against your neighbor" (Deut 5:20). Leviticus 19:17 expands this by commanding, "You shall not go around as a slanderer among your people." Numbers 12 records a time when Miriam and Aaron spoke despairingly of Moses because of his wife.

> Miriam and Aaron spoke against Moses because of the Cushite woman whom he had married, for he had married a Cushite woman. And they said, "Has the LORD indeed spoken only through Moses? Has he not spoken through us also?" And the LORD heard it." (Num 12:1–2)

The text does not record a response from Moses, other than saying, "The man Moses was very meek, more than all the people who were on the face of the earth" (v. 3). God's response was immediate:

> And suddenly the LORD said to Moses and to Aaron and Miriam, "Come out, you three, to the tent of meeting." And the three of them came out. And the LORD came down in a pillar of cloud and stood at the entrance of the tent and called Aaron and Miriam, and they both came forward. And he said, "Hear my words: If there is a prophet among you, I the LORD make myself known to him in a vision; I speak with him in a dream. Not so with my servant Moses. He is faithful in all my house. With him I speak mouth to mouth, clearly, and not in riddles, and he beholds the form of the LORD. Why then were you not afraid to speak against my servant Moses?" And the anger of the LORD was kindled against them, and he departed. When the cloud removed from over the tent, behold, Miriam was leprous, like snow. And Aaron turned toward Miriam, and behold, she was leprous. (Num 12:4–10)

Though 'leprosy' is the traditional translation of the Hebrew word *ṣā ra ʿ at*, it is not referring to what is now called leprosy. What we know as leprosy (Hansen's disease) did not reach the Middle East until New

Testament times at the earliest.[26] *Ṣā ra ʿ at* refers not only to a wide range of skin diseases, but also to mildew on clothes and the walls of houses.[27] White blotches of skin, hair loss accompanied by reddish-white spots, and spots on garments and walls are all called *ṣā ra ʿ at*. There is no known disease that affects not only people but also clothes and walls.

What is the link between skin, garments, and walls that they could all be diagnosed with *ṣā ra ʿ at*.? They all mark a boundary between inside and outside. They are the outer surfaces covering something whose essential significance is within. Priests were intensely concerned with boundaries between sacred and secular, clean and unclean, permitted and forbidden. "Decay in a boundary, whether it be skin, clothes, or walls, is to the priestly mind a sign of disorder within."[28]

Moses warned the children of Israel,

> Take care, in a case of leprous disease, to be very careful to do according to all that the Levitical priests shall direct you. As I commanded them, so you shall be careful to do. Remember what the LORD your God did to Miriam on the way as you came out of Egypt. (Deut 24:8–9)

The connection is made here between leprosy and Miriam's punishment for her derogatory words against her brother.[29] She spoke ill of someone and was marked with leprosy, as someone that was not safe to be around. That is what malicious words do, they make you unsafe to be around, for by your words you are a destroyer of the community God has called together by his word.

Not only are we to avoid derogatory words, but we are also to avoid deceptive words. Deceptive words of flattery that lay a trap to ensnare your neighbor in order to deceive or defraud must be avoided as well (Prov 29:5). Words that are deceptive, demeaning, derogatory, and malicious tear the fabric of society, damage relationships, and destroy trust, and without trust, no society can survive. Jesus warned, "I tell you this: every thoughtless word you speak you will have to account for on the day of judgement. For out of your own mouth you will be acquitted; out of your own mouth you will be condemned" (Matt 12:36–37, REB). Words

---

26. Wenham, *Number*, 128.

27. Elmer A. Martens, "1971 צָרַע (ṣāra ʿ) be diseased of skin, leprous," 777.

28. Sacks, *Leviticus*, 190.

29. It is a mystery to me why only Miriam was struck with leprosy when it was both Aaron and Miriam who had criticized Moses.

are powerful. Words are holy. "Death and life are in the power of the tongue, and those who love it will eat its fruits" (Prov 18:21). There is already enough death in this world; use your words to give life.

## Loving Your Neighbor in Deeds

Writing about America in the 1830s, French political philosopher and historian Alexis de Tocqueville found that he had to use a newly coined word for the phenomenon he encountered and saw as one of the dangers in a democratic society. The word was *individualism*. He defined it as "a mature and calm feeling which disposes each member of the community to sever himself from the mass of his fellows and to draw apart with his family and his friends," leaving "society at large to itself."[30] Tocqueville believed that democracy encouraged individualism. He feared that as a result, people would leave the business of the common good entirely to the government, which would become ever more powerful, eventually threatening freedom itself.

Since the day Cain killed Abel (Gen 4:1–16), we humans have tried to hide from the command to love our neighbor by asking, "Am I my brother's keeper?" While we may not be responsible for our neighbors, we most certainly have a responsibility to them. We are responsible to love them and to act justly toward them, for "the thoughts of the righteous are just; the counsels of the wicked are deceitful" (Prov 12:5) and "To do righteousness and justice is more acceptable to the LORD than sacrifice" (Prov 21:3). Leaders who follow the path of wisdom laid out in Proverbs will not forsake their neighbors (Prov 27:19) nor will they procrastinate to help when a need arises. "Do not say to your neighbor, 'Go, and come again, tomorrow I will give it'—when you have it with you" (Prov 3:28).

Proverbs teaches us to love our neighbors by respecting not only their person, but also by honoring boundaries around time, space, and money. Simple and common sense actions like not wearing out your welcome and respecting the quiet times of the day go a long way. Consider these verses: "Let your foot be seldom in your neighbor's house, lest he have his fill of you and hate you" (Prov 25:17) and "Whoever blesses his neighbor with a loud voice, rising early in the morning, will be counted as a cursing" (Prov 27:14).

---

30. Tocqueville, *Democracy in America*, 407.

When it comes to money, remember that neighbors and money are a volatile mix (Prov 6:1–3). If you have ever had someone invite you to dinner and then make their multilevel marketing presentation, you know the feeling of violation that happens when you cease being a person in a caring relationship and become a commodity for economic exchange. We should be generous and benevolent in gifts of compassion, as well as cautious, ethical, and professional in all economic and business transactions with our neighbors. For example, if your neighbor is an automotive mechanic, do not try to get a free auto repair from him because he is your neighbor. Pay for his service, and do not attempt to gain economic benefits at your neighbor's expense.

## Conclusion

Proverbs places much emphasis on the key relationships you have in your life. Your spouse, kids, parents, friends, foes, and neighbors all play leading roles in your life as a leader. It is too easy to see these relationships as things to juggle while leading or as intrusions into your leadership position when they are, in fact, the critical element in your identity as a human being. The idea is that if you are a healthy human being with healthy relationships, you will be a healthy leader and able to lead God's people with wisdom and compassion.

# 8

## The Lazy and the Diligent

The hand of the diligent will rule, while the slothful will be put to forced labor.

—PROVERBS 12:24

SOLOMON STARTED WELL, BUT he did not end well. While renowned for his wisdom, he did not stay true to it (1 Kgs 3:16–28; 10:1–13). He turned away from the LORD and followed the path of folly (1 Kgs 11). His life teaches us one big lesson: No matter how good things are or how smart you may be, you must never stop guarding your heart (Prov 4:23). Solomon dropped his guard, lost sight of wisdom, and heeded the voice of Folly. He may be the fullest exposition of folly in all of scripture. How did this wisest of all men become such a fool? Was he tricked? Was he seduced? He was eventually tricked, deceived, and seduced, but his journey into folly began elsewhere. It began the day he let go of diligence and became slothful. He would soon discover that laziness is a deadly destroyer (Prov 18:9).

Solomon is not the only one who did not finish well. Dr. J. Robert Clinton, a prominent scholar and author in the field of leadership and Christian ministry, conducted extensive research on more than 1300 ministers and concluded that more than 70 percent of Christian leaders do not finish well.[1]

Finishing well means different things to different people, each painting a distinct mental image of what it means to cross the finish line in triumph. When I speak of finishing well, I mean finishing well in my journey with God, faithful to Christ to the end, becoming more like him every day, fulfilling his purpose in my life, and hearing from him, "Well done, good and faithful servant." This quest to finish well stretches beyond the boundaries of personal faith. I also want to finish well with the people around me, the ones who have graced my life and whose lives I have touched. My wife, children, grandchildren, friends, neighbors, colleagues, and all those I've had the privilege to lead. I aim to leave a mark, a trail of joy and meaning in their lives so that when the sun sets on my days, they will be better off for having known me. Finishing well also entails my continual growth as an individual, persistently fostering self-improvement and nurturing the seeds of growth and maturation that breathe new life into the person I am continually becoming. This includes making plans that extend beyond the present to include my later years, ensuring, as much as is within my power, that I finish life with a heart filled with gratitude and joy. Such a quest to finish well, multifaceted and profound, shapes the legacy I want to leave behind and the future I want to pursue.

After diving into the lives of leaders from different walks of life, including those from biblical times and modern Christian leaders, Dr. Clinton uncovered intriguing patterns and traits that contribute to leaders finishing well. He discovered that people who finish well maintained a personal and vibrant relationship with God right up to the end. They enjoyed intimacy with Christ and sought moments of inner renewal. They were disciplined in crucial areas and continued to grow with a positive learning attitude. They surrounded themselves with meaningful relationships and sought guidance from important mentors throughout their journey, and they embraced a deep and growing awareness of God's call on their lives. These characteristics will not surprise you if you've spent time reading and rereading Proverbs.

The key to developing and maintaining these qualities is diligence. In this chapter, you'll discover how laziness and diligence can make all the difference in the world when it comes to living and finishing well.

---

1. Clinton, "Finishing Well," 1–3.

## The Lazy

Lazy. Just say the word. What image comes into your mind? A lazy dog? A lazy bum? A lazy man riding the couch? A deadbeat refusing to do his job? Some layabout refusing to lift a single finger to help. A disheveled slob and his disordered life? A couch potato hurling Cheetos down his throat while channel-surfing his life away? Did you picture an indolent freeloader living off the labor of others? A ne'er-do-well with a ready excuse as to why he is not working? A wastrel throwing away time, money, and opportunity? Did you imagine that good-for-nothing-bum of an in-law? A laggard dragging his lazy feet across the floor? Did you see a lazybones so lethargic he barely feeds and dresses himself? Did you think of that slacker who goes to great lengths to avoid anything resembling work? Or the clock jockey riding every minute until the shift is over so he can go home for the day with no concern for productivity?

We have so many colorful ways to refer to "the lazy" because we loathe laziness. Perhaps we secretly identify with the prefect of studies in James Joyce's *A Portrait of the Artist as a Young Man,* who walked into the classroom where Father Arnall was teaching Latin and asked, "Any lazy, idle loafers that want a flogging in this class?" We, too, may secretly want to flog any lazy, idle loafers we find.

We despise laziness for a reason. It is destructive (Prov 18:9). The Hebrew word for lazy ( ʿāṣēl) is used fourteen times in Proverbs, and it is always translated as "sluggard" in the English Standard Version.[2] It can also be translated as sluggish or slothful. This indolence is destructive because it gives way to the ever-encroaching powers of sin and death, seeking to overrun all of creation:

> I passed by the field of a sluggard, by the vineyard of a man lacking sense, and behold, it was all overgrown with thorns; the ground was covered with nettles, and its stone wall was broken down. Then I saw and considered it; I looked and received instruction. A little sleep, a little slumber, a little folding of the hands to rest, and poverty will come upon you like a robber, and want like an armed man. (Prov 24:30–34)

Slothfulness is a denial of the life that is meant to be lived; it is satisfied with passively watching life and consuming its fruits, but it will not lift a hand to contribute to what makes life good and meaningful. The

---

2. Prov 6:6, 9; 10:26; 13:4; 15:19; 19:24; 20:4; 21:25; 22:13; 24:30; 26:13,14,15,16

sluggard only takes. He never gives. This sloth manifests itself in at least three ways: a lack of initiative, distraction, and complacency.

## Lack of Initiative

The freeloading couch potatoes and lazy little loafers mentioned above share one common trait. Their hands refuse to work (Prov 21:25). Sure, they have desires, good ideas, and hopeful wishes, but they will not take the necessary action. They ignore the power of moving little by little, inch by inch, and minute by minute, even though wisdom cries out to them,

> Go to the ant, O sluggard; consider her ways, and be wise. Without having any chief, officer, or ruler, she prepares her bread in summer and gathers her food in harvest. How long will you lie there, O sluggard? When will you arise from your sleep? A little sleep, a little slumber, a little folding of the hands to rest, and poverty will come upon you like a robber, and want like an armed man. (Prov 6:6–11)

Yet, they refuse. They inflict poverty upon themselves (Prov 10:4–5). Their dreams are never fulfilled, their hopes are never acted upon, and their visionary words remain empty wind because they do not take action; they only have idle words.

This passage does not say poor people are lazy; it says lazy people inflict poverty on themselves. Scripture is clear that we are never to despise the poor:

> If among you, one of your brothers should become poor, in any of your towns within your land that the LORD your God is giving you, you shall not harden your heart or shut your hand against your poor brother, but you shall open your hand to him and lend him sufficient for his need, whatever it may be. (Deut 15:7–8)

Poverty is far more complex than an individual's work habits. Economic power structures, exploitation, lack of educational opportunities, systemic issues, and a host of other problems contribute to poverty (Prov 13:23). Those made poor by circumstance and exploitation are to be protected. We are commanded to be generous with them while we work with them to gain economic and social justice. These poor have been made poor by powers and circumstances beyond themselves. The lazy, on the other hand, make themselves poor. They inflict poverty, lack, deprivation, and sorrow upon themselves and those they lead.

Lazy leaders are big with their words but small with their deeds. They are idle dreamers (Prov 13:4). These lazy leaders idly dream of someday or someplace that will be different, never realizing "the eyes of a fool are on the ends of the earth" (Prov 17:24) but "the soul of the diligent is richly supplied" (Prov 13:4). They waste the time, resources, gifts, and opportunities entrusted to them. Darren was such a leader. He regularly talked about all his dreams for what his church would become. He also always complained about not having any leaders in his church to help him. When I visited his church, I was surprised to meet several very capable people who demonstrated a willingness to be equipped to serve others. I mentioned this to Darren and asked him, "What are you doing to develop these people?" I was hoping to encourage him. Well, I obviously hit a nerve with him. He replied, "I am tired of all these people telling me how I should be doing my job. I know what I am doing." It seems others had also observed what I saw and had offered similar encouragement. Unfortunately, Darren would have none of it. "The sluggard is wiser in his own eyes than seven men who can answer sensibly" (Prov 26:16).

It is almost impossible to help lazy leaders because an arsenal of lies and half-truths defends this stronghold of laziness. For every reason you give, there's an excuse given by the lazy leader for ignoring your good counsel. Sloth works its deepest advantage here. Truth is no longer seen, heard, or recognized. Nor is it desired, for it is easier to be comforted by lies than to be confronted with truth. The months and years have nothing to show but emptiness because these lazy leaders have wasted their resources.

Darren had managed to attract a few people with undeveloped capacity. Unfortunately, "Lazy people don't even cook the game they catch." If he followed wisdom and led wisely, he would have more than excuses, for "the diligent make use of everything they find" (Prov 12:27, NLT). Sadly, things for Darren never changed, and he had trouble all through life with this issue. Indolent leaders seem to have the same problems all the time. It may be a new year, a new job, a new church, or a new city, but before you know it, the new thing will be covered over with thorns and weeds because of the slackness of the leader. It will always be the same excuses, the same accusations of blame on others. "The way of the lazy is overgrown with thorns, but the path of the upright is a level highway" (Prov 15:19, NRSV).

If a lazy leader does work, it is only because he is forced to do so. "The hand of the diligent will rule, while the lazy will be put to forced labor" (Prov 12:24, NRSV). The slothful do not work because work is good and fulfilling and righteous: They work because they are forced to. Slothfulness has driven initiative and ambition from them, seducing their hearts and lulling them to bed; this time not as the foolish youth who thinks he will have sensual pleasures (Prov 7:1–27), but now as one who just loves sleep, for "As a door turns on its hinges, so does a sluggard on his bed" (Prov 26:14). This is the person who sleeps through every opportunity, and they suffer for it.

Stan was such a person. His supervisors gave him every opportunity to grow as a person and improve in his career. Yet, no matter what was offered to help Stan, he always had a "reason" why he could not do it and a complaint that the organization was not doing enough for him. The breaking point came when Stan's "reason" for not participating in the monthly team conference calls was that they were too early in the morning, and he needed to sleep. The meetings were at 8:00 a.m., and Stan was in his forties. He was let go after that. Proverbs had warned him, "Laziness will bring on a deep sleep, and a person of idleness will suffer hunger" (Prov 19:15, LEB). But he did not listen. Some ministry leadership positions can have so much flexibility that you can justify slack work hours, long lunches, and prolonged periods of unproductive behavior if you are not highly self-disciplined.

Anyone who depends on leaders with a slack work ethic will ultimately be disappointed, "Like vinegar to the teeth and smoke to the eyes, so is the sluggard to those who send him" (Prov 10:26). These lazy leaders procrastinate, cut corners, never finish tasks, and fail to follow through on promises. You cannot depend on them.

Lazy leaders do, however, excel at making excuses (Prov 22:13). These are the leaders who take the credit when things go well and pass the buck when things go wrong. When their plans fail, it is always someone else's fault. They will not take responsibility for themselves. They expect others to do their jobs. Sometimes they will not even feed themselves; they may put their hand in the bowl but are too lazy to put the food in their mouth (Prov 19:24; 26:15).

Lazy leaders don't see the connection between work and reward. "The sluggard does not plow in the autumn; he will seek at harvest and have nothing" (Prov 20:4). The lazy leader may have many dreams, but "Despite their desires, the lazy will come to ruin, for their hands refuse to work" (Prov 21:25, NLT). When leaders neglect to act on their responsibilities, the consequences are destructive, for entropy and decay happen automatically in the absence of leadership. Some leaders destroy with their actions; the lazy leader destroys by his inaction, for "Whoever is slack in his work is brother to one who destroys" (Prov 18:9).

The lack of initiative is the easiest manifestation of sloth to identify. The other two manifestations are more cunning, more subtle, and more difficult to identify and remedy. Proverbs 1:32 points them out, "For the simple are killed by their turning away, and the complacency of fools destroys them." Sloth seeks to turn you away from wisdom through distraction and complacency.

## Distracted

Laziness is not necessarily inactivity. In fact, some of the laziest people you will ever meet are always busy. Yet, their busyness leads neither to productive results nor to any life-giving presence. They are driven to distraction by their fear of boredom, thinking boredom is caused by a lack of activity. Danish philosopher Soren Kierkegaard defined boredom as a sense of emptiness and examines it not as an absence of stimulation but rather as an absence of meaning. People experience boredom because of their inability to pay attention to and glean meaning from life. I think this explains why it is possible to be both overstimulated with busyness and yet still bored with life.

If boredom is truly the absence of meaning, it cannot be cured by activity. At best, these activities are a drug-like diversion that masks but does not cure the emptiness. Yet, it is diversions we seek to soothe our lack of meaning. And like all drugs, our bodies build a tolerance that requires more of the drug to achieve the same benefit. This results in busyness. Busyness reduces life to a series of activities or tasks to accomplish rather than moments filled with meaning. Busyness distracts you from life so that you are no longer meaningfully present in life, nor are you able to experience any meaningful presence in your life.

For Kierkegaard, busy people experience this sense of emptiness because their activities are not directed towards some particular good. In *Works of Love*, he compared the busy person to a person who sows and harvests grains in order to once again sow and harvest grain over and over again. The busy person fills the barns with what they have harvested, and yet nothing is made from the grain; nothing good comes from all the activity. Just busyness. The busy person sows and harvests and rests upon these gains, only to begin again, for "busyness harvests over and over again." There is nothing gained, nothing produced, no one benefited, no purpose fulfilled. It is just an endless cycle of busyness.[3]

Busyness may be the surest way to lull yourself into a trance of passivity and distraction. Sure, you may show up for your obligations, but you are absent to the people around you. Ever moving, fidgeting in mind as well as body, you are driven to distraction, never finding the joy of being present with others, or with yourself. You have mistaken the act of doing for the act of being. You have chased the wind and reaped the whirlwind.

Our cultural obsession with hyperactivity has become so prevalent that busyness has become a status symbol.[4] Yet, when the outcomes of this overly active lifestyle are weighed in the balance, they are found wanting, for they are what Proverbs calls "worthless pursuits."

> Whoever works his land will have plenty of bread, but he who follows worthless pursuits lacks sense. (Prov 12:11)

> Whoever works his land will have plenty of bread, but he who follows worthless pursuits will have plenty of poverty. (Prov 28:19)

These verses highlight the two paths you can choose: You can do something productive like work your land, or you can spend your days in worthless pursuits and idle fantasies. To say it another way, "The discerning sets his face toward wisdom, but the eyes of a fool are on the ends of the earth" (Prov 17:24). It is the folly of laziness to spend your days in activities that are empty and cannot produce any advantage or benefit. These two verses are not speaking of the poor who could produce were he or she not exploited by the powerful (Prov 13:23). The individual here, unlike the exploited poor, has plenty of opportunity to enjoy the fruits of his labor; yet his opportunities for achievement are wasted while he pursues activities that are empty and without meaning. He is chasing the wind. His laziness is not one of the body, it is a laziness of the mind. He lacks judgment, not energy.

The consequences of his worthless pursuits are twofold. He has a lack of sense (Prov 12:11) and an abundance of poverty (Prov 28:19). The word here for sense (lēb) is used over 600 times in the Old Testament. It can be translated as mind, sense, understanding, courage, and skill, but its most

---

3. Kierkegaard, *Works of Love*, 247.
4. Bellezza, et al., "Conspicuous Consumption," 2016.

common translation is heart.[5] When not referring to the blood pumping organ, "heart" is the richest biblical term for the totality of one's inner essence, being, or substance.[6] Wasting your life chasing vain and empty activities not only leaves you without sustenance (Prov 28:19), it leaves you without substance (Prov 12:11). The leader who chases worthless pursuits may have the appearance of productivity and project a fashionable style, but it's a tale of folly "full of sound and fury, signifying nothing,"[7] for upon closer inspection, you will find only chains of sand and a vacuous soul. Substance is the missing part. Leaders, above all people, must be people of substance. Chasing the wind only leads to destitution and deprivation of soul.

## Complacency

The laziness addressed in Proverbs extends beyond just a leader's work ethic; it also encompasses the leader's heart condition in the battle against sloth; a heart condition of apathy, listlessness, slackness, deception (of self and others), and ultimately treachery. In Christian theology, sloth is listed along with lust, gluttony, greed, anger, envy, and pride as one of the Seven Deadly Sins. You may have a solid work ethic, but you will still have a deadly confrontation with sloth if you are a leader. Your battle with sloth will be just as real as your battles with the other deadly sins.

Sloth is a strange passivity that pushes you down. It is a deeply rooted cynicism that responds to every spiritual challenge with "What for?" or "Why bother?" It makes your life a spiritual wasteland by poisoning your spiritual energy at its very source, the inner person of the heart, and induces a particular carelessness about life and spiritual things. Sloth convinces you that not changing is desirable. This apathy is the initial pathway to sin because sloth persuades you to drop your guard and not care that the guard has been lowered.

The desert fathers referred to sloth as the "noontime devil" because apathy for their spiritual condition would peak as they practiced their spiritual disciplines in the noonday heat of the desert sun. The cool morning air gave way to stifling heat, and the sun seemed intent on slowly draining all life and vigor. It was common for these desert fathers

---

5. 469 times in the English Standard Version

6. Bowling, "1071 לָבַב (lābab) ravish." 466.

7. Shakespeare, *Macbeth*, 179.

and mothers to feel swallowed by sloth, despair, and despondency in the noontime heat of the day.

You do not need to be a desert monk to experience this noontime devil. Sloth is the despair that falls upon you in the middle, between the beginning and the completion of a journey, a project, or a goal. Sloth is that feeling of hopelessness and failure you feel in the middle when you want to give up and hide under the blankets. It is that urge to find a short-cut or a way out, to flee your current situation, and to convince yourself things would be better "if only." It is that voice telling you, "It is hopeless. Why bother?" Numbness envelops your inner core. Sure, you may be go-ing through the motions, but you feel the disconnection between your inner and outer world. Life has become a tedious anxiety of the heart. Carelessness works in you to destroy your focus. Hope is deferred, and your heart is made sick (Prov 13:12).

The result of sloth is faintheartedness The Church Fathers considered faintheartedness the greatest danger to the soul, for you are unable to see the light or even to desire it. Faintheartedness beats you down, convincing you that you no longer desire change. Everything is reduced to pessimism. It is a demonic power that fills life with darkness by flooding it with lies and half-truths. Faintheartedness is the suicide of the soul.

As strange as it may seem, it is sloth and faintheartedness that fill the heart with a *lust for power.* If God is not the Lord and Master of my life, then I become my own lord and master—the absolute center of my own universe, and I begin to evaluate everyone and everything in terms of *my needs, my ideas, my desires,* and *my judgments.* Everyone and everything are reduced to commodities for my personal happiness and self-fulfillment. This lust for power is a fundamental depravity in my relationship with others, for it seeks their subordination to me, not God. My attempts to subordinate others to myself may be expressed in the urge to command, control, or dominate others, or it may be expressed through indifference, contempt, lack of interest, lack of consideration, or a lack of respect. "It is sloth and despondency directed this time at others; it completes spiritual suicide with spiritual murder."[8]

When this sloth, faintheartedness, and lust for power control my life, my words become mere idle talk. Of all creation on earth, human-kind alone is endowed with the gift of speech. The Fathers saw this as the "seal" of the Divine Image in man because God himself is revealed as

---

8. Schmemann, *Great Lent,* 34.

Word. Being a supreme gift, it is also a supreme danger; life and death are in the power of the tongue (Prov 18:21).

We may use words to express love, give life, and build hope, or we may use our words to steal, kill, and destroy. With our words, we make covenants that heal and restore, and with our words, we betray and destroy. Words inspire, and words poison. With them, you can proclaim truth or spread lies. When our words deviate from God's original design and purpose, they become idle, bringing judgment upon ourselves,

> And I tell you this, that you must give an account on judgment day of every idle word you speak. The words you say now reflect your fate then; either you will be justified by them or you will be condemned. (Matt 12:36–37)

You can see why laziness is not something to be toyed with or tolerated. I hope you see now that laziness is not about low energy. Low energy may be a physical condition caused by genetics, diet, stress, exhaustion, allergies, and a host of other issues. Laziness is a deeper spiritual condition that seeks to nullify your life, numb your spiritual vitality, and rob you of your calling and destiny. This slothfulness is a complete abdication of your role in creation, a surrender of your glory as an image-bearer of God, and a destruction of all your vital relationships.[9]

Laziness and sloth are about far more than a personal work ethic; they are also spiritual struggles with which we must be fully engaged against. Over the years, I have had seasons of deep despondency where I felt no hope or even the desire to hope. When I began to learn from the desert fathers about the noonday devil, it liberated my mind from the condemnation I was feeling. I began to realize I was despondent, not because I was lazy but because I was in a battle. Learning to recognize this was liberating and empowering. Since then, when I have spoken with other leaders about this despondency and soul battle, many have confessed similar experiences. No wonder Proverbs warns leaders about the dangers of slothfulness and offers diligence as the antidote to this sickness that affects the mind, the body, and the heart.

9. See Schmemann, Great Lent, for a fuller discussion on this topic.

## The Diligent

I mentioned above that ministry leadership can have so much flexibility that you can be lazy and unproductive if you want to be. You can spend your days chatting with people, drinking coffee, and enjoying long lunches under the guise of "spending time with people," or wasting countless hours surfing the internet under the guise of "doing research for a sermon." Paradoxically, ministry leadership is also so demanding that you can justify becoming a workaholic because the job is never finished. Workaholism is not the solution to laziness; it is simply another dysfunctional behavior that reveals an internal disorder.

Workaholism, or ergomania if you prefer the technical name, refers to the excessive and compulsive devotion to work, especially as a symptom of a mental disorder.[10] Workaholism is not the same as working long hours or loving your work. It is the compulsion or the uncontrollable need to work incessantly because of internal pressures not external needs. Engaged workers are driven to work because they find it intrinsically pleasurable while workaholics are driven to work because they feel an inner compulsion to work due to guilt, anxiety, anger, or disappointment. Workaholics have persistent thoughts about work when not working and they work beyond what is reasonably expected (as established by the requirements of the job or basic economic needs) despite the potential harm to their relationships and health.

Researchers from the Department of Psychosocial Science at the University of Bergen in Norway created a work addiction scale with the following seven criteria as to the likelihood that an individual possesses a work addiction: 1) You think of how you can free up more time to work; 2) You spend much more time working than initially intended; 3) You work in order to reduce feelings of guilt, anxiety, helplessness and/or depression; 4) You have been told by others to cut down on work without listening to them; 5) You become stressed if you are prohibited from working; 6) You deprioritize hobbies, leisure activities, and/or exercise because of your work; and 7) You work so much that it has negatively influenced your health. Answering "often" or "always" to any of these could indicate you struggle with workaholism.[11]

I do have to admit, after answering "often" or "always" to each of the seven statements, I felt like saying, "Hi I'm Jeff, and I'm a workaholic." I

---

10. American Psychological Association. "Workaholism." 2016.

11. Andreassen, "Workaholism." 1–11.

am still on the journey with you. In today's world, where exhaustion is a status symbol and "hustle" is glorified, workaholism is celebrated as a strength not a weakness. After all, workaholics tend to be inventive, action-oriented, altruistic, compliant, and modest people. This makes it very easy to overlook the fact that they are also typically nervous, impulsive, and sometimes hostile. If you are going to follow wisdom and lead wisely, you will need to discover the alternative to both laziness and workaholism. In Proverbs this path is called diligence.

The Hebrew word translated as diligent (ḥārûṣ) is used five times in Proverbs (10:4; 12:24, 27; 13:4; 21:5). It carries the idea of being decisive, sharp, and cutting through things to make a pathway. The consequences of both sloth and diligence are succinctly captured in Proverbs 13:4: "The soul of the sluggard craves and gets nothing, while the soul of the diligent is richly supplied." The sluggard desires success, prosperity, and all the good things of life and leadership, yet they get none of it, for "the desire of the sluggard kills him, for his hands refuse to labor" (Prov 21:25).

The dreams and desires of the sluggard do not inspire him to action; rather, they torment him to death. His desires are a frustration to his soul. Whereas the manifestations of sloth are life-negating forces, diligence is life-affirming. Diligence nurtures life while sloth destroys it. Diligence develops plans to accomplish the good, while sloth brings only decay. Diligence empowers the leader to think and act like an adult, while sloth enslaves its captive in a prison of childishness. The leader who gives way to sloth diminishes over time, while the leader given to diligence grows and increases and is well supplied.

Just as sloth seeks to subjugate your vital life forces to death and decay, diligence seeks to subjugate your life forces of body, soul, and spirit to love for God and others. It is the persistent exertion of an intentional effort to bend the affections and will toward love and obedience. It is what overcomes the lethargy of sloth, for diligence trains and summons the will to trudge through the swamp of despair, to show up every day, to take the next step, and to do the next right thing.

When I was a young church planter, I would spend hours preparing my sermons. I would dig deep into the text, read widely, and craft the best sermon I could. Even though I was a bi-vocational pastor with a young, growing family, I would spend many hours every week working on my sermons. Then on Sunday morning, I would look at the fifteen or twenty individuals who attended our church and think, "Is it worth all this work?" Little did I know at the time, but sloth was tempting me with a little sleep, a little slumber, a folding of my hands to rest. Somehow, God worked into my heart a deep conviction that preaching the word of God and feeding the people of God were worthy of all my diligence. So, I kept at it.

That act of diligence set a course for my life that has led me to where I am today. It shaped the values, convictions, and practices that have been with me ever since those days of small beginnings. It all started there, but it did not end there. I have since learned that "the soul of the diligent is richly supplied." Those countless hours of diligently laboring in the scriptures have been a rich supply of spiritual strength that has sustained me for decades.

## Start Where You Are With What You Have

The diligent start where they are, and they make use of whatever they have (Prov 12:27). The wise leader understands she is held accountable and will seek to maximize the resources entrusted to her. Jesus makes this point in the parable of the talents (Matt 25:14–30). While the foolish and slothful leader diminishes the value of everything and everyone, the wise and diligent leader does the opposite by seeking to increase their value.

Starting where you are and with what you have begins with yourself. Diligent leaders have what world-renowned psychologist Carol Dweck calls a "growth mindset."[12] Dweck discovered through decades of research that success in almost every area of human endeavor is influenced by how we think about our talents and abilities. She persuasively demonstrates how people with a fixed mindset—who believe that abilities are fixed—are less likely to flourish than those with a growth mindset—who believe that abilities can be developed. The growth mindset teaches that what you have inside of you is your starting point not your end point. In other words, what you have right now is a foundation to build upon, not a ceiling that caps your potential. Whatever you have can be developed into something more. Diligent leaders are infused with this type of growth mindset, and it governs how they see both themselves and those they lead.

Consider how differently slothful and diligent leaders treat the people entrusted to their oversight. The slothful leader complains about a lack of quality in the people he leads. In contrast, the diligent leader

12. Dweck, *Mindset*, 2016.

accepts people as they are but doesn't leave them that way. The diligent leader develops ways to help others grow, regardless of their starting point. King David demonstrated diligent leadership when he escaped from Saul to the cave of Adullam,

> And everyone who was in distress, and everyone who was in debt, and everyone who was bitter in soul, gathered to him. And he became commander over them. And there were with him about four hundred men. (1 Sam 22:2)

David took this group of distressed, indebted, and discontented individuals and transformed them into "David's mighty men" (2 Sam 23:8–38). Diligent leaders know if you cannot find people the way you want them, take people the way you find them. Help them become the best version of themselves. You will be surprised by what you discover buried inside these earthen vessels.

The sluggard looks at what he lacks, while the diligent looks at what he has. Consider Moses. He was brought up in the house of Pharaoh (Exod 2:1–10), and "instructed in all the wisdom of the Egyptians, and he was mighty in his words and deeds" (Acts 7:22). He had power, he had position, he had influence, and he was not afraid to act. Certainly, he had the resources to liberate the children of Israel. Yet, when he saw an Egyptian beating a fellow Hebrew, he killed the Egyptian and buried him in the sand (Exod 2:11–12). He "supposed that his brothers would understand that God was giving them salvation by his hand, but they did not understand" (Acts 7:25). The Israelites did not understand, but it appears that Pharaoh did, for he now sought to kill Moses (Exod 2:15).

Moses fled to Midian. This son of Pharaoh's daughter was now a resident alien, living in a foreign land (Exod 2:22). Forty years went by (Acts 7:30), and Moses was stripped of everything. He no longer had his position in Pharaoh's house and was cut off from his people. He didn't even own the flock he was tending. It belonged to his father-in-law. Then the Angel of the Lord appeared to Moses in a burning bush (Exod 3:2). Moses turned to see this bush that burned but was not consumed. God called to him out of the bush, "Moses, Moses!" Moses replied, "Here I am" (Exod 3:3–4). He then discovered he was standing on holy ground before the "God of Abraham, the God of Isaac, and the God of Jacob." Moses hid his face, for he was afraid to look at God (Exod 3:6).

> Then the Lord said: I have surely seen the affliction of my people who are in Egypt and have heard their cry because of their

taskmasters. I know their sufferings, and I have come down to deliver them out of the hand of the Egyptians and to bring them up out of that land to a good and broad land, a land flowing with milk and honey, to the place of the Canaanites, the Hittites, the Amorites, the Perizzites, the Hivites, and the Jebusites. And now, behold, the cry of the people of Israel has come to me, and I have also seen the oppression with which the Egyptians oppress them. Come, I will send you to Pharaoh that you may bring my people, the children of Israel, out of Egypt. (Exod 3:7–10)

Moses began a series of arguments with God as to why he was not qualified for the task to which he was being called. Moses argued, "Who am I that I should go to Pharaoh and bring the children of Israel out of Egypt?" (Exod 3:11).

God replied, "I will be with you." (Exod 3:12)

Then Moses said, "If I come to the people of Israel and say to them, 'The God of your fathers has sent me to you,' and they ask me, 'What is his name?' what shall I say to them?"

God said to Moses, "I am who I am." And he said, "Say this to the people of Israel: 'I am has sent me to you.' Say this to the people of Israel: 'The Lord, the God of your fathers, the God of Abraham, the God of Isaac, and the God of Jacob, has sent me to you.' This is my name forever, and thus I am to be remembered throughout all generations" (Exod 3:13–15).

God then instructed Moses to go to the elders of Israel with the message that God would bring them out of Egypt, and they would listen (Exod 3:16–18a). God then instructed Moses to go to Pharaoh. God promised Moses that he would stretch out his hand and strike Egypt, and the Israelites would plunder the Egyptians (Exod 3:18–22).

But Moses kept arguing with God all the way into chapter 4. God seemed to have stopped listening to his arguments because the next thing God said to Moses was, "What is in your hand?" (Exod 4:2). Moses was holding his shepherd's staff, just a long piece of wood with a hook on one end. While useful for walking and tending sheep, it had limited applications beyond that. Certainly, to overthrow the power of Egypt and liberate the children of Israel from slavery was not among its uses. Well, not until God got involved with it. Moses was about to get a new perspective on what was possible. He was about to expand his growth mindset. God told him to take the staff in his hand, for with it he would perform the signs that would liberate the people (Exod 4:17).

The only thing Moses had was a walking stick and an encounter with God, and that was enough to overthrow Egypt and deliver the children of Israel. God can use a walking stick, a widow's jar of oil (2 Kgs 4:1–7), or a boy's lunch (John 6:1–15). God can use anything offered to him except an excuse. Start where you are with what you have, then watch what God does.

## Value Hard Work

Dreams are essential for leadership, but they are not enough. It is easy to have big dreams and big words, but what is needed is big action. Inspiring photographs with leadership slogans are not enough; your dreams must move from your heart to your head for thought and to your hands for action. Lazy leaders are filled with dreams, visions, and words, but "despite their desires, the lazy will come to ruin, for their hands refuse to work" (Prov 21:25, NLT). "In all toil there is profit, but mere talk tends only to poverty" (Prov 14:23). Wise leaders are people who take action because they work for their dreams (Prov 13:4).

As we will see in another chapter, words do have their place in leadership, but these words must be met with actions equal to them, for "wise words bring many benefits, and hard work brings rewards" (Prov 12:14, NLT). The issue is that your hands must be more active than your mouth because "a slack hand causes poverty, but the hand of the diligent makes rich" (Prov 10:4).

Diligence and excellence are the pathways to promotion. Solomon tells us, "Do you see a man skillful in his work? He will stand before kings; he will not stand before obscure men" (Prov 22:29). Wisdom teaches us that even the lowest servant can achieve great reward through diligence, for "a servant who deals wisely will rule over a son who acts shamefully and will share the inheritance as one of the brothers" (Prov 17:2). Diligent leaders rise to the top (Prov 12:24; 22:29). Jesus taught us that if we are faithful in small things, God entrusts us with more important things (Matt 25:14–30; Lk. 16:10–12). "Work hard and become a leader; be lazy and become a slave" (Prov 12:24, NLT).

This call to diligence includes not only how we work but also how we rest. You must be diligent in your self-care; honor a sabbath period every week. I realize we have been freed from the law, and we are no longer bound to observe laws governing sabbath rituals. But while we may not be bound to the sabbath as a matter of law, the sabbath remains for us a gift of grace, and like all gifts, it can be received or ignored. This one we ignore at our own peril. To set aside a 24-hour block of time every week, on which you stop your work and rest, is a powerful act of obedience that silences twin voices. The first voice tells us, "You are a slave, and your only value is what you produce." The second counters, "You are like God, everything depends on you. You cannot take time away or things will fall apart."

The diligent work of rest and renewal moves beyond a weekly sabbath to also include your daily habits that restore your body and mind through rest, diet, exercise, and sleep, as well as your emotions through meaningful connections and joyful play. You will have so many demands and expectations placed upon you as a leader that you will need to work hard to protect your rest. But it is as essential as all other forms of hard work. The alternative is not good. Working yourself to exhaustion and an early grave is not virtuous. It is stupid. So, stop it. Take time to sharpen the axe because "using a dull ax requires great strength, so sharpen the blade. That's the value of wisdom; it helps you succeed" (Eccl 10:10, NLT).

## Value Good Planning

Finally, diligent leaders understand the value of good planning (Prov 21:5; 3:21–26). While you may have weak administrative abilities, this is no excuse for poor planning. Wise leaders develop the skills for good planning. Many leaders deceive themselves with a misguided half-truth that says, "There are leaders, and there are managers. I am not a manager. I am a leader," as though this justifies inept planning and poor management. You must manage if you are a leader. You cannot get around it. You may have a great vision, but if you cannot plan your work and work your plan, you only have a fantasy in your mind, not a vision for your life.

According to an old military saying, "Amateurs talk about strategy and tactics; professionals talk about logistics."[13] The quote is frequently used in various contexts beyond military strategy, highlighting the importance of planning, organization, and resource management in achieving success in business, sports, and other activities. I cannot tell you how many times I have had someone tell me, "I am a strategic leader," and yet they do not accomplish anything strategic because they give no thought to logistics. Wise planning is needed if you are a leader. Period. The good news is

13. The quote is often attributed to General Omar Bradley, a senior officer of the United States Army during World War II. Unfortunately, due to the unclear origin, it's not possible to provide a single authoritative citation for the quote.

that if you have a growth mindset, you can improve your ability to develop and execute plans. You can grow in this area by reading books, attending a seminar, enrolling in a management course, or finding a mentor.

## Getting Started

Diligent leadership leads to greater favor (Prov 11:27), prosperity (Prov 10:4; 13:4), and honor (Prov 12:24; 22:29). The good news is that you can develop diligence as a personal characteristic. If you fight battles with laziness, own it. Face your reality with daily discipline to bring yourself under the rule of wisdom. Find a few people who are wiser than you in this area and learn from them. You may want to find a mentor or hire a professional coach to help you conquer this monster. Whatever you do, take action. You cannot defeat sloth with inaction.

If you have fallen victim to workaholism and the belief that your only worth is found in your labor, then let God begin to set you free from this tyranny.

Wherever you are in this journey toward wise leadership, start where you are. Do not condemn yourself because you "are not there yet." You may be a long way away from your goal, but like the children of Israel, you possess your promised inheritance a little bit at a time, going from glory to glory and from faith to faith (2 Cor 3:18).

Your journey to becoming a wise leader is long. If you keep going you will keep growing. The daily acts of obedience cause an incremental increase in wisdom. Your goal is to hear the Master say, "Well done, good and faithful servant" (Matt 25:14–30). Your work is done well, and you are good and faithful; your *doing* and your *being* are in harmony. This is what it means to follow wisdom and lead wisely.

Diligence must not be reduced to a puritanical Protestant work ethic,[14] for this virtue is about far more than yielding to capitalism's enchantment with mammon[15] or defending self-reliance and free markets.[16] It is about our struggle with a ruling spirit of the present age.[17] This power seeks to reduce all of creation to some form of an economic calculus. It is a principality that seeks to induce within the heart a lethargy of spirit

---

14. Weber, *The Protestant Ethic*, 2012.

15. McCarraher, *Enchantments of Mammon*, 2019.

16. Hirschfeld, *Aquinas and the Market*, 2018.

17. Wink, *The Powers that Be*, 1999.

that deadens all longing and desire for the eternal and the divine while enthroning meaningless activity and mindless consumption. In an age where busyness has replaced meaningfulness, where we are always connected but never present, where every moment is packed to overflowing yet we remain bored and numb, and where our social media platforms crowd out our lives and yet we long for human connection—in this age—in this present darkness—we need leaders who show the way and lead the way in the battle against faintheartedness, the unnamed evil of our age.

# 9

# The Wise Leader's Use of Money

IN MY EARLY DAYS of leadership, it was common for the older, wiser leaders to regularly warn us young leaders to safeguard our lives against the temptations of money, sex, and power. Being preachers with a sense of humor, these elders used alliteration, and in the spirit of Solomon, they added a fourth: "For three temptations ministry is destroyed, yea even unto four: Beware of gold, girls, glory, and goofing off." We called these the "g-forces"—our humorous way to remember the dangers of money, sex, power, and a poor work ethic.

G-force, or gravitational force, describes the forces experienced during rapid acceleration, deceleration, or high-speed motion. A person on the ground experiences 1 g, but in situations like fighter jet maneuvers, pilots can face several times the force of gravity, measured as 2 gs, 5 gs, or more. For example, a pilot experiencing 4 gs feels a force four times their body weight. In intense scenarios, like a top-fuel dragster accelerating to 99 miles per hour in 0.86 seconds, the driver experiences 5.3 gs. Astronauts on the Space Shuttle feel 3 gs during launch and reentry. However, our bodies have limits; we can endure 3 gs for an hour, 5 gs for two minutes, and no more than 9 gs for a few seconds. At 9 gs, the body feels nine times heavier; blood rushes to the feet, and the heart can't pump hard enough to get blood to the brain. Your vision narrows to a tunnel and then goes black. If the acceleration doesn't decrease, you will pass out and finally die.

So, when Han Solo talks about making the "jump to light speed," he implies that the *Millennium Falcon* is about to jump from its current speed to a whopping 186,000 miles per second. Accelerating from 0 to 186,000 miles per second in 5 seconds would push Han back so forcefully that he would become a large splat on the vinyl upholstery.[1] Jumping to light speed without worrying about g-forces works great in the movies. But in the real world, g-forces cannot be ignored. Astronauts, race car drivers, and fighter pilots must undergo intense training and preparation to deal with them.

Like these high-velocity roles, ministry leadership also has its own g-forces that will destroy your ministry if not guarded against. As my elders warned, such temptations commonly take four main forms. Elsewhere in this book, we have already examined three of these temptations: the allure of lustful desires (girls), the thirst for power and fame (glory), and the lure of idleness and sloth (goofing off). The fourth temptation (gold) emerges when one craves wealth for its own sake, becomes consumed by greed, or is slack in their financial stewardship. In this chapter, we will focus on the wisdom found in Proverbs concerning the proper stewardship of wealth, material resources, and money for leaders.

## Money in the Scriptures

Before the introduction of coinage in the late eighth century BCE, the medium of exchange in commercial transactions was a modified form of barter. In ancient Israel, goods or livestock were often exchanged in barter. These goods or livestock probably took on a monetary function as a primitive form of money. For instance, if Asher had a cart to sell and Josiah had some shoes, the exchange might be facilitated by quantifying the goods or livestock as the appropriate price for each item. Shoes might be worth five units of goods or livestock, while a cart would be worth 10 units. Asher could "buy" shoes from Josiah for five such units; in turn, Josiah could "buy" a cart from Asher for ten such units. In time, actual coins, such as silver pieces, would be substituted for the units of goods or livestock.

This monetization might be in view in Genesis. When Abimelech restored Sarah to Abraham, he paid him "sheep and oxen and male and female slaves," which were said to be the equivalent of "a thousand pieces of

---

1. Cavelos, *Star Wars*, 2000.

silver" (Gen 20:14–16). Likewise, Judah attempted to pay for the services of a prostitute by sending her a young goat from his flock (Gen 38:17, 23). Over time, standardized and portable commodities were employed, such as metal bars, ingots, and jewels. Eventually, coined money legally authorized by governments became the standard.[2] At its most fundamental level, money is simply a medium of exchange, whether the money designates livestock, precious metals, or minted coins as the standard of value.

Basically, wealth in turn refers to the accumulation of things of value (such as real estate or goods), which can be exchanged for money; the money measures the amount of wealth. Wealth can also refer to purchasing power, again where money is the currency. Spiritually, wealth is something you can have but not serve. Jesus clearly warned, "No one can serve two masters, for either he will hate the one and love the other, or he will be devoted to the one and despise the other. You cannot serve God and money" (Matt 6:24). The King James Version translates that last line, "You cannot serve God and mammon." The term mammon[3] (*mamónas*) is used in the Greek New Testament. However, it is worth noting that the Greek word is borrowed from Aramaic, and the Greek text simply transliterates the Aramaic noun. The Aramaic probably comes from the root *'aman* meaning "to trust," while mammon indicates "that in which one trusts." The word, while not used in the Old Testament, is used in Jewish writings, in the sense of resources, gain, compensation, ransom, or even a bribe. In general, mammon carries an ignoble sense; it is often called unrighteous, and it is a target of ethical censure or admonition. The Aramaic is used rather than the Greek,[4] most likely due to its untranslatable ethical and religious nuances.[5] While most modern translations construe mammon as "money" or "wealth," we do well to keep in mind the untranslatable implications of mammon. As "that in which one trusts," mammon inevitably becomes the master if we acquire it for its own sake. We end up trusting in mammon, serving it, rather than trusting in God and serving him.

Howard Dayton, the former CEO of Crown Financial Ministries, sorted 2,350 Bible verses on money into a topical index, arranged

---

2. Betlyon and Powell, "Money," 647.

3. Also used in Luke 16:9, 11, 13.

4. Such as ἀργύριον (*argyrion*: money, e.g., Matt 25:18, 27; Luke 19:15, 23) or χρῆμα (*chrēma*: money, wealth, property, e.g., Acts 4:37; 8:18, 20).

5. Hauck, "Μαμωνᾶς," 4:388.

alphabetically, ranging from bribes and budgeting to taxes and work.[6] It seems the Bible has a lot to say about money. Perhaps the Bible talks so much about money because we think so much about money. One recent study found that the average American worries about money six times a day. The study polled 2,000 Americans, split evenly by generation, to uncover how Americans feel about their finances. Millennials worry about money the most—an average of seven times a day.[7]

Money can be a force for good, as seen in buying property or providing for basic needs (Gen 23:9, 13; Deut 2:6, 28). It can be used for noble purposes like giving offerings or supporting God's work (Deut 14:22–26; 2 Kgs 12:4–15), paying taxes (Matt 17:27; 22:19–21), or paying wages (2 Kgs 12:15). Money can serve the purposes of God (Matt 25:14–30), or be wielded wrongly, leading to usury, bribery, or attempting to buy spiritual power (Ps 15:5; Acts 8:18, 20).

The nature of money itself is not evil, but the human heart can be easily swayed. Our misguided beliefs can be deceptive, and our misuse of money can be destructive. While money is neutral, the human heart is not. Jesus warns us: "Take care, and be on your guard against all covetousness, for one's life does not consist in the abundance of his possessions" (Luke 12:15).

Scripture seeks to set our hearts into a proper relationship with money. Neither loving nor despising it, we are called to see money as a valuable tool for serving God and others. But be warned, the love of money is a powerful seducer of the heart, and like all seductions, this inordinate love lodges first in the mind, producing an arsenal of arguments to guard what it most adores, and reason falls prey to the seductive charm of wealth, until finally mammon is enthroned as an idol in the heart.

## Love of Money as Sin in the Bible: An Overview

The first sin in Israel to cause a national defeat was over money. Joshua 7:1–26 records the defeat of Israel at the battle for Ai. God had promised the children of Israel victory over their enemies. Yet, at Ai they suffered their first national defeat. Joshua cried out, "Alas, O Lord GOD, why have you brought this people over the Jordan at all, to give us into the hands of the Amorites, to destroy us?" (Josh 7:7). To which the LORD replied,

6. Dayton, "Bible on Money." 2021.
7. DigitalHubUSA. "American Worries." 2022.

"Get up! Why have you fallen on your face? Israel has sinned; they have transgressed my covenant that I commanded them; they have taken some of the devoted things; they have stolen and lied and put them among their own belongings." (Josh 7:10–11). After an inquiry as to who could have done such a thing, it was revealed that Achan was the guilty one. He confessed to Joshua, "Truly I have sinned against the LORD God of Israel, and this is what I did: when I saw among the spoil a beautiful cloak from Shinar, and 200 shekels of silver, and a bar of gold weighing 50 shekels, then I coveted them and took them." (Josh 7:20–21).

Judas Iscariot is infamous for his betrayal of Jesus, an event recounted in all four gospels (Matt 26:47–56; Mark 14:13–50; Luke 22:47–53; John 18:3–11) and foretold by Jesus himself (John 6:70–71). Judas walked with Jesus as a close companion. He heard the words and saw the miracles of the savior. He shared in the ministry of Jesus. He was one of the twelve apostles chosen by Jesus. Yet, although called to be an apostle, greed filled his heart (John 12:5–6; 13:29). His greed reached its apex when he agreed to betray Jesus for thirty pieces of silver, the price of a slave (Matt 26:14–16; Zech 11:12–13). He accomplished this heinous act by leading the soldiers and officers of the chief priests and Pharisees to the garden, where he identified and betrayed Jesus with a kiss. After the deed was done, remorse overwhelmed him. Consumed by guilt, Judas returned to the chief priests and elders and threw down the thirty pieces of silver he had received, desperately trying to undo his terrible act. In anguish, he went and hanged himself (Matt 27:3–5; Acts 1:18–20), leaving a tragic legacy of betrayal and sorrow.

The first recorded sin of the early church was over money. Acts 4:32–37 offers a glimpse into the remarkable love, unity, and devotion among the early believers. These believers "were of one heart and soul, and no one said that any of the things that belonged to him was his own, but they had everything in common" (Acts 4:32). The apostles gave witness to Jesus with great power. Great grace was upon all the believers (Acts 4:33). "There was not a needy person among them, for as many as were owners of lands or houses sold them and brought the proceeds of what was sold and laid it at the apostles' feet, and it was distributed to each as any had need" (Acts 4:34–35). For example, Barnabas "sold a field that belonged to him and brought the money and laid it at the apostles' feet" (Acts 4:36–37). Although free to do as they wished with their property, both before and after the sale, Ananias and Sapphira agreed to deceive the apostles and the community about the price of a field, and so Ananias placed only a part of the proceeds at Peter's feet. But Peter asked Ananias, "Why has Satan filled your heart to lie to the Holy Spirit?" and further described his crime as lying to God not to human beings (Acts 5:1–5). Ananias and Sapphira's gift-giving was not motivated by the Holy Spirit; instead, theirs was a sinful pretense motivated by self-glory, for which God's subsequent judgment was death (vv. 5–10).

The author of Hebrews tells us, "Keep your life free from love of money, and be content with what you have, for he has said, 'I will never leave you nor forsake you'" (Heb 13:5). We are also told: "The love of money is a root of all kinds of evils. It is through this craving that some have wandered away from the faith and pierced themselves with many pangs" (1 Tim 6:10). In 2 Timothy 3:1–5 the lovers of money rank with those who are lovers of self: proud, arrogant, abusive, disobedient to their parents, ungrateful, unholy, heartless, unappeasable, slanderous, lacking in self-control, brutal, unloving of what is good, treacherous, reckless, swollen with conceit, and dedicated to pleasure rather than God. The passage concludes: "Avoid such people." It is not money but the love for money that is the problem. This was the problem with the Pharisees. They cloaked their love of money with religious piety (Luke 16:14).

## Setting the Heart Towards Wisdom: Money and Wealth in Proverbs

Proverbs has a lot to say about money, wealth, riches, and poverty. Often the terms "wealth," "money," and "riches" are used interchangeably, but there can be subtle differences in their connotations and contexts (Prov 8:18; 10:15; 13:7; 18:11; 22:1,16).

Wealth in Proverbs generally refers to material possessions, resources, and abundance. To have wealth (*hôn*) is to own possessions desirable in a society (Prov 1:13; 3:9; 6:31; 8:18; 10:15; 11:4; 12:27; 13:7, 11; 18:11; 19:4, 14; 24:4; 28:8, 22; 29:3). It encompasses a broader concept beyond just monetary assets and includes possessions like land, livestock, and other forms of tangible and intangible wealth. We see this reflected in the variety of words used in Proverbs to describe wealth (*ʿōšer*, 'wealth', 11:16, 28; 13:8; 14:24; 22:1, 4; *hôn*, 'wealth', 10:15; 11:4; 12:27; 13:7, 11; 18:11; 19:4, 14; 28:8, 22; 29:3; *môtār*, 'abundance, plenty', 14:23; 21:5; *ḥōsen*, 'wealth, treasure', 15:6; 27:24; *taʿanûg*, 'luxury', 19:10; *ʾôṣār*, 'treasure',

10:2; 15:16; 21:6, 20; and *ḥayil*, 'wealth,' 13:22).[8] Proverbs often emphasizes the importance of acquiring wealth through diligence, wisdom, and righteousness.

While money is often associated with wealth, it represents a narrower aspect of material prosperity. In Proverbs, money is often depicted as a means to achieve wealth or as a tool to facilitate transactions and economic activities. When Proverbs talks about money, it is typically as silver (Prov 2:4; 3:14; 7:20; 8:10, 19:10:20; 16:16; 17:3; 22:1; 25:4,11; 26:23; 27:21) for silver was the usual standard of trade.

The term "riches" in Proverbs typically refers to an abundance of material wealth or possessions. It signifies an accumulation of resources, both tangible and intangible, that exceeds what is necessary for basic needs. The pursuit of riches is often cautioned against in Proverbs due to the potential dangers of greed, arrogance, and misplaced priorities.

While these terms can overlap in meaning, Proverbs offers wisdom and guidance regarding the acquisition, use, and stewardship of wealth, money, and riches. The emphasis is often placed on the importance of integrity, generosity, and the search for wisdom alongside material prosperity. The book encourages individuals to prioritize righteous living, the well-being of others, and a balanced perspective on wealth and possessions.

The message in Proverbs seems to be positive toward the right use of money: "The blessing of the Lord makes rich, and he adds no sorrow with it" (Prov 10:22). Proverbs says that God desires that we use wealth to provide for our needs (Prov 30:7–9), care for the poor (Prov 14:21), do good deeds (Prov 3:27), and even leave an inheritance to our children and grandchildren (Prov 13:22). However, the challenge for us is that Proverbs does not present a single and harmonious view of this matter. Rather, the wisdom of Proverbs is contextual and addresses a multiplicity of situations. It is thus hard to generalize a single teaching about money and wealth. Proverbs states the blessings of wealth gained by hard work and wise living yet warns against the dangers of riches that seduce the heart. The accumulation of wealth through criminal activities, exploitation, and get-rich-quick schemes is denounced. Poverty is lamented when inflicted by oppression, exploitation of the powerless, or self-inflicted by laziness and folly.

---

8. Whybray, *Wealth and Poverty*, 11.

## Agur's Prayer

Interestingly, the only prayer recorded in Proverbs reflects this complexity concerning poverty and wealth. The prayer is attributed to Agur, whose sayings or oracles are evidently famous, worthy of inclusion in Proverbs, since they are mentioned at the start of Proverbs 30. Here is Agur's prayer regarding wealth.

> Two things I ask of you; deny them not to me before I die: Remove far from me falsehood and lying; give me neither poverty nor riches; feed me with the food that is needful for me, lest I be full and deny you and say, "Who is the LORD?" or lest I be poor and steal and profane the name of my God. (Prov 30:7–9)

Commentators are divided about what the two requests are. Does the prayer make a request about lying and wealth, namely "remove far from me falsehood and lying" and "give me neither poverty nor riches"? Or does this prayer make two requests in asking for equanimity regarding extremes in wealth in two kinds: "Give me neither poverty nor riches." One commentator takes the problem a step further. Although Agur explicitly indicates that he is asking for two things, nevertheless he prays for three: no falsehood, no poverty or riches, and sufficient food.[9]

Without being dogmatic about it, I propose that "remove far from me falsehood and lying" is introductory, and the two requests are (1) do not give me poverty and (2) do not give me riches. The introductory request shows Agur's wisdom, regarding wealth, the subject matter of his petitions. Through vain speech and words of deception, one forgets God when life is too easy and turns away from God when life is too hard. Thus, Agur makes an anticipatory statement, as to the need to be preserved from the falsehoods and lying that accompany the ills of extreme wealth or poverty. After all, "falsehood and lies" (v. 8) are mentioned as temptations associated with both wealth and poverty. The explanatory clauses (v. 9) disclose Agur's real admonitions, concerning the hazards of wealth and poverty, which is the theme of this prayer: "lest I be full and deny you" (the hazard of wealth) and "lest I be poor and steal and profane the name of my God" (the hazard of poverty). Agur's prayer is rooted in his dependence upon God and his desire to honor the Lord. He will do nothing to do violence or to bring disgrace upon the name of God. The right use of wealth brings credit to God. This is basic to a life lived under God's loving care.

9. Murphy, *Proverbs*, 229.

## Rich and Poor Character Types

Proverbs displays a surprising range of attitudes toward riches. While sometimes riches are presented as desirable (Prov 10:4, 22; 21:17), "the rich" as a character type describes a particular kind of wealthy person, with whom the wise do not wish to be identified and of whom Proverbs has nothing good to say (Prov 10:15; 18:11, 23; 22:2, 7, 16; 28:6, 11). For instance, the rich barricade themselves with their wealth (Prov 10:15), they speak harshly (Prov 18:23), and they are inclined to act as lords by dominating the poor (Prov 22:7), thus forgetting that the one Lord is their real maker (Prov 22:2). Virtue has its reward; the virtuous may be expected to become rich (Prov 10:22). Nevertheless, the virtuous person is never described as a "rich man"—since this character type is devalued. Some proverbs recommend contentment with just "a little" (Prov 15:16; 16:8); others approve of the ambition toward prosperity (Prov 11:25; 24:3–4). Some proverbs speak of wealth as ephemeral (Prov 23:4–5), while in others, wealth is apparently the ultimate reward for the righteous and hard work (Prov 10:4, 22; 11:24, 25; 28:19). In Israelite society, wealth was considered a blessing (Deut 8:18). But Proverbs warns that we consider the inner influences of riches upon the heart and that wealth be handled with caution. "Nowhere else in the Bible do we find this investigation into the character of the one who is 'blessed' with riches."[10]

The poor in Proverbs are the destitute; they possess nothing at all. Whether their plight is due to their own limitations the malice of others, or circumstances beyond their control, they are powerless and vulnerable. In accordance with the words of wisdom in this book, it is a moral and religious duty to show compassion towards them.

Proverbs refers to disasters that may occur in life and exhibits a fundamental anxiety about life's precariousness. Wealth can sprout wings and fly away (Prov 23:5), for "riches do not last forever" (Prov 27:24). However, the proverbs in question also demonstrate a belief that poverty can generally be avoided by hard work, together with contentment with one's lot (Prov 10:4; 28:19). Generosity to the poor is required (Prov 11:24; 22:16), and it's important to acknowledge that wealth can be a mixed blessing (Prov 13:8; 19:6). It is not so unconditionally desirable

---

10. Murphy, *Proverbs*, 263

that it should overshadow all other aspects of life (Prov 11:4; 15:16–17; 16:8).[11]

## Leadership and Money

> If you haven't been faithful with worldly wealth,
> who will trust you with true riches?
>
> —Luke 16:11 CEB

Leaders face accelerated levels of pressure and temptation because of their position and power. They can be led to exploit resources for personal profit and manipulation. Let's step back from Proverbs for a moment and look at a few other biblical passages on leadership and money. This will help us grasp the teachings of Proverbs about money and leadership.

Exodus 38:21–31 provides an excellent glimpse into how Moses handled the financial and material resources entrusted to his oversight. The section begins, "These are the records of the tabernacle, the tabernacle of the testimony, as they were recorded at the commandment of Moses, the responsibility of the Levites under the direction of Ithamar, the son of Aaron the priest." The passage goes on to list the specific amounts of gold, silver, and bronze that were collected and how they were used. The word translated "records" (*pāqad*) means "to see to," or "tend to" for the purpose of fulfilling an assigned task. The core sense of this verb has to do with fulfilling an obligation in a leadership role.[12] Moses demonstrates the importance of detailed accounting, lest one come under suspicion of having personally appropriated some of the gold, silver, or bronze. Moses was not accused of financial mismanagement. Nothing indicates that he needed to provide such strict and independent accounting. Yet, this proactive stance gives the passage its force. There must be clear and transparent accountability, not due to some accusation that needs to be countered but because this is the right thing to do.

This financial integrity was part of Moses' defense when he faced the most dangerous challenge to his leadership (Num 16:1–50). Korah, Dathan, and Abiram, along with two hundred and fifty well-known leaders of the congregation, denounced Moses and Aaron, claiming, "You have gone too far! For all in the congregation are holy, every one of them, and

---

11. Whybray, *Wealth and Poverty*, 60–61.
12. Merrill, "Authority," 2014

the LORD is among them. Why then do you exalt yourselves above the assembly of the LORD?" (Num 16:1–3). Each faction felt that they had been passed over in the allocation of leadership positions. The irony of their challenge is unmistakable. They pose as egalitarians and say that everyone should be a leader. What they really mean is: "I should be a leader."

These rebels illustrate the perennial threat of the ambitious person who foments discontent against a leader, accusing the leader of being a self-seeking tyrant. Enflamed by ambition, these rebels opposed Moses in the name of freedom, but they really wanted power. In response, Moses told the LORD, "Do not respect their offering. I have not taken one donkey from them" (Num 16:15). As a leader, you will face similar challenges. When accusations are made, you will be glad that financial integrity is part of your defense. As Jethro told Moses, leaders must be people of ability, who fear God, are trustworthy, and hate dishonest gain (Exod 18:21).

Samuel is another example of financial integrity. In his farewell address, he told the Israelites, "Listen: I have done everything you asked of me and have placed a king over you. The king will lead you now. I am old and gray, though my sons are still with you, and I've been your leader since I was young until now. So I'm here: Tell the truth about me in the presence of the Lord and his anointed. Have I ever stolen someone's ox? Have I ever taken someone's donkey? Have I ever oppressed or mistreated anyone? Have I ever taken bribes from someone and looked the other way about something? Tell me the truth. I will make it right." The people answered, "You haven't oppressed or mistreated us, and you've never taken anything from anyone" (1 Sam 12:1–4, CEB).

Building on the Old Testament, the New Testament gives a demanding list of qualifications for church leaders, who are "not given to wine, no striker, not greedy of filthy lucre; but patient, not a brawler, not covetous" (1 Tim 3:3 KJV). Servants of the church must be serious, "not double-tongued, not given to much wine, not greedy of filthy lucre" (1 Tim 3:8 KJV). Overseers "must be blameless, as the steward of God; not self-willed, not soon angry, not given to wine, no striker, not given to filthy lucre" (Titus 1:7 KJV). The apostle Peter tells pastors, "Feed the flock of God which is among you, taking the oversight thereof, not by constraint, but willingly; not for filthy lucre, but of a ready mind" (1 Pet 5:2 KJV). Recall the Pauline warning against false teachers, teaching "things which they ought not, for filthy lucre's sake" (Titus 1:11, KJV). Notice how the King James Version makes use of the Old English phrase, "filthy lucre."

Lucre comes from the Latin word *lucrum*. *Lucrum* meant gain, advantage, profit, wealth, or riches. We derive "lucrative" from this word.

Filthy lucre underscores this grave and severe temptation for ministers of the gospel. The corrupting power of money leads ministers to compromise, and they may make shameful and dishonest gain by peddling the word of God for money. When love for money corrupts your heart, you cease serving others out of love and begin using people for personal gain. You have commodified both redemption and relationships for the sake of economic advantage, and this is a filthy thing to do.

Moses, Jethro, Samuel, and the church ministers in the Pastoral letters of the New Testament, point us to leadership that transcends the allure of material gain and prioritizes the well-being of those under our care. Leaders must keep a watchful eye on the treacherous appeal of mammon, for the love of money is a cunning foe, ever ready to ensnare the noblest of hearts. Mammon will whisper in your ear, deceitfully urging you to exploit your position for personal gain, to show favoritism to the rich while the poor and powerless stand neglected, and to sway under the weight of influential donors. This is why you must be free from the love of money, for as a leader, you will have more opportunities than most to yield to the voice of mammon.

## Bribery: The Story of a Donor

This brings us to issues of bribery and its more subtle relative, lobbying. Bribery entails offering, giving, soliciting, or receiving any item of value to influence the actions of those entrusted with public or legal responsibilities. Lobbying, on the other hand, is the act of lawfully attempting to influence actions, policies, or decisions. The ethical lines between bribery and lobbying can often become fuzzy. And it's not just politicians, police, and judges who are lobbied or bribed. Pastors can also face donors who leverage their economic resources to gain influence and guide church decisions.

For example, Gil was a staff pastor in a large church in the American South. Most of the congregation was politically conservative. Gil shared many of their social and political concerns. However, during a presidential election, Gil concluded that he could not, in good conscience, support the Republican candidate. He voted for the Democrat. Though Gil kept his vote private, somehow, news of it began to spread and became a major scandal in the church. Members demanded that Gil be fired. A large donor in this prosperous church confronted the senior pastor while holding a check worth several thousand dollars, and he said, "If you ever want to see another one of these, you will fire Gil immediately."

Does this qualify as bribery? Was this an acceptable act of lobbying? Donors certainly have the right, and even the obligation, to withhold contributions when they observe ethical, moral, legal, or theological aberrations or misconduct. However, the pastor voted as a private citizen exercising his right to vote according to his conscience. While maybe not illegal, did the donor cross an ethical line in demanding that this staff pastor vote for a particular party or lose his job? Thankfully, the senior pastor did not succumb to these demands.

The pressure to keep donors happy is real. This is why you must have firm biblical and ethical convictions about money and its use, or you run the risk of selling yourself to the highest bidder. In Proverbs, there's wisdom that renovates the heart, renews the mind, and guides the hands in the wise use of money.

## Money and the Leader's Heart

> Honor the LORD with your wealth and with the firstfruits
> of all your produce; then your barns will be filled with
> plenty, and your vats will be bursting with wine.
>
> —PROVERBS 3:9–10

Agur's prayer (Prov 30:7–9) shows us how to pray about wealth. The advice about sacrifice (Prov 3:9–10) shows us how to use wealth as worship to honor the Lord. From these passages, we see that wealth is both a subject of prayer and an object for worship. The word "honor" *(kabbēd)* stems from the root *kābēd*, meaning "to be heavy," and signifies esteem for a person. Such a person has value and social weight or prominence.[13] The phrase could be expressed in this way: "Show that the Lord is great," "Show that the Lord is wonderful," or "Show how much you respect the Lord."[14] God's greatness and worth are declared not merely with words but by the concrete act of presenting tribute to him "from your wealth" *(mēhônekā;* see 1:13),[15] the first fruits of "all your produce." This is the only

13. Waltke, *Proverbs 1–15*, 247.

14. Reyburn and McG. Fry, *Handbook*, 75.

15. Waltke, *Proverbs, Chapters 1–15*, 247–48.

place where Proverbs alludes to ceremonial worship. These instructions echo a text in Deuteronomy that specifies what is due in support of the Levites. The Israelites were instructed to give the priests "the firstfruits of your grain, of your wine and of your oil, and the first fleece of your sheep, you shall give him" (Deut 18:4). Abundant blessings are promised for those who comply with God's directive: "Then your barns will be filled with plenty, and your vats will be bursting with wine (Prov 3:10; cf. Deut 28:8; Mal 3:10–12). We show the greatness of God when we honor him with our wealth, trust in him, show compassion to the poor, and treat others justly (Prov 3:27–35).

First fruits (rē 'šît) were offered by the worshippers in Israel at their yearly harvest festival, sometimes called the Festival of Weeks (Lev 23:15–21). The word rē 'šît may designate the first fruit of the womb (Gen 49:3; Deut 21:27; Pss 78:51; 105:36) or of the crops (Hos 9:10); as such it symbolizes "the best" (cf. Num 18:12–13; Ezek 48:14; Amos 6:6). In the arena of worship, offerings refer to the best of material things, such as of dough or grain (Num 15:20; Deut 18:4; 26:2, 10; 2 Chr 31:5; Neh 10:38; Ezek 44:30). Here, in this passage (Prov 3:9–10), the offering is expanded to include "all your produce" (Lev 23:10). This includes crops, as 3:10 suggests, and revenue in general (Prov 3:14; 8:19; 10:16; 14:4; 15:9; 16:8).[16] The first fruits are "the first part of the harvest that is given to God."[17] In other words, the first thing to do with produce is to honor God with it. This act of worship orients your heart toward God and opens the pathway of God's provision (Prov 3:10).

For all its warning against the dangers of money, the Bible does not discount or repudiate money in and of itself. In fact, it is just the opposite. Consider, for example, Deuteronomy 8:18: "You shall remember the LORD your God, for it is he who gives you power to get wealth, that he may confirm his covenant that he swore to your fathers, as it is this day." The Lord gives the power to get wealth, that he may establish his covenant. The issue is not that you possess wealth, the issue is wealth possessing you.

The promise of provision in Deuteronomy 8:18 is hemmed in before and after with warnings against self-exaltation and forgetting God as the source and owner of all things: "Beware lest you say in your heart, 'My power and the might of my hand have gotten me this wealth'" (Deut

---

16. Waltke, *Proverbs, Chapters 1–15*, 247–48.
17. Reyburn and McG. Fry, *Handbook*, 75.

8:17); and "if you forget the LORD your God and go after other gods and serve them and worship them, I solemnly warn you today that you shall surely perish" (Deut 8:19). God instituted a system of sacrifices and offerings to safeguard the heart by ritualizing worship, repentance, gratitude, humility, generosity, and community.

In the religious systems of the Ancient Near East, sacrifices were an attempt to placate the gods, earn their goodwill, and thus enlist their power. In scripture, sacrifice is something else altogether. The God revealed in the Bible is simultaneously the transcendent supreme power and creator of all things, and yet he acts on behalf of the powerless, be they slaves in Egypt, or the widow, orphan, and stranger in Israel, or the broken, the sinful, and the alienated in the gospels. This God does not need to be bribed or placated to show goodwill or to act on behalf of those in need. His very nature as love vouchsafes his goodness (1 John 4:16). He does not need sacrifices to bend his will toward us, for "The LORD is good to all, and his mercy is over all that he has made" (Ps 145:9).

This understanding that God does not need sacrifices is central to the message of the prophets. Samuel asked, "Does the LORD delight in burnt offerings and sacrifices as much as in obeying the LORD? To obey is better than sacrifice, and to heed is better than the fat of rams." (1 Sam 15:22, NIV). God declared through Hosea, "I desire steadfast love and not sacrifice, the knowledge of God rather than burnt offerings" (Hosea 6:6). Through Isaiah, God says, "The multitude of your sacrifices—what are they to me?" says the LORD. "I have more than enough of burnt offerings, of rams and the fat of fattened animals; I have no pleasure in the blood of bulls and lambs and goats. When you come to appear before me, who has asked this of you, this trampling of my courts? Stop bringing meaningless offerings! Your incense is detestable to me. New Moons, Sabbaths, and convocations—I cannot bear your worthless assemblies." (Isa 1:11–13, NIV).

In Psalms, we read, "If I were hungry, I would not tell you, for the world and its fullness are mine. Do I eat the flesh of bulls or drink the blood of goats?" (Ps 50:12–13). Even after his disastrous affair with Bathsheba and the murder of her husband, David cried out, "O Lord, open my lips, and my mouth will declare your praise. For you will not delight in sacrifice, or I would give it; you will not be pleased with a burnt offering. The sacrifices of God are a broken spirit; a broken and contrite heart, O God, you will not despise" (Ps 51:15–17).

The Psalms and the prophets were not criticizing the institution of sacrifices. They were condemning the belief that one could purchase divine favor and power while acting disdainfully, cruelly, unjustly, or callously toward God and others.

If God does not need sacrifices, why offer them? The answer is quite simple. We offer sacrifices to reorient our wayward hearts and to eliminate the obstacles of sin that have lodged there, which prevent us from loving God and others. Let me illustrate with examples of tithes and burnt offerings. The tithe was intended to accomplish good by expressing gratitude to God (Gen 14:18–20; 28:22), providing for the poor (Deut 14:28–29), supporting the priests and Levites (Num 18:21; 2 Chr 31:4), and building the social pillars of society through the tithe meal (Deut 14:23). In other words, the tithe was offered that poverty could be alleviated, worship and instruction maintained, public goodwill fostered, and humility and gratitude cultivated in the heart of God's people.

The burnt offering was something altogether different. At first glance, burnt offerings seem to serve no practical purpose, and this can be jarring to our modern pragmatic values. The entire animal was consumed—it just went up in smoke. In the agricultural world of the Old Testament, these were costly offerings. Perhaps a modern equivalent would be something like this: Suppose a local church asked its members to bring a large cash-only offering and then gathered in the parking lot and threw the offering in a bonfire while the whole congregation celebrated as thousands of dollars of cold, hard cash went up in smoke. Can you imagine the response? The media coverage would not be positive. I can imagine the outcries would be like those Mary faced when she poured out her expensive ointment on Jesus, "Why this waste? This money could have helped the poor" (John 12:1–8). And, like Judas, we normally say this not because we care for the poor but because we love the money.

The extravagant wastefulness of burnt offerings is precisely their point. The extravagant wastefulness breaks the heart's enmeshment with the deceptions of wealth. It frees the heart to truly value what is valuable and liberates it from avarice and the never-satisfied craving for more. When the heart is held captive to the deceitfulness of wealth, the word of God is unproductive in your life, and your perspective is distorted.[18] This is why you are to guard your heart above all things (Prov 4:23). When the love of money rules your heart, you know the price of everything, but you

18. Mark 4:1–20.

do not know the value of anything. Affluence can dull the senses, making you forget where you came from and from whom you have received all that you have. Honoring the Lord with your wealth helps keep your heart from this deception (Prov 3:9–10).

God does not want your money; he wants you. But to get you, he must first get your money because for us humans, our hearts go where our money goes. Jesus makes this explicit in Matthew 6:21, "For where your treasure is, there your heart will be also." First comes your money, then your heart. Most fundraising efforts get this backwards. Fundraisers normally appeal to the heart, with emotionally moving presentations about all the good they will do, if only the donor will make a significant contribution. Such appeals can raise a lot of money. However, these appeals miss the central point of the gospel. God is not seeking to develop a large cadre of philanthropists and do-gooders. He wants to cultivate sons and daughters who love God and others from a pure heart, free from avarice and economic exploitation.

Honoring the Lord with your wealth liberates your heart from the love of money. Money then ceases to be an object of worship and becomes an offering for worship. This act of worship dethrones a ruling power of this present age and enthrones God as ruler of the heart and source of all good things, for "Whoever trusts in his riches will fall, but the righteous will flourish like a green leaf" (Prov 11:28). You cannot have spiritual renewal without financial reform.

## Money and the Leader's Head

Financial experts point out that what causes one person to be successful with money and another to give up in hopelessness is a specific "money mindset." The premise is straightforward yet profound: Your beliefs concerning money, self, and the world fundamentally influence the trajectory of your life. These beliefs act as the architects of the decisions you make, either propelling you toward financial advancement or holding you back. When this "money mindset" is shaped by wisdom, it raises the standards of financial success to mean more than financial freedom and economic prosperity. Now, the right use of money includes caring for the poor, alleviating suffering, correcting injustice, and establishing righteousness. Wisdom recalibrates how you think about money. It liberates you from the love of money and transforms money into a tool for doing good.

## Wise Leaders Think Differently About Money

Wise leaders are not looking for a lucky break or a winning lottery ticket, for they heed the timeless counsel: "Wealth gained hastily will dwindle, but whoever gathers little by little will increase it" (Prov 13:11). Instead, wise leaders set a high standard of excellence to be skillful in their work (Prov 22:29), mindful that "a slack hand causes poverty, but the hand of the diligent makes rich" (Prov 10:4). These wise leaders are diligent in their savings (Prov 13:11), honest in their dealings (Prov 16:11; 20:10, 23), and truthful in their words (Prov 12:22). They live within their means and manage debt wisely (Prov 22:7) while making use of whatever they have, for "whoever works his land will have plenty of bread, but he who follows worthless pursuits will have plenty of poverty" (Prov 28:19).

While disciplined and diligent with money, the wise leader is not miserly, for she understands the power of generosity. Generosity is a spiritual act of sabotage against the forces of greed and the antidote to the craving disease. "One gives freely, yet grows all the richer; another withholds what he should give, and only suffers want" (Prov 11:24). This wise leader understands the renewing dynamics of generosity for "Whoever brings blessing will be enriched, and one who waters will himself be watered" (Prov 11:25); and "Whoever has a bountiful eye will be blessed, for he shares his bread with the poor" (Prov 22:9); and "Whoever is generous to the poor lends to the LORD, and he will repay him for his deed" (Prov 19:17). The wise leader is relentless in the pursuit of generosity.

I have spent decades working with leaders and churches throughout Europe, the Middle East, Central Asia, North Africa, and the United States. During these years, I have known gifted and well-trained leaders who have limited their life and fruitfulness because of their wrong-headed approach to money. I have also known leaders who are far less gifted but who have embraced a biblical view towards money, and they are blessed because of it. The truth is, I have never known a generous person who is not blessed. Billy Graham is credited with saying, "If a person gets his attitude toward money straight, it will help straighten out almost every other area in his life." My experience leads me to the same conclusion.

## Interlude: On Economics

In "Capital in the Twenty-First Century," French economist Thomas Piketty examines the dynamics of wealth and income inequality in capitalist societies, particularly focusing on historical trends and the potential consequences for the future. The book extensively analyzes historical economic data from various countries spanning several centuries. Sounds exciting, right?

Well, this apparently complex book became a surprising runaway bestseller in 2014. The Guardian declared it to be among the one hundred best books of the twenty-first century.[19] An impressive feat for an 800-page tome, which argues that the market economy tends to make us more and less equal at the same time: more equal because the market spreads education, knowledge, and skills more widely than in the past, but less equal because when the rate of return on capital (such as investments, property, and other assets) exceeds the rate of economic growth, wealth and income inequality tend to increase. He asserts that this pattern is inherent to capitalist systems because the accumulation of capital tends to concentrate wealth in the hands of a few. This increase in inequality is "potentially threatening to democratic societies and to the values of social justice on which they are based."[20]

Like any discussion of economics, this book sparked extensive debate among economists and policymakers. The key point for our purposes relates to economic inequality. These inequalities tend to increase over time with economic fluctuations. Though Piketty deals with capitalism, economic inequalities can plague society regardless of the economic system. This happened in biblical times. Debt might involve selling yourself into slavery as the only way of guaranteeing food and shelter (Deut 15:12–18). Families might be forced to sell their ancestral inheritance (Lev 25:23–34). The result would be a society in which, over the course of time, a few would become substantial landowners while many became landless and impoverished. The solution in ancient Israel involved a periodic restoration of fundamental liberties. Every seventh year debts were to be released, and Israelite slaves were set free. After seven sabbatical cycles, the Jubilee year arrived. This was to be a time when, with few exceptions, ancestral land returned to its original owners (Lev 25:1–55).

---

19. The Guardian, "The 100 Best Books of the 21st Century." 2019.
20. Piketty and Goldhammer. *Capital*, 571.

We, of course, are not the ancient Israelites, and we have not instituted these types of national policies. But we should still contend for economic justice in our day in whatever way is most pragmatic and just.

Don't get me wrong. I think the free-market economy is the best system we know for alleviating poverty through economic growth. However, the free-market economy is better at producing wealth than at distributing it equitably. When left unfettered and unregulated, as Piketty discusses, wealth tends to accumulate in a small handful of individuals. The spiraling accumulation generates inequality, the exploitation of labor, and environmental degradation. I am not arguing for one economic system over another. Rather, I advocate an overarching moral ethic that governs any system of power in order to protect the powerless and restrain the powerful. All power systems will, by nature, seek more power, and the more powerful the system becomes, the more it wields its power to protect and expand its power until it has consumed both its victims and itself.

Scripture teaches us to control our impulses to safeguard the future. Rest every seventh day. Place spiritual, not material, values at the heart of society. Fight poverty. Pursue justice. Treat employees decently. Care for the widow, the orphan, and the stranger. Treat others with dignity. Work for long-term sustainability, not short-term economic growth. To escape the enchantment of mammon, we need to regard wealth less as the accumulation of money and more as the accumulation of the power to do good, honor God, and serve others so that all may flourish.

Wealth is a form of power, and as such, the wise leader will use this power to do justice and benefit others. Any fool or knave may have great riches, but "riches do not profit in the day of wrath, but righteousness delivers from death" (Prov 11:4). The biblically informed leader shaped by wisdom knows that to have a more just society where all members of that society can flourish cannot happen without economic reform. This will include regulations that protect the powerless and constrain the powerful. Wise leaders have a fierce commitment to justice that includes honest and fair wages and the elimination of economic exploitation of the powerless, remembering that "the field of the poor may yield much food, but it is swept away through injustice" (Prov 13:23, NRSVue).

## Wise Leaders Think Money is a Wonderful Servant But a Terrible Master

"Do not toil to acquire wealth; be discerning enough to desist. When your eyes light on it, it is gone, for suddenly it sprouts wings, flying like an eagle toward heaven" (Prov 23:4–5). While Proverbs has no problem with money and no use for laziness, it does counsel against toiling for wealth. Proverb 23:4–5 recognizes how fleeting money can be and how seeking it can make it disappear. So, while Proverbs does condemn the pursuit of wealth as an end in itself, it does not condemn the possession of wealth. What Proverbs does is condemn wealth gained by wickedness (Prov 10:2; 11:4, 18; 21:6); and warn against the dangers of wealth gained hastily, "A faithful man will abound with blessings, but whoever hastens to be rich will not go unpunished" (Prov 28:20); "Wealth gained hastily will dwindle, but whoever gathers little by little will increase it" (Prov 13:11). Proverbs seeks to cultivate leaders who are fully devoted to God, who do not trust in their minds (Prov 28:26) or their money, but rather in the Lord, and they seek him first in all things (Prov 16:20; 28:25; 29:25; 28:1). As Jesus said, "No one can serve two masters, for either he will hate the one and love the other, or he will be devoted to the one and despise the other. You cannot serve God and money" (Matt 6:24).

## Wise Leaders Know Money Can Do a Lot, But It Cannot Do Everything

Money is a tool, not the goal, of the wise leader. While it has limitations and dangers, money also makes possible very positive outcomes. Let's face it, we all need money because money makes it possible to live and enjoy life (Prov 10:22; 14:24). Wealth also makes it possible to leave an inheritance for your children (Prov 13:22). And money makes it possible to help the poor and needy (Prov 10:15). To honor the Lord and meet your needs, leaving a legacy and alleviating poverty. are all worthy uses of money and only truly possible when the love of money has been overthrown in the heart. These are some of the good things you can do with money.

Money can do a lot, but it cannot do everything. Proverbs identifies at least four limitations of money and wealth. First, while money can bring a feeling of success, it cannot satisfy your deepest needs (Prov

11:4; 15:16–17; 16:8; 17:1). Second, wealth cannot be relied upon because it can fly away from you. "Do not toil to acquire wealth; be discerning enough to desist. When your eyes light on it, it is gone, for suddenly it sprouts wings, flying like an eagle toward heaven" (Prov 23:4–5). Third, wealth can seduce you with a false sense of independence from God (Prov 30:7–9), a false sense of security (Prov 11:28), or a false sense of pride (Prov 18:11). Finally, money can give you fake friends and real enemies, but it cannot give you loving relationships (Prov 13:8; 14:20–21; 19:4, 6–7).

## Money and the Leader's Hands

Money and relationships are a dangerous mix. The sage of Proverbs warns leaders about the dangers of financial entanglements (Prov 6:1–5). As a leader, you are given incredible levels of trust by those who follow you. You must take extreme caution to never fall for the temptation to convert that sacred trust into a profitable economic situation for yourself. A leader I admired and trusted called me one Saturday morning. It felt like such an honor that he would think of me and call. He asked about my family and how things were in the ministry. It sounded great. I was young and new in ministry. It felt like a father in the faith calling to check on me. Then the conversation turned. He began talking about the health supplements he was using and how they worked wonders for him. He asked if I would like to try them. He then said if I liked them, I could make money by selling them to my friends, family, and people in the church. What I thought was a friendly conversation now felt dirty, like some sort of violation. I was being asked to use my ministry and relationships to make money. And this being a multilevel marketing scheme, he would make money too. Over the years of my pastorate, people have tried to recruit me to use my role to sell insurance, Amway, and health supplements—to all of which I said no (though I did need the money). I was struggling to provide for my family. But I was also a pastor, and that sacred calling had to be protected from the deceptive lure of "filthy lucre."

Financial integrity for leaders also includes our expense accounts. We may never embezzle thousands of dollars, but we should also be diligent in the small things. For example, my denomination has an annual Pastors' convention. All churches are asked to provide funds for the pastor to attend. We are there to be refreshed, see old friends, make new friends, and "do the business of the church." If my church pays for me to go and I spend all my time at the pool, am I committing fraud? Am I taking a vacation at the church's expense? I suppose if you are on the verge of burnout and exhaustion, and your church would support you to go and sit by the pool, then do it. That is okay. If you are not in burnout and just taking advantage of your church's generosity, then you are on a slippery slope. This is why Proverbs is so vocal about financial integrity in leadership. You are given great trust as a leader, and you must guard it vigilantly.

We expect our leaders and churches to have the highest standards. Unfortunately, churches and ministries are regular victims of financial fraud and mismanagement. According to a recent study, $45 billion is lost each year due to ecclesiastical crime, fraud, and financial mismanagement. Some cases make the news. Many do not. Sadly, most financial fraud in churches and nonprofit organizations goes unreported.

The Association of Certified Fraud Examiners defines fraud as "any intentional or deliberate act to deprive another of property or money by guile, deception, or other unfair means." Fraud experts warn us that, of all the ways scammers can steal your money, the most difficult fraud to combat is that kind that uses your faith against you. Law enforcement officials call this "affinity fraud," targeting victims through a common bond. Because churches are typically close-knit affinity groups, the wise leader needs to be vigilant in protecting the flock from being financially fleeced. Protecting the church from being defrauded seems to have been needed in Paul's day as in ours. Paul told the Corinthians, "For we are not like so many others, hucksters who peddle the word of God for profit, but we are speaking in Christ before God as persons of sincerity, as persons sent from God" (2 Cor 2:17, NET). Huckster preachers existed long before television, direct mail, and the internet. Wise leaders protect the flock of God from financial fraud—this is part of the job.

## Wise Leaders Practice Accountability to God and Others

Accountability begins with God. He is the owner of all things, and we are ultimately stewards of what he has entrusted to us. Faithfulness as a steward brings favor and promotion, for "a servant who deals wisely has the king's favor, but his wrath falls on one who acts shamefully" (Prov 14:35). This can even exalt you above those with family connections. "A servant who deals wisely will rule over a son who acts shamefully and will share the inheritance as one of the brothers" (Prov 17:2).

Trust can cause organizations to grow slack in their accounting practices "since we trust one another." Trust is good, but trust with accountability is better. It is a safeguard for everyone. This is the meaning of the old Russian proverb, made famous in the English-speaking world by Ronald Reagan when discussing nuclear disarmament with the Soviet Union: "Trust, but verify."

Transparency and accountability are to be celebrated because they increase trust in leadership. This means you should follow standardized accounting practices.[21] Implementing internal policies and controls is another way to embrace accountability. While you would like to trust everyone who volunteers or works for your organization, you cannot assume you are immune to human frailties. Internal bookkeeping controls and policies are the first steps to reducing the risk of fraud. Look, I get it. Accounting, bookkeeping, budgets, and tax regulations are not necessarily the most exciting aspects of leadership, but doing the boring stuff will save you the unwanted drama of a financial scandal. These practices provide accountability and build trust, and this is wise leadership.

## Wise Leaders Practice Gratitude to God and Generosity to Others

Proverbs does not teach you how to live "the good life;" it teaches you how to live a better life. Pay attention to the word "better" in these verses. "Blessed is the one who finds wisdom, and the one who gets understanding, for the gain from her is better than gain from silver and her profit better than gold" (Prov 3:13–14). Wisdom is "better than jewels, and all that you may desire cannot compare with her" (Prov 8:11). Wisdom's "fruit is better than gold, even fine gold, and my yield than choice silver" (Prov 8:19). "Better is a little with the fear of the LORD than great treasure and trouble with it. Better is a dinner of herbs where love is than a fattened ox and hatred with it" (Prov 15:16–17). "Better is a little with righteousness than great revenues with injustice" (Prov 16:8). "How much better to get wisdom than gold! To get understanding is to be chosen rather

---

21. This might sound obvious, but you'd be surprised how many organizations do not adhere to the latest accounting standards in the industry. Generally accepted accounting principles (GAAP) will protect you and your organization.

than silver" (Prov 16:16). "It is better to be of a lowly spirit with the poor than to divide the spoil with the proud" (Prov 16:19). "Better is a poor person who walks in his integrity than one who is crooked in speech and is a fool" (Prov 19:1). "What is desired in a man is steadfast love, and a poor man is better than a liar" (Prov 19:22). "A good name is to be chosen rather than great riches, and favor is better than silver or gold" (Prov 22:1). "Better is a poor man who walks in his integrity than a rich man who is crooked in his way" (Prov 28:6). Wisdom, understanding, the fear of the Lord, love, righteousness, humility, integrity, steadfastness, and a good name: These constitute true wealth and success for leaders, not gold, silver, and the outward trappings of success.

## Wise Leaders Pursue God's Righteousness When Handling Both Poverty and Wealth

There is one consistent message in Proverbs that should govern our behavior with respect to poverty and wealth: Respond righteously. Throughout this chapter we have seen how the wisdom offered in Proverbs will help you navigate the turbulent waves of economic uncertainty. We are admonished: "Know well the condition of your flocks, and give attention to your herds, for riches do not last forever" (Prov 27:23–24). This is why, as we have seen, the only prayer in Proverbs contains this line: "Give me neither poverty nor riches; feed me with the food that is needful for me" (Prov 30:8).

Poverty is taken for granted in Proverbs. The poor are a fact of life. It is significant that in Israelite Wisdom Literature, the poor become a special object of care due to their relationship with the Lord. Both rich and poor were created by God, and so mockery of the poor is blasphemy against God (Prov 14:31; 17:5; 22:2). Proverbs 19:17 makes the relationship between the Lord and the poor explicitly clear: "Whoever is generous to the poor lends to the LORD, and he will repay him for his deed." God is bound by his compassion to the poor and he will fight for them, "Do not rob the poor, because he is poor, or crush the afflicted at the gate, for the LORD will plead their cause and rob of life those who rob them" (Prov 22:22–23). We who are entrusted by God with the responsibilities of leadership are called to champion who God champions, and he champions the poor, "Whoever despises his neighbor is a sinner, but blessed is he who is generous to the poor" (Prov 14:21). "Whoever gives to the poor will not want, but he who hides his eyes will get many a curse" (Prov 28:27). "Whoever multiplies his wealth by interest and profit gathers it for him who is generous to the poor" (Prov 28:8). "Whoever oppresses the poor to increase his own wealth, or gives to the rich, will only come to poverty" (Prov 22:16).

Throughout Proverbs, we have heard multiple voices speak. Among these voices are kings, fathers, mothers, Lady Wisdom, the wise, farmers, and at least two unknown characters named Agur and Lemuel. All those who speak in the book have material possessions. The voice that is inevitably missing in the book is that of the poor.[22] Like the poor in society, the poor in Proverbs are voiceless. However, this is not because Proverbs seeks to silence or avoid the poor. In fact, it does just the opposite. Proverbs calls us to "speak up for those who cannot speak for themselves; ensure justice for those being crushed. Yes, speak up for the poor and helpless, and see that they get justice" (Prov 31:8–9, NLT). Wise and godly leaders must contend for economic justice.

God's design is that people will prosper through hard work and a just society (Prov 10:4). This is why we must always fight against economic systems that perpetuate injustice on the poor and powerless (Prov 13:23). God takes economic justice seriously. In Ezekiel 16:1–58 we see that God judged Sodom, Samaria, and Jerusalem for, among other things, their opulent self-indulgence and neglect of the poor and needy, "Behold, this was the guilt of your sister Sodom: she and her daughters had pride, excess of food, and prosperous ease, but did not aid the poor and needy" (Ezek 16:49). Psalm 9:18 reminds us, "For the needy shall not always be forgotten, and the hope of the poor shall not perish forever." Wisdom calls us to more than sound financial management. Wisdom calls us to economic justice.

I recently spent a few days in downtown Seattle hanging out with my daughter. Recent riots and the global pandemic had taken a toll on the Emerald City. The scars of recent riots were everywhere. I was sad to see businesses closed due to the COVID-19 pandemic. I was heartbroken to see stores boarded up for protection against rioters. I was grieved to see peaceful protests seeking social justice hijacked by criminals, claiming violence as their right. Cries of the Spirit for economic, social, and criminal justice were drowned out by the screams of fascist agitators and provocateurs of both the radical right and the extreme left.

22. Whybray, *Wealth and Poverty*, 113.

As distressing as all of this was, the most distressing thing was the overflowing crowds of homeless people. Every street seemed populated by the unhoused. Overpasses were serving as shelters from the elements. Green spaces, intended to beautify the city and give respite to the city-dweller's soul, had become homeless camps full of weather-beaten tents, make-shift sheds, and stolen shopping carts. The words of Proverbs 21:13 were echoing in my mind, "Whoever closes his ear to the cry of the poor will himself call out and not be answered."

I was broken by their condition and overcome by a sense of help-lessness in the face of such overwhelming need. What could I do to fix homelessness, poverty, drug addiction, and mental illness? What could anyone do? I was powerless in the face of such desperation. Not knowing what to do, I did nothing. Even when a homeless man asked me, "Can you help me get something to eat?" I did nothing.

Homelessness is a complex problem with a multitude of contributing factors that include the lack of affordable housing, unemployment, personal crises, mental illness, family and societal alienation, drug and alcohol addiction, antisocial behavior, economic injustice, bad luck, bad choices, and even the voluntary choice to remain homeless. These factors all merge together in lockstep to beat down, dehumanize, and alienate our fellow image-bearers of God.

I was overwhelmed by the immediacy of the perfect storm we face as a society. Health care, race relations, immigration, social injustice, police and legal reforms, poverty, and economic inequality—all summoning us to a day of reckoning. I simultaneously felt like throwing my hands up in surrender, running to the mountains to hide, and jumping into this mess to make a difference.

I was also haunted by the words of Jesus in Matthew 25:31–46. This is the passage where Jesus tells us he will judge nations based on how they treat the poor, the hungry, the foreigner, and the prisoner. His words disturbed my thoughts, "Inasmuch as you did it to the least of these, my brothers, you did it to me." I have always wrestled with this passage, which depicts God judging the nations. Individual judgment I understand, but how will God judge nations? Do we get in the "individual judgment" line. Then once we are judged individually, do we go to the "nation judgment" line? What if I am a dual citizen? Do I get into the line for the United States and then Canada? Lame, I know. But those questions were running through my mind as I tried to understand the words haunting me.

Early the next morning, I was sitting in my hotel room, drinking coffee, and thinking about these societal ailments and the judgment of nations, without reflecting on their connection. I bounced between the two, like flipping between channels on the television, when suddenly they snapped together like two magnets. God will judge the nations on how they treat the poor, the sick, the powerless, the accused, the incarcerated, and the stranger (those "other" than "us" in nationality, ethnicity, race, gender, socioeconomic status, and religion), because it requires the whole nation to solve these challenges.

The whole nation is accountable because no individual or group can fix poverty, homelessness, race relations, criminal justice, and health care. The entire spectrum of human participation is necessary to bring about justice and healing. The full spectrum from liberals to conservatives, free markets to government taxation and regulation, for-profit businesses and not-for-profit institutions. All are needed: families, churches, synagogues, mosques, community centers, private initiatives, and government programs—all working together for economic, social, legal, and healthcare justice.

Economic and social justice, healthcare, judicial reform, and protecting the stranger and the powerless are more than just current pressure points in society. They are the cries of Jesus to the nations. This is not a liberal thing, a conservative thing, a political thing, or a religious thing. It is a human thing. And Jesus takes it personally, "For inasmuch as you have done it unto the least of these, my brothers, you have done it unto me."

## Conclusion

Mammon is a ruling power of this present age. It transforms creation's goodness into a lifeless abstraction of monetary value. This is an enthusiastic cult of insatiable consumption, enslaved to a filthy god. In the early days of the Christian movement, another young leader who was seeking to follow wisdom and lead wisely was instructed, "Now godliness with contentment is great gain. For we brought nothing into this world, and it is certain we can carry nothing out. And having food and clothing, with these we shall be content. But those who desire to be rich fall into temptation and a snare, and into many foolish and harmful lusts which drown men in destruction and perdition. For the love of money is a root of all kinds of evil, for which some have strayed from the faith in their greediness, and pierced themselves through with many sorrows" (1 Tim 6:6–10, NKJV). More than likely, there will be a report on the news this week about another minister exploiting the flock of God because of greed. By following the wisdom of God, you can ensure that it will not be you.

# 10

# The Wise Leader's Use of Words

Death and life are in the power of the tongue, and
those who love it will eat its fruits.

—PROVERBS 18:21

MOST OF THE STUPID things I have done as a leader have involved words.
Come to think of it, most of the stupid things I have done in every area
of life have involved words. I have lived Proverbs 18:6: "A fool's lips walk
into a fight, and his mouth invites a beating." Even as a child, my father
had his own proverbial saying for me, "Son, don't let your alligator mouth
overload your hummingbird back." Little did I know then how important
his advice would be as I grew older. I was always spouting off, speaking
far beyond the boundaries of my knowledge and experience. When not
showing off my ignorance, I could be found giving my opinion about
every subject that came into my head. In the words of the King James
Version, "A fool utters all his mind" (Prov 29:11). My rash words were
like sword thrusts (Prov 12:18). It's almost like Solomon was thinking of
me when he wrote, "Do you see a man who is hasty in his words? There is
more hope for a fool than for him" (Prov 29:20). I did a lot of damage to a
lot of people that I loved. Some of that damage has been healed. Some of

the damage has left scars. Some of the damage is still present. Death and life really are in the power of the tongue.

Perhaps this is why Proverbs says more about words than any other subject. Within its 915 verses, at least 244 are dedicated to speech. It's adorned with words like listen, hear, say, speak, voice, and word, as well as references to the organs tied to speech: ears, lips, mouth, and tongue. If we were to add scriptures mentioning lies, deceit, false witness, flattery, slander, and gossip, the list would stretch even further. The book devotes so much attention to words because the sages understood their power and influence.

Given how words have been my biggest enemy, I continue to pray, "Set a guard, O LORD, over my mouth; keep watch over the door of my lips!" (Ps 141:3). My journey to discovering the power of words began during a season where God seemed to give me and my words his undivided attention. It was not a pleasant experience, but the results were worth it. Before this happened, I did not think about the consequences of what I said. Afterward, I not only thought about the consequences of my words, but I also felt their impact. I became aware that my words were giving life or death. Scripture verses about words began to linger in my mind. This went on for months. Then, one morning I said something really stupid to my wife in front of one of our kids. I knew as the words came out of my mouth that I should shut up. But I didn't.

Embarrassed, I confessed to my wife, "I think God wants to heal my diarrhea of the mouth." And again, as those words came out of my mouth, I wished I would just shut up or at least say this in a more appropriate way. I had a lot to learn when it came to words. The first lesson I needed to learn was to be quiet, for "even a fool who keeps silent is considered wise; when he closes his lips, he is deemed intelligent" (Prov 17:28), and "too much talk leads to sin. Be sensible and keep your mouth shut" (Prov 10:19, NLT).

While keeping silent was a good discipline, staying silent was not an option. Learning to keep quiet helped me break free from a destructive relationship with words. This allowed me to learn to love words and to build a healthy relationship with my words. This is what Proverbs 18:21 is talking about when it says the tongue has the power of life and death, and those who love it will eat its fruit. The "it" we are to love is the tongue, an idiom for words.

The word used in Proverbs 18:21 for love (ʾāhab) also means to desire, to breathe after, or to delight in. It can refer to love of many kinds, including the love of parents (Gen 22:2), the love between a man and woman (Gen 24:67; 1 Sam 18:20), and loving food (Gen 27:4). It is used both to describe God's love for humans (Deut 4:37) and humans loving God (Deut 6:5). It can also refer to a beloved friend, which is distinct from a companion and more intimate, as where Abraham is called the friend of God (Isa 41:8). The deep friendship between Jonathan and David is described not with the noun *rēa'*, (friend, companion), as might be expected, but with the verb *'āhab*: "The soul of Jonathan became attached to the soul of David, and Jonathan loved ('*āhab*) him as his own soul" (1 Sam 18:1; compare 1 Sam 20:17). It is this latter option that is captured in the Revised English Bible's translation of Proverbs 18:21: "The tongue has power of life and death; make friends with it and enjoy its fruits." Words had been my enemy. Now, words needed to become my friend.

Making friends with my words meant that I needed to honor, respect, cherish, desire, and delight in what they are and what they do. I had to respect their potency for both death and life and cherish their ability to create bonds of love and affection. I needed a deep, intimate, and personal relationship with words, and like all such relationships, this begins with listening.

## Learning to Listen

If there were ever a leader who did not need to listen to his people, it would be God. He is, after all, God. He knows everything. Yet, again and again, God hears our cries and is moved to act on our behalf. When Hagar fled from Sarai, the angel of the LORD appeared to her and told her to name her son Ishmael "because the LORD has listened to your affliction" (Gen 16:11). Ishmael means "God hears." Later, when Abraham prayed for Ishmael, God responded, "I have heard you" (Gen 17:20) and promised that Ishmael would be the father of a great nation.

When the Israelites were enslaved in Egypt, the LORD said, 'I have surely seen the affliction of my people who are in Egypt and have heard their cry because of their taskmasters. I know their sufferings" (Exod 3:7). Their afflictions and groans ascended to God and moved him to action. In 1 Kings, God listens to Solomon's prayer for wisdom (1 Kgs 3:1–15). Then, after completing the temple, God appears a second time to him (1 Kgs 9:1–9), saying, "I have heard your prayer" (1 Kgs 9:3). In 2 Kings, Hezekiah is facing an attack from the Assyrians (2 Kgs 18–19). He cries out, "Incline your ear, O LORD, and hear; open your eyes, O LORD, and see; and hear the words of Sennacherib" (2 Kgs 19:15–16). God replies through the prophet Isaiah, "Your prayer to me about Sennacherib king of Assyria I have heard" (2 Kgs 19:20). Later, when Hezekiah is sick and on the verge of death (2 Kgs 20:1), he cries out once again to the Lord, and the Lord replies, "I have heard your prayer" (2 Kgs 20:5). Both Solomon and Hezekiah had profound experiences of God listening to them. Interestingly, both Solomon and Hezekiah play a central role in the composition of the book of Proverbs (Prov 1:1; 25:1). Perhaps their encounters with the God who listens influenced their instructions that leaders should also listen.

This God who listens and sees is the model of leadership we are to imitate. He has created us for this purpose. Proverbs 20:12 tells us, "The hearing ear and the seeing eye, the LORD has made them both." Take this to heart, for your first job as a leader is not to lead but to listen.

My experience with a colleague named Carl is an example. I was leading a meeting when I said something that was not very clear. Carl took it to mean something very different from what I meant. I was not aware of the misunderstanding at the time, but I was about to find out. Carl stewed until he went into a rage. Before the night was over, he was pounding his finger into my chest and yelling at me with some very choice words. I managed to stay out of enemy mode[1] and just listened to him as he railed against me. This ugly outburst ended when he stormed away, still raging at me. Carl did not need my explanations or defense. He needed to be seen and heard. By refraining from reacting with anger or self-defense, I managed to find a place in Carl's heart. My soft words turned away his wrath. The next morning, Carl was ashamed of his behavior and offered his resignation. I replied to him, "Carl, now you know how I will treat you on your very worst day. Can you see your way to trusting me just a little in this situation so that we can move forward?" I then refused to accept his resignation. We talked openly and honestly for a long time. Both Carl and I laid our hearts before God and one another. We listened and God did an amazing work. Carl has gone on to become a dear friend and trusted colleague. Carl showed me that in a world where everyone has been categorized and commodified, the ability to see and hear is a revolutionary act of transformational leadership.

---

1. Wilder, *Enemy Mode*, 2022.

Listen to God

> Let your heart hold fast my words; keep my commandments,
> and live. Get wisdom; get insight; do not forget, and do
> not turn away from the words of my mouth.

—PROVERBS 4:4–5

The Hebrew Bible is filled with commandments, laws, and ordinances. It would seem logical to conclude that the rich vocabulary of biblical Hebrew would also contain the verb "obey." However, it does not. While there are 613 commandments in the Law of Moses, there is no word in biblical Hebrew that means "to obey." The Hebrew word used as the appropriate response to God's commandments is *shema*. It is one of the keywords, if not *the* keyword, of the Old Testament. It is almost impossible to translate this crucial term because of its many shades of meaning. It can mean "to hear," as when Adam and Eve "heard the sound of the LORD walking in the garden" (Gen 3:8), or "to listen, or pay attention, or heed," as when Abram "listened to the voice of Sarai" (Gen 16:2). It can mean "to understand" as when God put a stop to the building of the tower of Babel, "Come, let us go down and there confuse their language, so that they may not understand one another's speech" (Gen 11:7). It can also mean, "to heed" or "to do what someone else wants," as in Genesis 21:12, "Whatever Sarah says to you, do as she tells you, for through Isaac shall your offspring be named." It is in this last sense that it comes closest in meaning to "obey."

Obedience to God must be understood from a biblical perspective, for the biblical connotation is altogether different from obedience in general. To obey in ordinary parlance means to comply with a regulation or a command, as when we obey traffic laws, or a soldier follows orders. However, when we apply this understanding to our relationship with God, we run the risk of misunderstanding the relationship into which God is continually inviting us.

Don't get me wrong; there is nothing wrong with "obey" as a translation of this word. The problem has more to do with how we understand what it means to obey. By this misunderstanding, obedience seems like a slavish obedience to divine decrees. This creates a false, misguided concept of the Old Testament as a book of rules featuring a God with a short temper and harsh judgments for anyone who steps out of line.

Yet, the God of the Old Testament is the same God revealed in and by Jesus Christ. God did not get converted between the Old and New Testaments. Sadly, this misconception of the Old Testament God, and the term obedience, has deprived generations of Christians of the richness of the Hebrew Bible.[2]

The title "Old Testament" was coined by Melito of Sardis around 170 CE.[3] The word "testament" refers to "covenant." The New Testament, from the perspective of Christians, contains books of the new covenant while the earlier scriptures (i.e., the Hebrew Bible) contains the old covenant. Though he did not intend it, the term can imply "old and outdated." For this reason, some scholars suggest First Testament[4] as a better name. Others prefer Hebrew Bible while still others prefer Tanakh.[5] Keep in mind that what is called "scripture" in the New Testament refers to Old Testament texts. This term most often refers to specific quotes and passages rather than to books collectively. In the New Testament, the phrase "the Law and the Prophets" (Luke 16:16) is sometimes used to mean Jewish scriptures and, more generally, the previous revelation of God through them. The Old Testament is certainly not a deficient old work in need of a Christological makeover.[6] It is a rich and splendid revelation of God's faithfulness to Israel and the world, which has something to say to us today if we will only *shema*—listen, hear, and understand.

## Shema

The root $\check{s}^e ma$ ' is a key word in the book of Deuteronomy, where it occurs ninety-two times, usually indicating what God wants from us in response to his word. Its most well-known occurrence is in Deuteronomy 6:4, a passage known as the *Shema Israel,* and it serves as the most fundamental expression of the Jewish faith, "Hear, O Israel: The LORD our God, the LORD is one." God wants us to listen, to hear, to understand. The *Shema* calls us to a relationship for the goal is to "love the LORD your God with

---

2. I am grateful to John Goldengay and Walter Brueggemann for their prolific scholarship and for opening my eyes to the riches of the Old Testament.

3. Roberts, et al., eds. "Melito, the Philosopher," 8:759.

4. Goldingay, *The First Testament,* 2018.

5. Tanakh reflects the threefold division of the Hebrew Scriptures by using the first letters of each word Torah ("Teaching"), Nevi'im ("Prophets") and Ketuvim ("Writings") to form the title.

6. Goldingay, *Do We Need the New Testament?* 2015.

all your heart and with all your soul and with all your might" (Deut 6:5). *Shema* is not about blind obedience. If God wanted creatures who would blindly obey, he would not have created humans; he would have created soulless robots. God is not interested in slavish obedience or mindless adherence. He created us in his image as sons and daughters who can hear his voice and understand his commands so that we may know him. He is the God who invites us to come near, close enough to hear him and to know him and to love him. He does this out of his great love for us.

This is the same message we hear repeated throughout Proverbs. For example, "Let the wise hear and increase in learning, and the one who understands obtain guidance" (Prov 1:5); "Whoever listens to me will dwell secure and will be at ease, without dread of disaster" (Prov 1:33). Or these passages: "Hear, for I will speak noble things, and from my lips will come what is right" (Prov 8:6); "O sons, listen to me: blessed are those who keep my ways. Hear instruction and be wise, and do not neglect it. Blessed is the one who listens to me, watching daily at my gates, waiting beside my doors" (Prov 8:32–34). "Listen to advice and accept instruction, that you may gain wisdom in the future" (Prov 19:20). *Shema* appears thirty times in Proverbs and is a central command in the book.[7]

Our greatest problem lies in our failure to listen to God. We see this problem going back all the way to the Garden of Eden. God clearly instructed Adam and Eve, saying, "You may surely eat of every tree of the garden, but of the tree of the knowledge of good and evil you shall not eat, for in the day that you eat of it you shall surely die" (Gen 2:16–17). Although they heard God's command, their downfall came when they believed their eyes rather than their ears: "When the woman saw that the tree was good for food, and that it was a delight to the eyes, and that the tree was to be desired to make one wise, she took of its fruit and ate, and she also gave some to her husband who was with her, and he ate" (Gen 3:6). The consequences were immediate: Their eyes were opened, they knew they were naked, and they felt shame. This initial sin was all about what the eyes see; it is about appearances, and pursuing appearances always leads to shame. They had heard God's word but chose to believe their eyes. Now, their eyes were opened, and they did not like what they saw. They had followed their eyes, yet now they did not want to be seen. They tried to hide (Gen 3:9–10). Hiding is an immediate, intuitive

---

7. *Shema* appears thirty times in Prov 1:5, 8, 33; 4:1, 10; 5:7, 13; 7:24; 8:6, 32–34; 12:15; 13:1,8; 15:29, 31, 32; 18:13; 19:20, 27; 20:12; 21:28; 22:17; 23:19, 22; 25:10,12; 28:9; 29:24.

response to shame. Yet God came speaking, and you cannot hide from a voice.

The God who fills all of creation cannot be seen, but he can be heard. It is in the act of hearing that we are formed as the people of God. Abraham heard the call of God (Gen 12:1–9). The nation of Israel was told, "Hear, O Israel: The Lord our God, the Lord is one. And you shall love the Lord your God with all your heart and with all your soul and with all your mind and with all your strength." (Deut 6:4; Mark 12:30). Jesus said, "My sheep hear my voice, and I know them, and they follow me" (John 10:27). Elsewhere, he said, "My mother and my brothers are those who hear the word of God and do it" (Luke 8:21). Paul would later say to the Romans, "So faith comes from hearing, and hearing through the word of Christ" (Rom 10:17). No wonder David sang, "In sacrifice and offering you have not delighted, but you have given me an open ear" (Ps 40:6). The people of God are formed by listening to God.

The primary way we hear God is through the scriptures. We are people of the Book. "Whoever gives thought to the word will discover good and blessed is he who trusts in the LORD" (Prov 16:20). Proverbs 13:13 warns, "Whoever despises the word brings destruction on himself, but he who reveres the commandment will be rewarded." If we turn away from listening to God's word, even our prayer becomes an abomination (Prov 28:9). Regular reading, meditating upon, and studying the scriptures is essential for wise leaders. "Apply your heart to instruction and your ear to words of knowledge" (Prov 23:12). Proverbs 22:17 advises, "Incline your ear, and hear the words of the wise, and apply your heart to my knowledge."

God also speaks through the Holy Spirit. Wisdom and the Spirit of God are often linked in the Old Testament, for it is the Spirit who gives wisdom (Gen 41:38–39; Exod 31:3–4; Deut 34:9; Isa 11:2; Job 32:7–10). This wisdom from the Spirit is usually seen revealed in practical action (Gen 41:7–57; Exod 31:3).[8]

For me, such wisdom normally doesn't involve angelic visitations or audible voices. OK, it never involves those things. It does, however, involve slowing down long enough to listen to that "nudge" in my heart or that scripture that seems to stand out as I read the Bible. A friend of mine training to become a spiritual director taught me a powerful prayer. We began praying Psalm 46:10, "Be still, and know that I am God," followed

---

8. Hildebrandt, *Spirit of God*, 44.

by a moment of silence. We then prayed, "Be still, and know that I am," followed by more silence. Again, we prayed, "Be still, and know," followed by a longer silence, and a gradual sense of the divine presence came upon us both. Then we prayed, "Be still," followed by an increasing awareness of God's presence. Finally, we prayed, "Be." And we were filled with a profound sense of our being present in the divine presence. Slowing down does that for you.

You can also listen to God through his creation. Proverbs 1–9 reveals Wisdom's role in creation. Throughout these chapters she lifts her voice above the fray of conflicting voices vying for the reader's attention and summons us to listen to her in the midst of creation (Prov 1:11–14; 7:14–20; 9:13–18).

Proverbs 8:22–31 is one of the most beautifully crafted poems in all of scripture. This poem marks the pinnacle of Wisdom's speech in Proverbs (Prov 1:20–33; 4:5–9; 8:1–36; 9:1–6). According to her own testimony, Wisdom was God's first act of creation, and she sits preeminent at the very beginning of creation. She recounts God at work in carving, anchoring, stabilizing, establishing, circumscribing, securing, and setting the boundaries of creation, and she frolics in all God did. Every facet of creation is graced by her playful presence. She was at his side each day, his darling and delight, playing in his presence continually, playing over his whole world while delighting in humanity (Prov 8:30–31). This beautiful poem "is a tangible testimony to Wisdom's continued delight in creation; it is her ode to joy."[9]

And wisdom uses creation, including animals, to teach us about God. Consider, for example, Proverbs 6:6: "Go to the ant, O sluggard; consider her ways, and be wise." Leeches, ravens, eagles, serpents, ants, rock badgers, locusts, lizards, lions, and roosters are among our teachers in Proverbs 30.


## A Digression on Dogs

In line with this potent role of animals in Proverbs, let me tell you about three of my best teachers, all of whom happen to be dogs.

Noel was a scruffy little Schnauzer who taught me the power of welcoming people who may feel awkward and out of place. Kelly was a black Labrador Retriever who loved to sit with me for long periods of time. She

9. Brown, "Proverbs 8:22–31." *Interpretation*, (2009).

would rather be with me than with her own kind. She taught me about lingering in the presence of God and just being at peace and resting in the presence of the One who is Wholly Other. My current teacher is a tricolor Aussalier[10] named Millie. She has never met a stranger and she is a terrible guard dog because she thinks everyone is a friend who wants to rub her belly. While I will not be offering my belly to anyone for a rub, I do find myself regularly praying, "Lord, teach me to love people the way Millie does."

I realize dogs sometimes appear in negative contexts in the Bible, including in Proverbs 26:11, "Like a dog that returns to his vomit is a fool who repeats his folly," though they are not listed as ritually unclean animals. There is archaeological evidence from the skeletal remains found within the Eastern Mediterranean that the domestication of dogs did not happen until the Persian (559–331 BCE) and Hellenistic (323–30 BCE) periods within Israel.[11] The historical setting of the Old Testament ranges between 1500—400 BCE, and so this context predates the domestication of dogs in the area. Over time Jews began to view dogs more positively as can be seen in the second century BCE book of Tobit. Tobit, a devout and wealthy Israelite, living among the captives deported to Nineveh from the Northern Kingdom of Israel in 722/721 BCE, suffers severe reversals and he is finally blinded. Because of his misfortunes, he begs the Lord to let him die. But recalling the large sum he had deposited in faraway Media, he sends his son Tobias there to bring back the money, accompanied by the angel Raphael and the family dog: "The young man went out, and the angel went with him, and the dog came out with him and went along with them" (Tobit 6:1–2, NRSVue).

Other ancient authors began to observe that dogs know to elevate an injured leg, just as Hippocrates prescribed. They also observed that dogs know which plants to eat as medicine to induce vomiting if they have eaten something that upsets their stomach. Dogs also know to lick their wounds to ensure that they remain clean and heal quickly. Consequently, dogs began to be associated with healing, as physicians of the animal kingdom. Dogs appear in the cult of Asclepius, the Greek god of medicine, and the father of Asclepius, Apollo Kunegetes, was known as the "patron of dogs." Sacred dogs, living in the god's temples, would lick the injuries of the sick visitors. Their tongues apparently soothed and

10. A newly recognized breed, a cross between a miniature Australian Shepherd and a Cavalier King Charles Spaniel

11. White, "Dogs." March 29, 2022.

healed wounds. Perhaps this gives insight into the parable of the rich man and Lazarus (Luke 16:19–31). While the rich man could not be bothered to offer mercy and aide to this destitute man, a dog had compassion on Lazarus, providing company and licking his sores to bring relief and remedy. The dog was teaching compassion, but the rich man would not listen. I think dogs teach us to be better people. We should listen to them.

Another way we can listen to God is through his action in history. In the Hebrew canon, Joshua, Judges, 1 & 2 Samuel, and 1 & 2 Kings are joined with Isaiah, Jeremiah, Ezekiel, and the Twelve Minor Prophets and are referred to as the Former and Latter Prophets. What the Jews called the Former Prophets is now commonly referred to as part of the "historical books" of the Old Testament. These books are more than stories of people long dead. They are a prophetic record of the living God telling his story.

History is the crucible in the hand of God by which he makes known his judgments on the earth. History is quite literally "His Story." This link between prophets and history is seen in 2 Chronicles 9:29 and 12:15, which note that the acts of Solomon are written in the history of Nathan the prophet, in the prophecy of Ahijah, and in the visions of Iddo the seer, and the acts of Rehoboam are written in the chronicles of Shemaiah the prophet and of Iddo the seer. It is fitting that the historical books are linked together with the prophetic, for history reveals God just as does inspired prophetic utterance. It doesn't always look like it, but God does act in history. When he acts, people will say, "Surely there is a reward for the righteous; surely there is a God who judges on earth'" (Ps 58:11, NRSVue).

When Christianity took root in the Hellenistic world, Greek metaphysical categories gradually replaced Hebrew historical thinking. The God who reveals himself by his acts of salvation in the history of Israel slowly became the God who is seen to reveal himself through abstract concepts of truth, goodness, and beauty. While the Gospel can certainly be contextualized within a Hellenistic worldview, we should not lose sight of God's earthy and sometimes messy revelation in the history of Israel.

## Listen to Others

Let the wise hear and increase in learning, and the
one who understands obtain guidance.

—PROVERBS 1:5

How I hated discipline, and my heart despised reproof! I did not
listen to the voice of my teachers or incline my ear to my instructors.
I am at the brink of utter ruin in the assembled congregation.

—PROVERBS 5:12–14

As I write this, the United States has just completed one of its midterm
election cycles. It has been six days since the polls closed. Both the House
of Representatives and the Senate are almost equally divided between the
two parties. If you listen to the pundits, they will tell you this is another
sign of a deeply divided country. The problem is that we are not divided
because one half the country voted for the Republicans while the other half
voted for the Democrats. We are divided because we will not listen to one
another. When Aristotle said we humans are by nature political animals,[12]
he was referring to how we are social creatures who form societies by
working together to determine how we will live together; this involves ne-
gotiations as to how we will solve problems and advance the public good.
Unfortunately, politics today is something altogether different.

Disagreements and different perspectives are to be welcomed if we
can listen to one another with humility and openness to find common
solutions for "wisdom is with the humble" (Prov 11:2, NRSVue). This
kind of collaboration makes us better and stronger as families, communities, organizations, and a society. The pundits miss this when they say we
are divided because of who the citizenry votes for. That is a distraction,
for the solution certainly is not one-party rule. Nor is the solution to talk
over one another, and it certainly is not to dehumanize and demonize the
other. Silencing the opposition is always a move aimed at the accumulation of power. This is never about discovering the best way forward. That
can only be found when we learn to listen and learn from one another.
If you and I see things differently and we have an argument because we
are seeking the truth, then even if I lose, I still win because I have learned
some new truth, and I have grown because of it. But if I argue with you
for the sake of power, even if I win, I lose. I lose because I have diminished both of us.

Unfortunately, today's social media and newsfeed algorithms are designed to feed you a continuous loop of information that only reinforces

12. Aristotle, *Politics*, 4.

what you already think and believe. Before long, you live in an echo chamber that is little more than intellectual and spiritual inbreeding, which results in cognitive and emotional deformities. You need other well-informed perspectives to stay healthy. "Listen to advice and accept instruction, that you may gain wisdom in the future" (Prov 19:20). Sometimes listening to others is painful but "the ear that listens to life-giving reproof will dwell among the wise" (Prov 15:31). Remember: "the way of a fool is right in his own eyes, but a wise man listens to advice" (Prov 12:15). If I only listen to those with whom I already agree, I am not learning anything new, I am only having my opinion reinforced. If I listen to those who see and think differently, then I am learning and growing. My most profound relationships are with those who have told me the most challenging truths. Learning to listen means to listen to God and others, even when we do not like what either is saying. After all, "Whoever loves discipline loves knowledge, but he who hates reproof is stupid" (Prov 12:1).

In her book, *Team of Rivals: The Political Genius of Abraham Lincoln*,[13] Pulitzer Prize-winning author Doris Kearns Goodwin recounts how Lincoln used his extraordinary ability to understand the motives and desires of his former political opponents and to bring them together to create the most unusual cabinet in U.S. history, which saved the Union and won the war. Lincoln knew that to win someone to your cause, you must first reach their heart, and you do this by listening.

We should also listen to those who have gone before us. Listening to those who have gone before tells us not to neglect a good opinion, even if it comes from our father, mother (Prov 5:7; 23:22), the prophets and sages of Israel, or the mothers and fathers of the ancient church, or those who have walked the path before we arrived, be they alive now or long deceased. Listening to those who have gone before "means giving a vote to the most obscure of all classes, our ancestors. It is the democracy of the dead." It is the refusal "to submit to the small and arrogant oligarchy of those who merely happen to be walking about."[14]

Cultivating the habit of listening empowers you to gain wisdom (Prov 15:22). "Listen to advice and accept instruction, that you may gain wisdom in the future" (Prov 19:20), and "those who love discipline love knowledge, and those who hate correction are stupid" (Prov 12:1, CEB).

13. Goodwin, *Team of Rivals*, 2006.
14. Chesterton, *Orthodoxy*, 22.

Debbie and I had been married for a few years when she asked me, "How can you be such a good preacher and yet be such a terrible communicator?" Those words stung because they were true. I devoted my life to preaching the Word of God. Each week I devoted an average of twenty hours of study for each sermon. However, it takes more than good preaching to be a good leader. It takes a lot more.

I did not know how to lead people, and I was terrible at personal conversations. All I could do was preach. My solution to every challenge was the same: preach. Even in my marriage—well, until my wife reached her limit and put her foot down, saying, "Stop preaching to me and start talking with me." I had to learn a whole new way of communication in life and leadership. This new way of communication began with listening to others.

It was around this time that I heard someone observe that God gave us two ears and one mouth because he wants us to listen twice as much as we speak. I found it funny. Then, I found it helpful. Starting in my marriage and then in my ministry, I made the intentional effort to listen more than I spoke. I started to lead meetings differently by giving each member plenty of room to discuss and process decisions. We would only decide on an issue once everyone felt we had processed it thoroughly. While we did not always reach a unanimous agreement, we would always strive to fully understand each decision. This built trust, and trust is more important than agreement. I discovered that people need to weigh in before they buy in. Once they participate in the process, they own the decision. I learned that what I thought was resistance to my great ideas was just human nature and how people process things. I was learning to use words to build arenas of trust.

Proverbs 1:5 tells us, "A wise person will hear and increase in learning, And a person of understanding will acquire wise counsel" (NASB 2020). I discovered that if I wanted to flourish, I need to listen, learn, and grow (Prov 4:18; 9:9; 11:9), and when I make a mistake, or a gross failure, I must own it, make it right, and move on for "even if the righteous falls seven times," they get back up (Prov 24:15–16). When I learned to listen to others, an arena of trust was established where we could do life and ministry together. I was trained as a preacher. I was now learning to be a leader by learning to listen.

Listening leads to wisdom, so train yourself to listen to God who is above you, to those who are different from you, to those who have gone before you, to the wise who are around you, and even to your critics who may improve you. Just listen. If you learn to do this, you may even hear God speak in sheer silence (1 Kgs 19:12 NRSVue).

God calls us to "hear" (*shema*) so that he may establish his divine presence among us. The Jews referred to this divine presence as *Shekinah*, a word meaning "dwelling" or "settling." Though not used in the Old Testament, it is the word used in the Mishnah, Talmud, and Midrash to describe the glorious presence of God. The Old Testament mentions several places where the presence of God was felt and experienced, including the burning bush (Exod 3:1—4:17) and the cloud that rested on Mount Sinai (Exod 19:1–25; 24:16–17). The Shekinah was often pictured as a cloud or as a pillar of fire and was referred to as the glory of God (Exod 14:19–31). The Shekinah was also understood to be present in the Tabernacle (Exod 29:43) and the Temple in Jerusalem (1 Kgs 8:10–11). When the people of God hear God (*shema*), he makes known his presence among them (*shekinah*), and they experience peace, harmony, wholeness, completeness, prosperity, well-being, and tranquility (*shalom*). In the same way, when we learn to listen to one another, we create a place for people to be present in their fullness, and this produces a human community of peace, harmony, wholeness, completeness, prosperity, well-being, and tranquility. We do this by listening.

## The Words We Use

God created the universe with words. We create, and sometimes destroy, our social universe with words. We call our native language "our mother tongue" because it is the language that nurtured us, taught us, fed us, shaped our thoughts, and formed our opinions. Language is the air we breathe as social beings. That is the power of words. As indicated earlier, no book in the Bible offers such an extensive reflection concerning the possibilities and functions of language as Proverbs.[15] Words are the basis of creation, revelation, and a righteous life. They have the power of life and death (Prov 10:10–11, 14, 21; 12:6, 13; 11:9; 15:4; 18:7, 21; 25:18; 26:28).

---

15. Murphy, *Proverbs*, 259.

## On Promises and Lies

Of all creation on earth, humankind alone is endowed with the gift of speech. The Church Fathers saw speech as the supreme gift and the "seal" of the Divine Image in humankind because God revealed himself in Christ as the Word.[16] As we have seen, wisdom in Proverbs is associated with this creative Word. God upholds and sustains all of creation by the power of his Word and Wisdom.[17] We are created in his image, and our words also have power. Human cooperation and our victory over human unpredictability depend on our ability to give and keep our word. It is in making and keeping promises, in giving and honoring your word, that free human beings construct relationships of trust. And this trust enables us to create order out of chaos.

When we make a promise, we are using language in a unique way. We are using words not to describe but rather to create something that was not there before. For example, when a couple exchanges vows during a wedding, they are not describing their marriage; they are creating it. They perform their vows through their utterances; this is the power of giving your word. Giving and keeping your word allows us to cooperate freely and rely on one another. Your word rolls back and holds at bay the chaos of disorder and broken promises that seeks to dominate our world. Your words are always at work, building or destroying the arena of trust.

Being the supreme gift, words are also the supreme danger, for "like the glaze covering an earthen vessel are fervent lips with an evil heart" (Prov 26:23). Words can seduce hearts (Prov 7:21), deceive minds (Prov 21:6; 24:28; 26:23–24), and destroy lives (Prov 11:11–12; 12:6; 18; 25:23). It is easy to point to the spectacular failures of megachurches and global ministries. Sadly, they are too many to recount. The reality is that this destruction happens on a smaller but no less damaging scale every day. For example, Caleb, a friend of mine, fell into this trap. He was one of the most gifted and charismatic young leaders I knew. He had experienced incredible success in business, at times reaching executive levels of leadership in global brands (which you would recognize). Then, he had a conversion experience with Jesus. His testimony, together with his business success, opened doors for ministry. A dynamic speaker, he could spin a story and keep people on the edge of their seats. Then, he began to

16. John 1:1
17. Heb 1:3

embellish his stories. These embellishments became lies. Eventually, he was caught in such a web of deception that he lost his ministry, his job, his friends, and his reputation. All because of his words.

We can use words to fulfill and express love; to give life and hope; or to steal, kill, and destroy. With our words, we make covenants, and with our words, we can betray those closest to us. Words can save or kill, inspire or poison, proclaim truth or spread lies. Consequently, words must be rooted in righteousness (Prov 4:23–24; 8:6–8; 10:11, 31–32; 12:4; 23:16), knowledge (Prov 2:6; 10:13–14; 11:9; 15:2, 7, 14, 28; 20:15; 22:12, 20–21; 23:12), and wise counsel (Prov 13:20; 19:20; 22:17–18, 24–25; 27:17). When your words are used according to God's intent, they are powerful, active, and creative. When deviating from their divine origin and purpose, your words become *idle,* lazy, and worthless. And we will eventually give an account for them.[18]

The old saying goes: *Sticks and stones may break my bones, but words will never hurt me.* This is a great line, but it isn't true. Words matter whether they were spoken to us as children, in our youth, in our relationships, or in marriage. They have a lasting impact and the power to shape minds and cultures for they have the power to heal or to wound, to build up or to tear down (Prov 11:9–11; 12:18; 15:4; 16:24, 27–28; 25:15, 25). Our words bring reward or trouble, safety or destruction, war or peace (Prov 12:14; 13:2–3; 14:3; 15:1, 18; 18:6–7, 20; 21:23). No wonder Proverbs has so much to say about words. This great gift must be guarded with sound wisdom.

## Speaking Words of Life: Spencer

The life-and-death power of words were at work in Spencer, a colleague in ministry. Though a very gifted person, he had several rough years of ministry while serving under a verbally abusive leader. This kind of experience wears you down and makes you question yourself, your abilities, and your calling. Your mind churns with self-doubts: "Do people see me? Do they think I am just floundering and a failure?" Spencer had not heard many words of encouragement during this cruel season. While he patiently endured his situation, I was learning the importance of speaking words of life (Prov 10:20; 25:11–12). One day, when Spencer and I were together working on a project, I placed my hand on his shoulder and

18. Matt 12:36

said, "You know, Spencer, I am very proud of you. You have substance to you and a lot to offer; plus, you are a good man. I want you to know how much I respect you." These words were timely and well-suited for a man longing to hear them (Prov 10:32; 15:23; 25:11–12, 20). Spencer is not the kind of guy that cries, but tears came to his eyes. My words were like water and sunshine for seeds that had gone dormant during his cold winter of ministry (Prov 10:11; 18:4; 13:14). I watched him begin to break free from the bonds of death imposed on him through abusive words. He has gone on to serve with courage and confidence: leading, mentoring, and influencing people in over a dozen nations. I witnessed the power of words to bring beauty, value, nourishment, refreshment, and healing that day (Prov 10: 21; 12:18; 15:4; 16:24; 18:20).

Speech seems to be the surest indicator as to whether one is wise or foolish, for your words reveal who you are. "The mouth of the righteous brings forth wisdom, but the perverse tongue will be cut off. The lips of the righteous know what is acceptable, but the mouth of the wicked, what is perverse" (Prov 10:31–32). "The tongue of the wise commends knowledge, but the mouths of fools pour out folly" (Prov 15:2). Proverbs declares, "The heart of the righteous ponders how to answer, but the mouth of the wicked pours out evil things" (Prov 15:28). "The wise of heart is called discerning, and sweetness of speech increases persuasiveness" (Prov 16:21). "The heart of the wise makes his speech judicious and adds persuasiveness to his lips" (Prov 16:23).

Echoing the wisdom of Proverbs, the apostle James is explicit in his instructions to those who would be teachers "So also the tongue is a small member, yet it boasts of great exploits. How great a forest is set ablaze by a such a small fire!" (Jas 3:5). James says, too, about religion and the power of words: "If any think they are religious and do not bridle their tongues but deceive their hearts, their religion is worthless" (Jas 1:26).

## Doing a Ratner: Words Can Un-Do a Business

In the previous chapter, I mentioned 4 g-forces: girls, gold, glory, and goofing off. Now, I suppose we can add a fifth g-force: gab. Words can make or break your leadership. A single comment or ill-advised tweet sent in a moment of anger or poor judgment can bring you down. Just ask Gerald Ratner. Ratner inherited a small family jewelry business in 1984. Over the next six years, he built it into a multimillion-dollar empire with

2500 stores across Europe and the United States. Then, on April 23, 1991, he destroyed the business in 10 seconds with a single speech. He was speaking to 6,000 businesspeople and journalists at an Institute of Directors event when he said the words that caused his business to lose $800 million over the next few months. What did he say that was so awful?

"We also do cut-glass sherry decanters complete with six glasses on a silver-plated tray that your butler can serve you drinks on, all for £4.95. People say, 'How can you sell this for such a low price?' I say, 'because it's total crap.'"[19] The audience laughed.

Ratner explained he was successful in retail because he could give the masses of middle and lower-income a taste of the luxuries they craved to fulfill their fantasies of being among the pampered rich—all through the purchase of sherry glasses. As reported in the news the following day, Ratner's speech sounded as if it mocked the very people he served. And his words cost him dearly. He lost millions of dollars and was removed from the company he built. The company was rebranded, and "doing a Ratner" entered the British lexicon as a phrase referring to self-inflicted harm that ruins reputations—and sometimes, entire businesses.

Gerald Ratner learned a hard lesson. If you use words carelessly or foolishly, they will be your undoing (Prov 14:1). Proverbs tells us: "Whoever keeps his mouth and his tongue keeps himself out of trouble" (Prov 21:23). And: "A fool's mouth is his ruin, and his lips are a snare to his soul" (Prov 18:7). Your words are important, and someone is always listening.

When used wisely, words can be your most powerful tool as a leader to inspire vision, restore hope, and give direction to those you lead (Prov 9:1–12; 15:1). When you cultivate the power of your words others will trust you because your words are honest (Prov 6:16–17;12:19, 22; 16:10, 13; 17:4, 7, 20) and used with restraint (Prov 10:19; 13:3; 15:28; 17:27–28; 21:23), and they will inspire people to grow in knowledge and understanding (Prov 13:14; 15:2, 7; 16:21, 23).

Your words are the audible indicators of your heart's true condition.[20] Pay attention to what you say. Your words are the overflow of whatever is growing in your heart. Monitoring your words is the most reliable way of monitoring your heart. Inconsistent speech bears witness to a divided heart. It was only a few weeks ago that the wisdom in Proverbs called me out on this (again). I was frustrated with another leader to the point that

19. Ratner, *Rise and Fall*, 352.
20. Luke 6:45

I became angry with him. This anger took root in my heart and began to express itself in my words. I caught myself giving in to backbiting and using information to diminish this fellow leader. My words exposed my heart (Prov 11:12–13; 16:27–28; 17:9; 18:8; 20:19; 25:9–10, 23; 26:22). I had to set a watch over my words that I would not use them against him (Prov 6:12–15; 10:18). Yes, I needed to speak truth with him, but I also needed to use my words to express genuine gratitude and respect. I did this out of a profound sense of appreciation for my brother, without resorting to flattery to win favor or manipulate the situation, nor did I use it as a means to avoid the conflict (Prov 26:24–25, 28; 27:6; 28:23; 29:5).

I had to get my heart right toward my brother. Then, once my heart was in proper working order, we were able to begin a journey toward uprightness in our relationship. Learning to deal with disagreements, difficult people, and volatile situations has been a long struggle that I have worked to overcome. In the past, I would typically resist dealing with the problem until either the problem or I exploded. This was not healthy. I had to learn from Proverbs 28:23, "In the end, people appreciate honest criticism far more than flattery" (NLT). I have since learned that you show honor and respect to people when you speak honestly with them. Speaking the truth in love builds an arena of trust where people feel accepted and appreciated.

Learning to restrain your words means you should never use words to boast about yourself (Prov 27:2), badger others (Prov 19:13–14; 25:24; 27:15–16) or be argumentative (Prov 17:14; 26:7). Instead, your words should be thoughtful, calm, cool, and restrained (Prov 15:1, 28; 17:27–28; 18:13; 29:11, 20) because you are gentle and peaceable (Prov 12:16; 15:1, 8), even when correcting others (Prov 27:5–6; 28:23). Words do not need to be loud or forceful to be powerful. Gentleness in your words is powerful, for not only can a soft answer turn away wrath (Prov 15:1), but a soft tongue can break a bone (Prov 25:15).

While you can do much good with your words, be aware of their limitations (Prov 4:24). Words are no substitute for work (Prov 14:23; 25:14), nor can they alter facts (Prov 24:12; 26:23–28; 28:24). While words can persuade many, they are not always enough to compel a response (Prov 17:10; 29:19). Sometimes you need to build credibility with your actions before you start talking about your next great leadership focus.

As a young leader, I would get very excited about some issue or project. I would then build sermons to go with what I was excited about. Then, I would sit back and wonder why nothing happened. I gradually realized that people were skeptical about my words because they were doubtful about my actions. Sure, I could talk about my dreams, but could I produce results with my actions? I decided to stop practicing what I preached and start preaching what I practiced. For example, I knew fasting was an important part of prayer and spiritual growth. So, I began fasting one day a week. I did this for one year before I mentioned it in public. Then, when I talked about prayer and fasting, my words had weight because of the substance of my behavior. That Apache proverb I quoted in an earlier chapter is true: "It is better to have less thunder in the mouth and more lightning in the fist."

Wisdom will teach you to use the right words at the right time (Prov 10:32), even when dealing with fools. Sometimes you will need to respond to a fool, and sometimes you will need to keep silent (Prov 26:4–5). Most of the time, however, it is best not to waste words on fools, "Do not speak in the hearing of a fool, for he will despise the good sense of your words" (Prov 23:9), and "the instruction of fools is folly" (Prov 16:22).

By knowing the power of words, you can use them to produce good fruit (Prov 12:14; 13:2; 18:20–21). The good fruit of words is that they can restore (Prov 10:27; 25:12; 28:23), instruct, and persuade people to follow wisdom (Prov 15:7; 16:21, 23). Your words can encourage and strengthen those who are burdened (Prov 12:25; 15:23; 16:24) and rescue those who are perishing (Prov 14:25). Words are powerful.

## Communication and Leadership

Perhaps Proverbs mentions words more than any other subject because your success as a leader depends on your ability to communicate. Yes, leadership requires a clear sense of direction, a compelling vision of a preferred future, an overarching set of values, and a steady assurance during the turmoil of change and disruptions. However, it is communication that causes this sense of mission, vision, values, and steady assurance to shift from the leader to the community. It then becomes the fabric of a culture built around a shared mission, shared vision, shared values, and a shared steady assurance.

The word communication comes from the Latin verb "*communicare*," which means "to share," "to make common," or "to be in relation with." It is related to the words "common," "commune," and "community." It implies an act of "bringing together." It is impossible to be a great leader without being a great communicator. You may have a vision, but you are not leading if you cannot get others to share this vision. You may oversee a group of people, but if you cannot get them to share common values and convictions, you are not leading. Learn to love the power of the tongue. Make friends with it and enjoy its fruit. Then you will be able to teach those you lead the way they ought to go.

## The Leader as Teacher

When God called Moses to lead the children of Israel out of slavery in Egypt, Moses pleaded, "My Lord, I've never been able to speak well, not yesterday, not the day before, and certainly not now since you've been talking to your servant. I have a slow mouth and a thick tongue" (Exod 4:10, CEB). I suppose forty years of tending sheep in an isolated desert doesn't do much for building your vocabulary or cultivating eloquence. Moses entered his calling with a profound sense of unworthiness due to his inarticulate speech, yet when he reached the end of his leadership, we see a different man. Moses knows his time as leader is ending. He appointed Joshua as his successor. It would be Joshua, not Moses, who would lead the people across the Jordan into the Promised Land. Moses had achieved everything he was destined to achieve. There would be no more battles to fight or miracles to perform and no more prayers to offer.

Then we witness one of the great moments of personal transformation. It is what Moses did next that bears the mark of greatness: Moses, the liberator, miracle worker, and lawgiver, becomes "Moses, our teacher." For the final month of his life, Moses stood before the people and delivered the series of addresses we know as the book of Deuteronomy. The Hebrew title is *Devarim*, literally "words." He meticulously retraced the people's past and foresaw their future. He taught the people to see themselves as those on whom God had set his love, a chosen people consecrated by the very hand of God. He taught them that their existence bore witness to a transcendent purpose, they testify to something beyond themselves. A glimpse into his prayer, encapsulated in Deuteronomy 32:1–2, reveals his yearning:

> Give ear, O heavens, and I will speak, and let the earth hear
> the words of my mouth. May my teaching drop as the rain, my
> speech distill as the dew, like gentle rain upon the tender grass,

and like showers upon the herb. For I will proclaim the name of
the LORD; ascribe greatness to our God!

Moses the tongue-tied is now Moses the teacher. This transformative event reshapes our understanding of leadership itself. Moses demonstrates that the highest form of leadership takes place when the leader
becomes a teacher, when the leader realizes that true greatness is not in
what they do, but rather in what they help others do. Moses knew that his
greatest achievements would not last forever. The people he had rescued
would one day suffer exile and persecution again. The next time, though,
they would not have a Moses to do miracles. However, through his words,
he planted a strength in their souls that would sustain and renew them
like rain renews the tender grass.

When leaders become teachers, they wield the power to change
lives, for "the teaching of the wise is a fountain of life, that one may turn
away from the snares of death" (Prov 13:14). Teachers are the architects of
the future, and if you want to make lasting change, you too must do like
Moses and become a teacher. The leader as teacher uses influence, not
power, spiritual and intellectual authority, rather than coercive force, to
empower others and shape the future.[21] This is the ultimate power of wise
leaders, and it is a power conveyed through words.

Is there any greater accolade than hearing someone say, "You taught
me"? To hear one say, "I learned the ways of God from you," or "Your life
taught me how to live." This is higher praise than any award or monu-
ment can bestow. Teaching may include preaching, lectures, and lessons,
but it is far more than these. It includes mentoring, coaching, instructing,
and guiding; these pursuits shape the heart and mind. For the leader who
has walked the path of wisdom and embodied the righteous character
of the wise, their entire life becomes a university. The sage becomes the
classroom, the textbook, and the living example of wisdom encased in a
human life. This is the highest form of teaching, for while we teach what
we know, we reproduce what we are.

## Preaching the Word of God

While you are always teaching, you are not always preaching. But if you do
preach, do it well, for it is a fearful thing to handle the word of God. This
must be done with seriousness and devotion. The first step is to saturate

21. Sacks, *Leadership*, 241–44.

your life in the word of God. The prophets, Jesus, and the apostles were all preachers whose lives were saturated in the word of God. They are models for us to imitate.

What does it mean "to preach the word of God"? Fundamentally, preaching is the event by which God speaks through a human voice. To preach the word of God is to proclaim Christ and his kingdom in the power of the Holy Spirit, offering those who hear the opportunity to encounter God through the preached word. This is more than a good talk about Jesus, a book report about the Bible, or a discussion about the kingdom of God. Preaching is an experiential encounter with the risen and living Christ through the spoken word of God.

Preaching is exegetical but more than explanatory. It is biblical, but more than a Bible lesson. It is theological but more than a theological discourse. It is rhetorical but more than beautiful words. It is rational but more than an intellectual argument. It is emotional, but more than feeling. Preaching the word of God is spiritual. The sermon is infused with the life of God through the Holy Spirit; Jesus is manifest in the experience of the hearer. God breathes his life into the sermon, and the words become more than the words of a preacher; they become a word from God. This kind of preaching does not just happen. The preacher must be called by God, transformed by the Spirit, and sent out by Jesus as one called, anointed, appointed, and prepared for this task.

The preacher must be prepared for the fearsome task of proclaiming the word of God. If you are called to preach, devote yourself to the study of scripture. Learn to keep your heart soft and pliable before God. Cultivate your hunger for God. And learn to be humble when rejected and criticized. (Trust me, you will have plenty of opportunities to practice that last bit of advice.) I was told as a young pastor that I must have the mind of a scholar, the heart of a child, and the hide of a rhinoceros. That remains some of the best advice I have ever received for ministry.

If preaching the word of God is part of your calling as a leader, give yourself entirely to this task. It is a sacred calling. Do not use your preaching to ride your hobby horse or discuss your favorite subjects. Preach the word. Give yourself to be like Ezra, who "set his heart to study the Law of the Lord, and to do it and to teach his statutes and rules in Israel" (Ezra 7:10). Study the word. Know the word. Teach the word. Preaching is not the place for shallow and superficial talk. It is not a motivational speech, though it is motivating. Preaching is not pop psychology or self-help advice spoken in a loud voice. Preaching is unleashing the word of

God through a human vessel, a sacred mystery where the word of God comes through a human voice. When leaders preach the word of God under the Spirit's unction with faithfulness to the text and compassion for the people, something powerful takes place. We encounter God, and he encounters us. The preached word makes known the God who cannot be seen. Preaching with integrity creates an arena of trust for experiencing a life-transforming encounter with God.

## Conclusion

I would love to tell you that I no longer have trouble with my words. I could tell you this, but I would be lying. Just last night, I said something stupid to my wife. So, this morning I had to apologize and make things right with her. She, being a noble wife and a wise woman, continues to help me overcome my alligator mouth.

My goal for today is "Don't say anything stupid." So, I pray, "Set a guard, O LORD, over my mouth; keep watch over the door of my lips!" (Ps 141:3). My mouth needs a guard because my tongue remains a destroying fire, a dangerous beast, and a deadly poison (Jas 3:1–12). Yet, it also contains the power to bring life and blessing to others. By listening to Proverbs, I am learning to make friends with my tongue and enjoy its fruit. This is why I also pray every day, "Let the words of my mouth and the meditation of my heart be acceptable in your sight, O LORD, my rock and my redeemer" (Ps 19:14). Today is a good day to unleash the power of words to do good and produce life.

# 11

# Righteous and Wicked Leaders

BOTH PROVERBS AND MODERN leadership literature make one thing clear: Great leadership is complex and demanding. It takes years of practice and experience to master the leadership skills of communication, collaboration, adaptability, responsible management of resources and people, decision-making, healthy relationships, a growth mindset, and virtuous character. These skills are essential qualities for every great leader, but are they enough? Is something more needed to be a great leader?

In the early chapters of Genesis, we find a situation that called for extraordinary leadership. Let's turn our attention to that for a few minutes to see what God was looking for when he chose someone to overcome a challenge and save the day—not to mention the whole human race. It's the story of Noah and his call to build the ark.

Genesis 6:1–8 is, without a doubt, "the most demanding passage in Genesis for the interpreter. Every verse is a source of exegetical difficulty."[1] These two paragraphs leave me scratching my head,

> When man began to multiply on the face of the land and daughters were born to them, the sons of God saw that the daughters of man were attractive. And they took as their wives any they chose. Then the LORD said, "My Spirit shall not abide in man forever, for he is flesh: his days shall be 120 years." The Nephilim were on the earth in those days, and also afterward, when the

1. Mathews, *Genesis 1–11:26*, 320.

> sons of God came in to the daughters of man and they bore chil-
> dren to them. These were the mighty men who were of old, the
> men of renown.
>
> The LORD saw that the wickedness of man was great in
> the earth, and that every intention of the thoughts of his heart
> was only evil continually. And the LORD regretted that he had
> made man on the earth, and it grieved him to his heart. So the
> LORD said, "I will blot out man whom I have created from the
> face of the land, man and animals and creeping things and birds
> of the heavens, for I am sorry that I have made them." But Noah
> found favor in the eyes of the LORD.

Who were these "sons of God" and what's the deal with these
Nephilim? I think it unlikely that a completely satisfactory explanation
can be given for Genesis 6:1–4, but people have tried.

The verses in Genesis 6:1–4 that precede the flood story explain
its origins. God saw the evil and corruption of human beings (v.5). The
cause of the corruption of humanity is unclear. Some believe that it was
a result of the mating of the sons of God[2] and daughters of men, but we
are not told for sure. However, we do know that the flood was on its way.
The passage also mentions a race of heroes or giants (the Nephilim) (v.4).
These Nephilim could be giants or people of brute strength. Though the
etymology of Nephilim and the character of these "men of renown" are
debated,[3] one might regard them as contrasting figures; they are men of
strength or renown but not justice. Thankfully, these sons of God and
Nephilim are not really the point. The main point is that humanity had

---

2. Some interpreters claim they are angels, while others assert they are royal despots
or human judges, while others have taken a combination of the angel and human views
in which the human despots are demoniacs possessed by fallen angels. Some see them
as the descendants of Seth. Still others attribute 6:1–4 to pagan sources and argue that
the "sons of God" are the lesser gods of the Canaanite pantheon. So, we don't really
know who these "sons of God" are.

3. I am sorry to tell you, we don't know much about them. Even the etymology of
this word is uncertain (see Gesenius and Tregelles, *Lexicon*, 556. The Common English
Bible translates the word as "giants," while John Goldengay translates it as "the Fallen"
(see Goldingay, *Genesis*, 91) Other translations, such as the ESV, NRSV, NASB, and
NIV, have chosen to transliterate the Hebrew word into English as "Nephilim," which is
most likely safer. (see Milton C. Fisher, "1393 נפל," in *Theological Wordbook of the Old
Testament*, ed. R. Laird Harris, Gleason L. Archer Jr., and Bruce K. Waltke (Chicago:
Moody Press, 1999), 587.) The only other place the Nephilim appear is Numbers 13,
when the spies return to report what they saw when scouting the land of Canaan before
the Israelite invasion, "We saw the Nephilim (the sons of Anak, who come from the
Nephilim), and we seemed to ourselves like grasshoppers, and so we seemed to them"
(Num 13:33).

become completely corrupt, crossing every boundary established by God, including these sons of God and Nephilim—whatever they were—and judgment was coming.[4] The world was in chaos. There was a leadership crisis. Something had to be done.

As Proverbs indicates, God's judgment happens when he turns us over to the fruit of our ways, to reap what we have sown (Prov 14:14). In the Genesis story, humanity had rejected the ways of God and now they will "eat the fruit of their way and have their fill of their own devices" (Prov 1:29–31). Here, in Genesis, we are witnessing humans break every boundary of heaven and earth; consequently, the boundaries of earth and sky were about to be broken upon them, flooding the earth with judgment and destruction, a reversion to primeval chaos. If ever there were a time for heroes, for men of renown, this was it. But humanity was beyond self-help; not even the "the heroes that were of old, warriors of renown"[5] could save them. The corruption and violence that humanity had unleashed upon the earth could not be resolved by their corrupted offspring, who are men of violence. However, "Noah found favor in the eyes of the Lord" (Gen 6:8).

Unlike the world around him, "Noah was a righteous man, blameless in his generation. Noah walked with God" (Gen 6:9). No one else in the Pentateuch received such tribute; not Abraham, Isaac, Jacob, Joseph, Moses, or Joshua. When God had determined to blot out from the earth the humans he created, he also set in motion a plan of redemption so that humanity would not be utterly destroyed. That plan would be executed through Noah. We know nothing about Noah's ability as a carpenter, nor do we know of his skills in animal husbandry or his ability to navigate the turbulent waters of the flood. All we know of him is his character, showing us once again that character is destiny. And this brings us to Proverbs.

## Righteous Leaders

Proverbs seeks to develop leaders whose characters are shaped by wisdom. It is important to know, however, that the purpose of wisdom is not to be smart: The purpose of wisdom is to be righteous. After all, the world is filled with smart leaders, yet we still have a leadership crisis. Smart is not enough, for without wisdom smart people just create more elaborate

---

4. Especially when read in the fuller context of Gen 6:1—9:29.

5. Gen 6:4, NRSVue

ways of doing stupid things. This is why Proverbs aims to teach leaders wisdom, instruction, understanding, and insight that result in righteousness, expressed as justice and integrity. We find this in the opening verses of Proverbs as it lays out its agenda as a training regimen for leaders:

> The proverbs of Solomon son of David, king of Israel:
> For learning wisdom and discipline;
> for understanding insightful sayings;
> for receiving prudent instruction
> in righteousness, justice, and integrity;
> for teaching shrewdness to the inexperienced,,
> knowledge and discretion to a young man—
> let a wise person listen and increase learning,
> and let a discerning person obtain guidance—
> for understanding a proverb or a parable,
> the words of the wise, and their riddles.
> The fear of the Lord
> is the beginning of knowledge;
> fools despise wisdom and discipline.
> Proverbs 1:1–7, CSB

Most leadership books focus on either strategic or tactical aspects of leadership. These books line our shelves with advice on strategic planning and execution, communication, vision casting, building a team, or conflict resolution—and for a good reason. These are essential leadership skills. Proverbs, however, is different—for while the book does speak about many essential leadership skills, its primary focus is on the character of the leader, not just the skills of leadership. This is important because our world needs leaders who are more than efficient, articulate, and able to mobilize others to accomplish great tasks. Our world needs leaders who are righteous.

When I started out in ministry, I was focused on being effective and efficient. I wanted to build a great church, a large church, to validate myself as a man and as a leader. But God had other plans. He wanted me to be righteous, not just effective or efficient. Little did I know that God was about to take me to school and teach me a few lessons. God was about to spend a long time giving me his undivided attention. I ignored what he was doing in my heart and focused instead on every trick and trend that promised to increase church attendance. Despite my best efforts, nothing I did seemed to work.

My pride and selfish ambition were being dismantled, and my folly was on full display for everyone to see. As a young, self-conscious, insecure introvert, it was painful. When things didn't work, I blamed others. When people left our church, I said mean things about them. I am ashamed of it now. I had a lot to learn, and class was going to be in session for a long time.

My misguided ideals about ministry left me feeling barren. A continual loop played in my head, "You are a failure! You are not able to do this!" I felt both a deep shame at my inability and a driving ambition to prove that voice wrong. I would cry out to God for a breakthrough. As I was soon to discover, the breakthrough I needed would begin when something in me was broken. That breaking started with a church split.

People were leaving the church, and everything seemed to be falling apart. It was heartbreaking to see the fabric of a spiritual community torn apart. I cried out to the Lord, "Everyone is leaving!" and I heard these words in my spirit, "Do you want to leave too?" At that moment, I knew God was giving me a choice: I could either walk away from it or I could walk through it—with him. From the depths of my heart came the answer that echoed Simon Peter's answer to the same question: "Lord, where else could I go? You alone have the words of eternal life."[6] To which he replied, "Then follow me."

Through this experience, I learned that what God was doing in me was far more important than what he would do through me. My self-worth had been rooted in what I could produce. If I could not produce, I was nothing. Well, I was not producing, and I felt like I was nothing, just a waste and disappointment. Everything I believed about myself was being stripped away. Now, with nothing left to offer God but myself, I offered that to him. I stood before him empty-handed and barren, and he delighted in me. I began to discover the radiant joy of being loved by God for no other reason than that I exist. As I experienced this love, my heart began to overflow with love for God. This was a radical and liberating renovation of my heart, and through it I learned to love righteousness more than success.

6. John 6:60–71

## Righteousness

Righteousness is a complex yet central idea in the Old Testament.[7] Keep in mind that the Old Testament texts must not be read through the eyes of the Reformation controversies about "righteousness" and "justification" or even through Paul's letters to the Romans and Galatians. The Old Testament writers were not aware of the problems of the New Testament church, whether in the first or sixteenth century.[8] I do fear that since the Reformation, we Christians have fixated so ardently on the debate between righteousness by faith and righteousness by works that we may have overlooked a profound truth about righteousness itself. Reducing righteousness to a rigid set of legalistic standards or a simplistic slogan (about "Christ's imputed righteousness"), we risk stifling the potential for deeper growth in righteousness as a virtuous way of being.

Righteousness (ṣedeq, ṣĕdāqâ, ṣaddîq) lies at the heart of the Hebrew Bible.[9] The richness of the word can be seen in the various ways it is translated into English. For example, the Revised Standard Version renders ṣedeq, ṣĕdāqâ/ṣaddîq by a variety of words: acquittal, deliverance, honest evidence (Prov 12:17), integrity (Job 31:6), judgment, justice, prosperity, right, righteousness (most common), righteous deeds, righteous help, salvation, saving help, victory, vindication. The Jerusalem Bible, particularly in Isaiah 40–66 and the Psalms, often opts for the translation "integrity." These diverse renderings highlight the nuanced depths contained within the Hebrew word.[10]

God himself is often depicted as "righteous." This portrayal speaks to his essential nature of justice, fairness, goodness, integrity, and unwavering faithfulness that forms the bedrock of his relationship with his people. It serves as the cornerstone of his bond with his chosen ones and sets the standard against which all human conduct is measured. Righteousness encompasses God's intentions for both creation and the community in which he dwells. It is through righteousness that God brings forth order and prosperity in creation, fulfilling his purpose and demonstrating his redemptive will. The understanding that righteousness encompasses God's intentions for both creation and the community in which he dwells

---

7. Skinner, "Righteousness," 272.

8. Scullion, "Righteousness," 5:724.

9. It appears 523 times in the Hebrew Bible. Verbal forms 41 times, the nouns ṣedeq 119 times, and ṣĕdāqâ 157 times, the adjective-substantive ṣaddîq 206 times

10. Scullion, "Righteousness," 5:724.

invites us to explore the profound connections between religion, spirituality, and ecological stewardship. It deepens our comprehension of humanity's role in caring for and harmoniously dwelling within creation.[11] This truth resonates in the jubilant celebration of wisdom in Proverbs 8:22–31, as she rejoices in God's handiwork.

Righteousness is also used to describe human conduct aligned with God's will. However, the Old Testament resolutely reminds us that righteousness is not mere adherence to rules; it is a matter of the heart. Righteousness is meant to govern not only our actions but also our attitudes. To embody righteousness in action and attitude is to live in harmony with God's character and commands. It entails a moral existence imbued with integrity, honesty, and humility, coupled with the just and merciful treatment of others.

In other words, righteousness is about relationships more than it is about rules. It encompasses the pursuit of right order in creation and the cultivation of right relationships within the community where God dwells. Restoring and cultivating relationships that cause human flourishing is the aim of righteousness. However, a mistaken understanding of righteousness can lead to elevating external behavior over God's redemptive purpose. This can lead to a legalistic approach to religion, where people focus on following a set of rules rather than on restoring relationships. Let me illustrate with a story from the life of Jesus and the woman caught in adultery (John 8:1–11).

Imagine yourself as one of the men who stood ready to stone this woman for her sin. You stand there ready to do your duty, to obey the law of God to its fullest. The adulteress must be stoned (Lev 20:10–12). This woman violated God's holy law. To you, she also violated the community, the man (who is strangely absent), and herself. How, you might reason, can society survive if she goes unpunished? We must uphold the standard of our God, our nation, and our people. Her actions were an affront to the God of Abraham, Isaac, and Jacob. This assault could not stand. It was evil. You stand there ready, a stone in hand.

You do not know her name. It does not matter. You know her crime. You know her sin. She was caught in the very act of adultery. She is to you a nameless, immoral woman. An adulteress, a seducer of men. Those who go near her tread the very gates of hell. What has happened to our world? You wonder to yourself. Our morals are in decay. This must be stopped

---

11. Jorgenson and Padgett. *Ecotheology*, 2020.

here and now. You are not alone in your judgment. Others stand with you, ready and united, each with a stone in hand. Your stones would bury this assault on your values. Your stones would crush this nameless woman.

It was easier to do this as a crowd. You would all participate, but none of you would bear the guilt of knowing whose stone struck the mortal blow. It was better this way—a nameless seductress dispatched by a faceless crowd. You were only doing your duty to protect the honor of God.

Then this man steps in the way. He stands between your justice and the condemned woman. He kneels. At first, you think he is reaching for a stone to join you. But he did not pick up a stone. Instead, he wrote something in the dirt. We do not know what he wrote, but you can tell us what he said, for it destroyed something in you. You had been zealous from your youth to please God, to do what is right, and to live according to his Law. You wanted nothing to do with compromise.

By outward appearance, you were very successful in this pursuit. But, in the dark silent places of your heart, you knew better. Age has a way of revealing human frailties that youth so easily hides. Not the frailties of an aging body; you are not vain enough to care about grey, thinning hair. No, it is a much deeper frailty. More than your body aches, your soul aches. In spite of all your efforts, the painful broken places remain covered over but not hidden. They are there. You know it. And he knows it.

He spoke, and his voice was like that of many waters. Water for cleansing, water for healing, water for renewing. Water was again flowing from the rock. His words shake you to your core, "Let him who is without sin among you be the first to throw a stone at her." Every darkness in you flashed through your mind on full ignoble display. You are undone. You surrender. You cannot cast a stone at her without unleashing a thousand condemnations upon your own head. You are the guilty one. He knelt again and began to write. As he did, the stone fell from your hand, and you fell upon the rock. The woman was set free from her condemnation, and so were you. That is what righteousness does. It restores people to life.

When my relationships with others are broken because I allow unrighteousness to fester in my life, I am breaking myself off from the very presence that holds the power to heal and restore me. Righteousness as right relationships, as well as right behavior, aligns us in the divine order, forging a path of restoration before God and our fellow human beings. It is righteousness, the embodiment of our actions toward others, that establishes well-being within the community and forms the bedrock of an ethical community built upon mutual love and responsibility. When we are righteous, we treat others with honor, compassion, and justice. We build up others instead of tearing them down. We create a sense of community and belonging. We make the world a better place. We create a more just, equitable, and peaceful society. We help to build a world where everyone can thrive.[12] This clarion call to righteousness resonates through the Law and the Prophets,[13] and continues through to the New Testament, transcending time and summoning us to a steadfast commitment to walk the path of righteousness in all relationships.

Wisdom promises to form righteousness in us, accordingly, if we will listen to her voice and walk in her ways (Prov 1:2–6). Proverbs 2:1–22 expands on this theme. Wisdom calls out via conditional statements by the structure of "if. . .then."

> *If* you will receive my words (2:1–2),
> *If* you will call out for insight (2:3),
> *If* you will seek it like silver (2:4),
> *Then* you will understand the fear of the Lord (2:5–8),
> *Then* you will understand righteousness and justice and equity (2:9–15),
> *Then* you will be delivered from the forbidden woman and walk in the way of the good and keep to the paths of the righteous" (2:16–22).

I would love to tell you that after that church split everything fell into place and we all lived happily ever after. But I can't. What I can tell you is that God began cultivating righteousness in my life as an intentional process which began with my walk with God (Prov 15:29; 18:10). I began to guard my heart (Prov 4:23), my thoughts (Prov 12:5), and my words (Prov 8:8). Before, I loved the church I dreamed about. Now, I was learning to love the church I had. I used to daydream about ministering to multitudes. Now, I was learning to be faithful with the few entrusted to me. God was developing righteousness within me. Prioritizing relationships was outweighing the pursuit of achievements.

I used to think that success would make me feel secure and fulfilled. I thought it would fill the empty void in my life and make me happy. But as God worked in my life, my perspective began to change. I gradually realized that true security and a solid foundation for life come from

12. Elwell and Beitzel, "Righteousness," 1860.

13. See, for example, Is 24:16; 26:7; 53:11; Jer 12:1; 22:3; Ezek 3:20; 45:9; Amos 5:12; Zeph 3:5; Hab 2:4.

righteousness, not external success (Prov 12:3). Trusting in riches or power might seem tempting, but true security comes from taking refuge in the Lord and living a life of integrity, in right relationship with God and others (Prov 11:28; 16:8; 18:10; 20:7).

Embracing righteousness not only molds your character but also invites blessings into your life. The righteous are favored by God, guiding them away from death, adversity, and retribution (Prov 3:33; 4:18; 10:2, 6–7, 30; 11:8, 21; 12:21; 14:32; 15:9; 20:7). It instills a sense of security, productivity, and prosperity, infusing your days with happiness and honor (Prov 10:28; 12:12, 28; 13:21; 14:19; 16:31; 21:21). Though righteousness surpasses wealth in value, the righteous may also be granted riches as a form of recompense (Proverbs 11:4; 13:22; 15:6; 16:8). Constructing upright relationships becomes the key to abundance in God's economy. Righteousness nurtures generosity, empathy, and a willingness to extend kindness to others, particularly the less fortunate who cannot reciprocate. These deeds cultivate communal well-being and unleash divine blessings upon the entire society (Prov 12:26; 14:34; 21:26; 25:5; 28:12; 29:2, 7). Through the cultivation of righteousness, even your treatment of animals becomes a reflection of your compassion and virtue (Prov 12:10). Embracing righteousness not only invites blessings into your own life but also positively impacts those around you, creating a ripple effect of goodness and kindness in your community and beyond.

These are the things I began to learn after that day I felt God say, "Do you want to leave too?" No one would have blamed me for moving on. Yet, the right thing was to stay put. I was to stay put in relationship with God—not because of what I could do for him but because of what he was doing in me. I was learning to trust in the Lord and to experience God's presence and provision (Prov 10:6; 13:25).

The financial consequences of our church split caused stress. One day, at the supermarket, my daughter, Elizabeth, asked, "Dad, can we get a pineapple?" My heart broke. We had no money for a pineapple. The next day I came home to find a bag of groceries on the kitchen counter. To this day, I have no idea how it got there, but sitting on top of that bag of groceries was a huge pineapple. When my little girl asked, "Dad, can we get a pineapple?" her father in heaven heard her request. God made good on his promise. Our children are blessed by God (Prov 11:21; 20:7).

Righteousness is the divine mold to shape our lives. However, we humans seemed determined to break that mold and to fashion ourselves after something less than righteous, and this fills the world with iniquity, injustice, and idolatry. Leaders are to step into this chaotic disorder to heal what was broken, restore what was lost, and remember what was forgotten. Wise and righteous leaders are needed to overcome the chaos, disorder, confusion, violence, oppression, greed, exploitation, and lies unleashed by unrighteousness. Godly leaders do this not by violence or force, nor through positions of power, but by their indomitable lives expressed as justice toward others and integrity within oneself (Prov 1:3).

## Justice

> Evildoers have no understanding of justice, but those
> who seek the Lord understand it well.
>
> —PROVERBS 28:5 REB

Genesis 18:16—19:29 records the judgment that falls upon Sodom and Gomorrah. Yet, interestingly, the passage also contains the only passage in the Torah that explains why God singled out Abraham for a special blessing. The Lord asks, "Shall I hide from Abraham what I am about to do, seeing that Abraham shall surely become a great and mighty nation, and all the nations of the earth shall be blessed in him? For I have chosen him, that he may command his children and his household after him to keep the way of the LORD by doing righteousness and justice" (Gen 18:17–19). God chose Abraham to be the father of a great and mighty nation, and through this nation, all the nations of the earth would be blessed. And how was this blessing to the nations to be fulfilled? By Abraham and his offspring keeping "the way of the LORD." The "way of the LORD" is defined here as "doing righteousness and justice."

Justice (*mišpāṭ*) appears some 418 times in the Hebrew Bible. The idea provides a correct understanding of government, whether of humans by humans or of the whole creation by God.[14] Deuteronomy 16:20 is a key text demonstrating the centrality of justice for God's people: "Justice, and only justice, you shall follow, that you may live and inherit the land that the LORD your God is giving you." Although the idea encompasses equitable judgments in the courtroom, it is more than that. Justice is also about fair dealings in everyday social life, including the proper protocol

---

14. It is translated as justice (Exod 23:6), judgement (Exod 28:15), just (Job 35:2), rule (Exod 15:25), rules (Exod 21:1), decision (Deut 17:8), sentence (2 Kgs 25:6), manner (2 Kgs 17:33–34), and as right, or rights (Deut 21:17).

in all relationships. Justice prepares the people for right relationships in the promised land: relationships between the monarchy and subjects, employer and employees, business and customers, parents and children, the extended family, society, neighbors, enemies, and property owners and tenants—every one of these relationships is encompassed by the call to do justice.

God's throne is built upon the unshakable foundations of justice and righteousness (Ps 37:28; 89:14). As God's people, we are called to do justice as well (Mic 6:8). This means treating others fairly, regardless of their social status or circumstances. It also means standing up for the rights of the oppressed and the vulnerable. The Bible especially calls on us to defend those who are powerless and the victims of mistreatment, especially foreigners, orphans, widows, and all without political, economic, or social power. We are to be their champions, speaking up for them and fighting for their rights. Leaders are to be the central champions of justice, for "to do righteousness and justice is more acceptable to the Lord than sacrifice" (Prov 21:3).

Justice preserves well-being and sets right a disturbed or unjust situation. The aim of justice is not punishment or retribution but rather *shalom* (peace). As we discussed in an earlier chapter, the concept of *shalom* conveys peace, harmony, wholeness, completeness, prosperity, welfare, and tranquility. To work for justice means to work for *shalom* in every area of human existence. *Shalom* does not emerge from the absence of disagreement, conflict, or war. Rather, it arises from the profound interconnectedness of all things, where each part contributes to the wholeness and well-being of the entire system. *Shalom* is a state of rightful order, in harmony with the physical and moral laws governing the universe. God's intent for all leaders (political, civic, economic, religious) is that they work for justice—for *shalom* (Jer 21:12; Prov 24:10–12).

In *The World as I See It*, Albert Einstein speaks of "an almost fanatical love of justice" in Judaism, "which make me thank my lucky stars that I belong to it."[15] This devotion to justice as the cornerstone of faith answers the question, "Why are there so many Jewish lawyers?"[16] This "fanatical love of justice" is woven throughout the Hebrew Scriptures. We see it when Abraham tries to convince God not to destroy the people of Sodom: "Far be it from you to do such a thing, to put the righteous

---

15. Einstein, *The World as I See It*, 63.

16. Dershowitz, *Abraham*, 2015.

to death with the wicked, so that the righteous fare as the wicked! Far be that from you! Shall not the Judge of all the earth do what is just?" (Gen 18:25). We see it when Moses tries to convince God not to destroy the golden calf worshipping children of Israel (Exod 32:30–32). This quest for justice is evident in some of the intense encounters between the prophets and God, which are represented as courtroom dramas (Jer 12:1–13; Mic 6:1–8). This type of courtroom drama reaches its apex in the New Testament when Jesus Christ is called our advocate (1 John 2:1). An advocate is "one who is called alongside to help," and in this case, an advocate in the law-court[17] speaking on behalf of the accused.[18]

Religion has often been used to anesthetize pain and lull us into indifference to poverty, hunger, disease, and injustice. Such problems belong to the world order, so we reason. Our numbness and indifference convince us that we can only find joy by fleeing society, hiding in our religious subcultures. or awaiting the next world. While our faith may certainly comfort us in our affliction, it should also stir us to action against such evils (Mic 6:8). God does not want people to be beaten down by poverty, dehumanized by hunger, marred by oppression and sickness, blinded by ignorance, deprived of rights, or subjected to abuse. We are called to be God's agents in this world: "to keep the way of the LORD by doing righteousness and justice" (Gen 18:19). Alleviating poverty, curing disease, educating people, ensuring the rule of law, defending the rights of the defenseless, securing human rights: these are spiritual tasks no less than prayer, worship, and Bible study. It is into this fray that God calls leaders to lead with righteousness and justice.

Righteousness and justice are often paired together as in Deuteronomy 16:19: "You shall not pervert justice. You shall not show partiality, and you shall not accept a bribe, for a bribe blinds the eyes of the wise and subverts the cause of the righteous." When *mišpāṭ* and *ṣedeq/ṣĕdāqâ/ ṣaddîq* appear as a word pair, they form a particularly significant statement pertaining to the right ordering of society within God's covenant community.[19] In the Pentateuch, righteousness and justice are essential principles that define what it means to live ethically in this world. The Hebrew words *mišpāṭ* ("legal judgment, justice") and *ṣĕdāqâ* ("righteousness") are often used interchangeably and in the format of parallelism (e.g., Gen 18:19, 25). They are both forms of justice but different in

17. Smalley, *1, 2, 3 John*, 36.

18. Kruse, *John*, 72.

19. Hayes, "Justice, Righteousness," 467.

their logic. *Mišpāṭ* refers to the rule of law; everyone is to be treated by the same standard, and disputes are settled by right rather than might. *Ṣĕdāqâ* most often signifies a person's ability to uphold social well-being and exemplify unwavering faithfulness in their interactions with others. It is a virtue that nurtures the bonds of human connection, fostering an environment of trust and genuine concern for one another.

When *mišpāṭpāṭ* and *ṣedeq/ṣĕdāqâ/ṣaddîq* appear as a word pair in the prophets, they form a particularly significant statement about the right ordering of society within God's covenant community, as in Isaiah 28:17: "And I will make justice the line, and righteousness the plumb line; and hail will sweep away the refuge of lies, and waters will overwhelm the shelter." The prophets regularly call us back to what is important, as we see in Jeremiah 9:23–24, who speaks for the Lord: "Let not the wise boast of their wisdom or the strong boast of their strength or the rich boast of their riches, but let the one who boasts boast about this: that they have the understanding to know me, that I am the LORD, who exercises kindness, justice and righteousness on earth, for in these I delight" (NIV). God spoke through Jeremiah to the sons of King Josiah, "Do you think you are a king because you compete in cedar? Did not your father eat and drink and do justice and righteousness? Then it was well with him. He judged the cause of the poor and needy; then it was well. Is not this to know me? declares the LORD" (Jer 22:15–16). Josiah did justice and righteousness, judging the cause of the poor and needy, and God asks, "Is not this to know me?" In this context, the knowledge of God transcends mere thoughts or contemplation; it transforms into tangible action directed towards another individual. Through such just action, one comes to know God by participating in his concern for kindness, justice, and righteousness.

In Proverbs, righteousness and justice are paired together in 8:20; 18:5; 21:3; and with the addition of equity in 1:3 and 2:9, and they form essential qualities for wise leaders. Righteousness takes place in relationships and justice in actions. Righteousness is essential for leaders because leadership involves relationships, and these relationships can get messy. After all, we humans are a mixture of holy aspiration and unholy ambition. Leadership sets you in the middle of this convulsing mixture, and you discover things about yourself and others that you wish you did not know. It is here, in this messiness, this ugliness, that righteousness serves to set hearts back into order, back into right relationship.

Equally challenging is the need of leaders to make wise and just judgments. Metaphors about measuring devices, such as equal weights and measures, give central expression to the kind of justice God expects of his people and their leaders (Prov 16:11; 20:10, 23). Units of measure in the ancient world were largely based on practical standards: the length of an arm, a day's journey, how much a donkey could carry, and so forth. While convenient, this system lacked units of standardization. Some arms were longer than others, some donkeys could carry more. The history of weights and measures, therefore, becomes the story of seeking standards.[20] A central metaphor governs ideals of righteousness and justice: everyone and everything is measured by equal standards, for "partiality in judging is not good" (Prov 24:23). As a leader, you must treat everyone, even your critics, with equal standards. There is no room for favoritism or prejudice.

## Integrity

I was criticized a lot during that church split. Not all the criticism was deserved, but some struck me to the bones as being painfully true. I was not consistent, they said. I would say one thing with one group and then another to another group. I did not intentionally act in a way that was inconsistent or deceptive. I did not want to be wishy-washy. I think I was afraid. Maybe even cowardly. I was trying to protect my fractured self from further pain by avoiding conflict. I was afraid that if I disagreed with people, they would leave our church. This brings us back to Proverbs 1:1–3: "The proverbs of Solomon son of David, king of Israel: For learning wisdom and discipline; for understanding insightful sayings; for receiving prudent instruction in righteousness, justice, and integrity" (CSB). I needed integrity.

The Hebrew term translated as integrity (*mêšārîm* from the root *y-š-r*) refers to what is right and reasonable (Prov 1:3). It portrays a person with an upright, honorable, and straightforward demeanor, walking in the way of truth.[21] This root, *y-š-r*, is employed in various ways: literally, denoting a direct or even path, like Hezekiah's aqueduct (2 Chr 32:30), or metaphorically, "making a way straight" by removing obstacles, as when preparing for a royal visitor. God's work for his people is to "make

---

20. Elwell and Comfort. "Weights and Measures," 1298.

21. Lange, *Proverbs*, 44.

straight your paths" when we acknowledge him in all our ways (Prov 3:6). Similarly, the people's work for God is to "prepare the way of the LORD" (Isa 40:3). One with integrity looks straight ahead (Prov 4:25). Ethically, uprightness characterizes the blameless (Prov 11:5) and the discerning (Ps 119:128). It defines God's reign, ways, words, and judgments (Deut 32:4; Hos 14:10; Ps 111:8; Ps 119:137). Uprightness is rooted in the heart and mind (Ps 7:11; 11:2), exemplified by King David (Deut 9:5; 1 Kgs 3:6; 9:4). It leads to "right paths" (Prov 2:13; 4:11) and holds the idiom "to be right in the eyes (of a person)," gaining approval through keeping commands (Num 23:27; Jer 27:5). This uprightness signifies conforming to a moral standard, equating to equity, innocence, justice, integrity, justification, and righteousness (Isa 33:15; 45:19; Ps 98:9; Prov 8:6; 23:16). It also denotes fairness, the ability to make unbiased judgments (Ps 99:4; Prov 1:3; 2:9). Integrity can also refer to a texture without roughness; it's smooth to the touch like the flow of wine (Isa 26:7; Prov 23:31). Overall, integrity is the essence of fairness and the ability to make judgements free from discrimination or dishonesty (Ps 99:4; Prov 1:3; 2:9).

Equity, uprightness, and integrity are often used synonymously in Proverbs. Recall from our earlier discussion how Hebrew poetry is not like modern poetry.[22] Modern poetry often makes use of rhyming words while Hebrew poetry focuses on the rhyming of thoughts. Hebrew poetry accomplishes this "thought-rhyme" through a mutual correspondence of sentences or clauses called "parallelism:" there's synonymous parallelism, where the thought expressed in the first part of the verse is repeated in the second part (with different but equivalent terms) and antithetical parallelism, where the two parts contain opposite thoughts. Synonymous parallelism is common in Proverbs. Proverbs 2:7: "He stores up sound wisdom for the upright; he is a shield to those who walk in integrity;" and Proverbs 2:21: "For the upright will inhabit the land, and those with integrity will remain in it;" and Proverbs 17:26: "To impose a fine on a righteous man is not good, nor to strike the noble for their uprightness." These parallelisms show how equity, uprightness, and integrity describe the formation of character shaped by wisdom.

In speaking of his rule as king, Psalm 78:72 says: "David shepherded them with a heart of integrity; he led them with the skill of his hands" (CEB). This verse perfectly captures the kind of leadership we are to pursue. Every godly leader should seek to lead with integrity of heart and

22. Alter, *Biblical Poetry*, 2011.

skillful hands. Integrity of heart is a life-long journey to overcome the fractured condition of the human self. Sin and death shatter the inner self, leaving one to struggle against oneself. Righteousness heals the soul by restoring us to our true self, as one created by and for God. We are restored to relationship with God and our fellow humans and all creation. This overcomes the chaos and confusion of sin. Through a lifelong pursuit of the way of the Lord, integrity is restored. This integrity of soul is essential to resist the pressures of leadership.

Integrity is not something that happens overnight. When you opt for the path of wisdom, integrity begins to take shape within you (Prov 1:3). This is a journey, a gradual process. The essence of integrity is not forged in a day but must be chosen every day. When you choose to walk with integrity (Prov 2:6–7; 10:9; 14:2; 20:7), it will guide (Prov 11:3), protect, and deliver you (Prov 2:6–7; 2:21; 10:9; 28:18), and grant favor and blessings upon you and your children (Prov 16:13; 19:1; 20:7; 28:6). By heeding the counsel of wisdom, you become righteous, just, and integrous. This transformation empowers you to lead others to righteousness, justice, and integrity. And this is the ultimate success for any leader (Prov 19:1; 28:6, 18).

## Wicked Leaders

> Those who forsake the law praise the wicked, but
> those who keep the law strive against them.
>
> —PROVERBS 28:4

Toxic leadership is wicked leadership. The Hebrew word used in Proverbs for "wicked" (*rāšāʿ*) conveys the idea of one who is guilty of hostility toward God or people, one who is "in the wrong."[23] This wickedness is a violation of the rights of others through violence, oppression, greed, dishonesty, manipulation, and even murder. Wickedness is destructive both individuals and the community. It is the exact opposite of righteousness.

Forty-nine times in Proverbs *rāšāʿ* is placed in antithetic parallelism to *ṣedeq* (the righteous), and it is from this contrast that we get the clearest profile of the *rāšāʿ* kind of people.[24] The focus is on both the

---

23. Livingston, "2222 רָשַׁע (rāšaʿ) be wicked, act wickedly." 863.

24. Prov 3:33; 10:3, 6, 7, 11, 16, 20, 24, 25, 28, 30, 32; 11;5, 8, 10, 18, 23, 31; 12:5, 7, 10, 12, 21, 26; 13:5, 6, 9, 25; 14:19, 32; 15:6, 9, 28, 29; 17:15; 18:5; 21:12, 18; 24:15, 16;

quality of lifestyle and the results of these two contrasting ways of living. For example, "The LORD's curse is on the house of the wicked, but he blesses the dwelling of the righteous" (Prov 3:33), and "The wage of the righteous leads to life, the gain of the wicked to sin" (Prov 10:16). While the wicked turn their back on God, the righteous steadfastly cling to him. The wicked are characterized by oppression and deceit, whereas the righteous stand upright and are fervent advocates of truth. The contrast between the wicked and the upright is reiterated six more times in Proverbs (11:11; 12:6; 14:11; 15:8; 21:18, 29). The harsh judgment of the wicked in Proverbs is consistent with the judgments against leaders found in other sections of the Bible. For example, Jeremiah says, "For from the least to the greatest of them, everyone is greedy for unjust gain; and from prophet to priest, everyone deals falsely. They have healed the wound of my people lightly, saying, 'Peace, peace,' when there is no peace" (Jeremiah 6:13–14). The contrast between the wicked and the righteous in Proverbs is a reminder that there are two paths in life: the path of folly and the path of wisdom. The path of folly leads to destruction, while the path of wisdom leads to life. We choose which path we will follow.

To be called to lead God's people is a serious responsibility. It is not to be entered into lightly. The gravity of this task can be seen from the severe statements found throughout Proverbs. In chapter three we discussed how a person who will not address their immature ways may eventually become a fool, and once folly is lodged deep in the heart, this fool may become a mocker. We can go through a similar process in our leadership. Reflecting on my behavior during those years of trouble and testing, I see now that my leadership was immature and naïve. I had to face that. If I did not deal with my failings in leadership, I would have become entrenched in bad leadership. From there, I could have become a wicked leader. Thankfully, through Proverbs, the grace of God, and a lot of help from my wife and friends, I eventually began to deal with my issues and averted the dreaded outcome of wicked leadership.

Recall also from chapter three our discussion of wise and foolish leaders. Now we are talking about righteous and wicked leaders. Wise and foolish leadership describes how we lead, righteous and wicked leadership describes what our leadership produces. The wise leader produces the fruit of righteousness; the foolish leader produces the fruit of wickedness.

---

25:5, 26; 28:1, 12, 28; 29:2, 7, 16, 27.

I must warn you. The next few paragraphs are brutal, yet they underscore the gravity with which God regards the issue of toxic leadership. Wicked leaders are characterized by instability, destined for being cut off, ultimately leading to their own ruin and devastation (Prov 2:22; 3:25; 10:25, 30; 12:7; 13:9; 14:11, 32; 16:4; 20:26; 21:12, 18; 24:15–16, 19–20; 25:5; 28:1; 29:16). These individuals, distant from God and under a curse, evoke the Lord's displeasure (Prov 3:33; 15:8, 29; 21:12). Much like Samson and Saul, these wicked leaders "play the fool" (1 Sam 26:21 KJV). Their behavior, thoughts, and even their worship are deemed abominable (Prov 15:9; 21:27). Consequently, they are repugnant to humanity (Prov 24:9). The Lord thwarts their desires, leading their aspirations to futility (Prov 10:3, 28; 11:7, 23).

Their words are crooked, lying, deceptive, deceitful, and destructive (Prov 6:12; 10:32; 11:18; 12:5; 13:17; 15:1, 2, 4, 7, 28). Their hearts are devoted to schemes of evil (Prov 6:18; 12:12). These toxic leaders will not listen, and they will not learn (Prov 9:7; 15:5, 12, 31–32).

They exhibit violence and cruelty (Prov 10:6, 11; 21:7; 24:15–16), fueled by an inflated sense of pride and arrogance (Prov 10:20; 21:4, 29). These wicked leaders feed upon and listen to evil (Prov 17:4; 19:28; 29:12). They themselves are corrupt and a source of corruption for others (Prov 10:16; 17:23; 29:12, 16). Greed fuels their actions, they have no regard for the poor (Prov 14:21, 31; 19:17; 29:7). Instead, they mock the poor (Prov 17:5) and close their ears to their cries (Prov 21:13). They are merciless toward others (Prov 12:10; 21:10) and unsatisfied in themselves (Prov 13:25).

These wicked leaders cause trouble and destruction for the community and will ultimately be despised and accursed by the people (Prov 10:7; 11:10–11; 12:6, 26; 15:6; 17:11; 24:24–25; 28:12, 15, 28; 29:2) because they reap what they sow, bringing shame and disgrace upon themselves and others (Prov 11:31; 12:21; 13:5–6). They foment chaos, turmoil, destruction, and rebellion (Prov 17:11). What they dread comes upon them, and their way ends in trouble and death (Prov 10:24, 27; 11:8). Enmeshed in their own wickedness, the wicked tread a path of darkness, ultimately leading to their own ruin (Prov 4:19; 5:22; 11:5). They should be avoided at all costs (Prov 4:14).

Leadership and Violence

> Do not envy a man of violence and do not choose any
> of his ways, for the devious person is an abomination to
> the Lord, but the upright are in his confidence.
>
> —PROVERBS 3:31–32

References to violence appear throughout Proverbs (Prov 1:10–19; 3:31; 4:17; 10:6, 11; 11:16; 13:2; 16:29; 19:26; 21:7; 22:24–25; 24:2, 15; 26:6). To be a violent person (Prov 11:16) is to embody a ruthless cruelty, an intense ferocity, and an unrelenting harshness[25] towards others, often with the intention of asserting dominance or power through fear. Proverbs staunchly advises against the perils of violence, deeming it as both morally wrong and destined to usher in destruction, given its roots in hatred (Prov 10:12, 18).

The Hebrew word for violence (ḥāmās) can refer to physical violence, but it also has a broader meaning.[26] It can encompass wrongdoing, hurtful speech, harsh treatment, insolent wickedness, boisterous and unrestrained cruelty, and hatred characterized by violence and oppression.[27] This term can signify a potent and destructive force, giving rise to actions causing harm, devastation, or even death. This often implies a state of lawlessness, fear, and a deficit of moral restraint (Gen 49:5; Proverbs 3:31). It can also signify the ruin or desolation of an entity, territory, or people, highlighting the inherently violent nature of these deeds (Hab 2:8, 17). This concept also encompasses instances of injustice that infringe upon established norms, suggesting an intense and grievous injustice (Gen 16:5; Job 19:7). Furthermore, it can pertain to the plundering or looting of war spoils (Amos 3:10), as well as to the willful falsehoods of a malicious witness, especially in a legal context (Exod 23:1; Deut 19:16; Ps 35:11).

Violence pursues unjust gains through methods that are cruel, harmful, deceptive, oppressive, unrighteous, coercive, or abusive. It manifests in diverse forms, spanning physical, verbal, emotional, and structural realms. Physical violence stands as the most evident manifestation, encompassing actions like hitting, kicking, stabbing, and shooting. Verbal

---

25. Brown, et al., *Lexicon*, 792.

26. Redding, "Violence," 2014.

27. Gesenius and Tregelles, *Lexicon*, 288.

violence harnesses words to inflict harm or induce intimidation, encompassing insults, threats, and derogatory language. Emotional violence involves manipulating emotions to exert control or harm, encompassing tactics like gaslighting, guilt-tripping, and stonewalling. Structural violence operates through systems and institutions to perpetuate harm, encompassing phenomena like racism, sexism, and classism. All forms of violence are manifestations of hatred (Prov 10:12, 18). When hatred takes hold, it can fuel violent actions towards the target of that hatred. Additionally, violence can be employed as a tool for control or dominance. Those who perceive themselves to have power over others may resort to violence as a means to preserve that power.

Violence makes its first appearance in the story of Cain killing Abel (Gen 4:1–16). The scriptures do not tell us why the Lord accepted the offering of Abel but not of Cain. Many commentators have speculated, but the scriptures remain silent on the subject. Perhaps the more important truth is what the scriptures are not silent about. Immediately following this act of worship, Cain acts with violence against his brother Abel. Violence makes its appearance on the stage of creation. Before long, wrongdoing has covered the earth. By the time we reach Genesis 6, God looks at the earth he has made, and it is covered with violence (Gen 6:11–13).

We humans have a long history of doing violence, and we continually invent new ways of inflicting harm. The scars of our violence are carried by the Creator himself. One day we will look upon him and behold our war against God. We will ask him, "Where did you receive these wounds?" He will reply, "These are the wounds I received in the house of my friends."[28]

Violence has worked its way into the fabric of life and ministry. Take, for example, the story of Elisha and the boys who mocked his bald head. Elisha was called by God to become a powerful prophet. He succeeded Elijah as prophet and received a double portion of the spirit that was on Elijah (2 Kgs 2:1–18). More miracles are recorded during his ministry than for any other prophet in the Hebrew Scriptures. After his prophetic inauguration, Elisha supernaturally parts the river to walk to the other side (2 Kgs 2:9–14). He then miraculously heals a poisoned water source (2 Kgs 2:19–22). Then, while walking to Bethel, a group of little boys taunt Elisha because he is bald. Does Elisha laugh with them? Does he ignore them? No! He calls down a curse upon these children, then two

---

28. Zech 13:6

raging she-bears come out of the woods and forty-two boys are torn to pieces! The lamentation of forty-two mothers was heard that night, refusing to be comforted, for their sons were no more. Horrible and unimaginable violence was poured out on forty-two little boys merely because they acted like little boys.

Consider how the disciples reacted when the Samaritans did not receive Jesus.[29] They wanted to call fire down upon the whole village in punishment for their lack of hospitality and welcome for the Prince of Peace. Jesus rebuked their violence, telling them, "You do not know what manner of spirit you are of. For the Son of man did not come to destroy men's lives, but to save them."[30]

Violence generally evokes for people the specter of mass violence. War, genocide, school shootings, gangs, or street crime. We like to deceive ourselves by dwelling on violence in monstrous proportions; in this way, we can suppose that only evil people and sociopaths are such monsters. Unfortunately, the evidence does not support our claim. Monsters did not kill millions during the Holocaust; average people did. This was the jarring conclusion of Hannah Arendt's report about the trial of the German Nazi official Adolf Eichmann.[31] Arendt's 1963 book *Eichmann in Jerusalem* showed us the banality of evil. Eichmann was neither a fanatic nor a sociopath, but instead an average person—even a mundane man— who did great violence.

No matter how horrifying, we cannot afford to let mass atrocities numb our senses to the daily violence around us, even in church. Sexual and financial abuse are two of its more well-recognized expressions. We anesthetize ourselves by creating euphemisms, docile names to soften the reality and the blow. The pastor had "a moral failing" with a staff member or a parishioner. To say a pastor "had an affair" neglects the power imbalance at play. Ministers have enormous power within their congregation. People often turn to their ministers when they are most vulnerable. The power differential is immense. We should not fool ourselves with sanitized language. This is not pastoral misconduct; it is an abuse of power.

Violence in church is not only about sexual abuse and financial scandal. There are worrisome acts of violence done in churches—right in plain sight. Here are two examples of what I mean.

---

29. Luke 9:51–56
30. See Lk 9:55–56 KJV, NKJV
31. Arendt, *Eichmann*, 2006.

Let's set the scene. Pastor Hank is teaching about the love of God from 1 John 4:4–21. As he is reading 1 John 4:11: "Beloved, if God so loved us, we also ought to love one another," a cell phone rings. An embarrassed woman in the third row quietly retrieves her phone to whisper into the receiver, and then she hangs up. Meanwhile, the angry pastor stomps his way over to the woman. With a look of contempt, he demands she hand over her cell phone. She complies. The pastor slams the phone to the ground, shattering the device. Pastor Hank then marches back to the pulpit, turns back to the Bible, and continues reading with a smirk: "We love because he first loved us." No one is shocked. No one is outraged. Everyone sits quietly while the earth is covered in violence.

Another example is Pastor John, who interrupts his sermon to reprimand a man who has fallen asleep. "Son, don't go to sleep while I'm talking. Hey! Hey! Hey! Don't you lay your head back. I'm important. I'm somebody. Now, you might do your English teacher that way but I'm not teaching English. I'm teaching eternal life here." By now Pastor John has marched off the platform. He is standing directly in front of the sleepy man, demanding that he stand up. Pastor John's language could lead you to believe he is reprimanding a child or a young boy. No, this is a full-grown man who looks to be in his mid-forties. The pastor's language and behavior are calibrated to humiliate and inflict shame. Pastor John tells the man, "I love you. You know I love you? Have I convinced you? Yeah, you better nod your head yes. You stay awake, and you listen to me."

Pastor John is not done yet. Not by a long shot. After shaming the fatigued man, Pastor John notices a young couple who have not been in church lately. "Where have you been, Mr. Underwood? I noticed on the calendar I'm supposed to marry ya'll. What makes you think I'd marry you? You're one of the sorriest church members I have. You're not worth fifteen cents. And you want me to marry you to her? And you want to marry him? And he doesn't even know where he belongs. And you don't know where you belong." After telling this man he is not worth three nickels, the pastor berates his congregation and threatens to leave them if they don't like his behavior. He then goes after a mother named Brandi (Yes, he calls her name), telling her what a terrible job she has been doing as a mother and how messed up her children will become. He berates her, "Your children will turn on you if you don't hold up the standards of God."

Unfortunately, Pastor John is still not done. He then turned his wrath on the young man working the video room: "Are you all keeping the camera on me back there in the little video room? Good. We are having trouble in the video room. There is no one finer than young Cox back there. And he comes down here and spends hours in that thing. But he has a little attitude adjustment that we're going to fix. Mr. Cox, are you listening? Brother Cox, I can fix your attitude adjustment." Not content to berate young Mr. Cox, Pastor John must also berate Mr. Cox's mother. "Now, I don't care what your momma thinks or what your daddy thinks. And I don't have a better friend than your momma, but momma you get out of my way when I'm messing with that boy because I'm his preacher. I'm your preacher when I'm talking to you, but I'm his when I'm talking to him. And last I checked, he's a grown man!" The pastor goes on: "That video room ain't going to be a youth hang out! We might as well fix this thing. I don't know what I'm doing wrong. Now, if you don't know what you're doing wrong. Son, you don't care about what I want to do right. Because if you loved me, and you submitted to me, you'd know what my heart is and what my message is. And you wouldn't go about establishing your own kingdom in the video room!"

Finally, Pastor John is done pouring out his rage upon the congregation. He lets everyone know how he feels about this public shaming and berating of the congregation by wrapping up with, "I really feel good now." Shouts of "Preach It!" and "Amen!" can be heard coming from the congregation.[32]

Pastor John and his congregation form what is called a toxic triangle. A destructive leader, susceptible followers, and a conducive environment make a trio. This allows toxic leaders to charm, manipulate, mistreat, weaken, and ultimately destroy their followers.[33] Pastor John used his leadership position to commit acts of violence against the flock he was called to love and protect. These violent acts did not involve blood but instead harm to the heart and soul. These assaults are indeed types of violence. Violence has covered the earth.

These two examples may seem extreme, but what about the subtle but common occurrences bullying on the part of ministry leaders? Or the berating of staff and congregants? As a leader, you may be tempted to berate or disparage those who disagree with you. Resist this temptation toward violence. I once knew a pastor who openly stated he manipulated people "for their own good." You may think the end justifies the means,

---

32. Yes, this all of this is true, and it is the word for word transcript from a recorded church service.

33. Lipman-Blumen, *The Allure of Toxic Leaders*, 2006.

but it does not. Any act that manipulates or demeans—be it emotional, psychological, economic, or physical—is violence.

Abusive leaders seek to dominate the space for the sake of emotional attention. When leaders use fear to dominate, control, or destroy; and when they use their position of authority to manipulate, abuse, or defraud another, they are engaging in acts of violence. The spectrum of violent behaviors ranges from passive-aggressive acts of micro-aggression to physical, sexual, and emotional types of abuse (overt and covert) to violence on a grand scale through mobilizing followers to engage in acts of collective intimidation, sabotage, or war. Violence uses physical, material, economic, social, and emotional resources to dominate or destroy the other and exalt the self or the favored group. The consequence for the victim is the dehumanizing loss of personhood and identity. This dehumanization happens on a small scale with individuals, groups, and congregations or on a grand scale in religious, social, and cultural movements, which impact entire nations and peoples.

From the start (e.g., Prov 1:10–19), the book of Proverbs warns leaders to relentlessly avoid violence. Proverbs 4:10–17 warns not to "drink the wine of violence." Violence, like wine, can be intoxicating to a leader who breaks the boundaries of restraint and gives full vent to his or her spirit in anger (Prov 29:11; see also Prov 14:29; 15:1, 18; 16:32; 19:11; 20:2; 21:14; 22:24; 24:18; 27:4; 29:22; 30:33).

Violence is perhaps most seductive where it seems to provide an effective means to reach an end. In their fascinating study of the "virtuous violence theory," Alan Page Fiske and Tage Shakti Rai observe, "Most violence is morally motivated. People do not simply justify or excuse their violent actions after the fact; at the moment they act, people intend to cause harm or death to someone they feel *should* suffer or die." Fiske and Rai go on to explain how people are morally motivated to do violence. They rationalize that they can thereby create a new future, protect some point of pride or honor, or redress a grievance. They describe "virtuous violence" as actions in which the perpetrator inflicts suffering, pain, fear, distress, injury, maiming, disfigurement, or death while justifying these harms as the intrinsic, necessary, or appropriate means to accomplish a desired result. "Insults, taunting, and cursing often precede [physical] violence, and are motivated by the same relational intentions."[34] Walter Wink refers to this type of violence as "the

---

34. Fiske and Rai, *Virtuous Violence*, 15.

myth of redemptive violence;" this is a story of the victory of order over chaos by means of violence. This myth enshrines the belief that violence saves, that war brings peace, and that might makes right. This myth of redemptive violence is the real myth of the modern world, indeed, the dominant religion in our society today.[35]

Why did the Israelites keep turning away from YHWH to worship Ishtar, the Queen of Heaven?[36] What was the appeal? I've often wondered. Then I realized that Ishtar was the goddess of war and sex.[37] The old gods are not banished. They are still worshipped today. We may dress them differently or call the false god "Jesus," but Satan can be disguised as an angel of light. When leaders use subtle forms of violence to advance their purposes, others are diminished, the humanity of all is reduced, and the self is deformed. Violence again covers the earth.

Most likely, no one reading these words has directly participated in genocide or mass murder. But what about that tamed and domesticated violence that differs by degree but not in kind? What's the fundamental difference between the hatred of murder and the hatred that spews out sexual abuse, sexist insults, racial slurs, power ploys, and demeaning, dehumanizing comments—all intended to destroy or subjugate the other while exalting yourself? Jesus doesn't seem to think there is a difference (Matt 5:21–26).

In *Moral Man and Immoral Society*, Reinhold Niebuhr makes painfully clear a paradox. Upright citizens with strict personal moral codes will simultaneously comply with oppressive systems that undermine basic decency and leaders who perpetuate real harm and evil. As individuals, moral people believe they ought to love and serve each other and establish justice. However, when they act within racial, economic, and national groups, these same individuals take for themselves whatever their power can command.[38] Likewise, victimized groups (ethnic minorities, the powerless, the disenfranchised) suffer from group violence.

To exalt ourselves and our group usually involves dominating and subjugating "the other." This egoism, both collective and personal, dominates our world in every sphere (religious, political, economic). Racism, nationalism, xenophobia, sexism, and all forms of othering are manifestation of this urge for self-exaltation. Sadly, even our own homes

---

35. Wink, *The Powers that Be*, 1999.

36. Jer 7:18; 44:17–19, 25.

37. Moore, "Ishtar," 2016.

38. Niebuhr, *Major Works*, 156.

provide no refuge from dehumanizing motives. In Christ God overthrew and destroyed the body of sin (Rom 6:6) and created a new and unified humanity (Eph 2:15) called the body of Christ. The gospel silences our clamoring to exalt the self and subjugate the other. Such arrogance is not only inconsistent with the gospel; it is a denial of the gospel.

As leaders, we are called to follow the One who is gentle and lowly of heart. When we, his servants and shepherds, are like our Good Shepherd, perhaps the flocks entrusted to us will find rest for their souls.[39] The world has plenty of charismatic, powerful, strategic, transformational, empowering, and servant leaders. Yet, this is not enough. Something more is needed. Someone else is longed for. The great pantheon of leadership retains a vacant seat for a single good person: the wise leader who embodies righteousness, justice, and integrity.

Then, may it come to pass in our day too, that "I will give you shepherds after my own heart, who will feed you with knowledge and understanding" (Jer 3:15). The people of God will become a healed and healing people sent as God's agents of restoration into a world wounded by sin and ruled by death. We will bring the world as it is a little closer to the world as it ought to be. Wisdom calls us to participate in the drama of redemption; as people who bring blessings into the world as the redeemed community of God, living in righteousness, justice, and integrity. May "justice roll down like waters, and righteousness like an ever-flowing stream" (Amos 5:24). And may God raise you up to help lead the way.

---

39. Matt 11:28–30

# 12

## Cultivating the Habits that Cultivate Your Heart

LISTEN AS WISDOM CALLS to us:

> Now then, my children, listen to me;
> blessed are those who keep my ways.
> Listen to my instruction and be wise;
> do not disregard it.
> Blessed are those who listen to me,
> watching daily at my doors,
> waiting at my doorway.
> For those who find me find life
> and receive favor from the Lord.
> But those who fail to find me harm themselves;
> all who hate me love death.
> Proverbs 8:32–36, NIV

Wisdom calls to us, her children, to open our hearts, heed her voice, and follow her ways with unwavering devotion. She promises that those who diligently seek her will find life's richness and God's favor. But those who turn away from her guidance and despise her counsel will sow the seeds of their own destruction, for in rejecting Wisdom, they embrace death. The path of wisdom leads to life, abundance, and God's favor. We can choose to heed the voice of Wisdom and follow her ways. Or we can choose to turn away from her and follow our own foolish desires. Wisdom's ways are often challenging. But the rewards of following her are worth it. A life of wisdom is a life of abundance, joy, and peace.

As we near the end of our study, we have seen the transformative power of God's wisdom. We have seen how wisdom can forge men and women into pillars of righteousness, justice, and unwavering integrity. In this closing chapter, we will look at three case studies where wisdom prevailed through tumultuous trials, when the circumstances were complex, and the stakes were high. I will then leave you with three habits to ready your heart for Wisdom to make it a home.

## Wisdom at Work

First, let us unwrap the case studies. In these stories, we see the wisdom of God working her way through the complex fabric of human life. We gain insight into her ways and glimpse the marvel of her work, even in the most challenging of circumstances. Wisdom dances amidst the complexities of life, delighting in the human race (Prov 8:1–36).

## Joseph, a Man Tested and Refined

Joseph provides a compelling illustration of a leader who faced multiple trials and tests (Gen 37–50). Being his father's favored son, Joseph is hated by his brothers (Gen 37:3–4). God gives Joseph a dream that his brothers will bow before him, further fueling their hatred (Gen 37:5–8). Joseph has a second dream revealing that not only his brothers but even his father and mother will bow before him (Gen 37:9–11). Enraged, his brothers plot to kill him, but they are convinced to sell him to human traffickers. To cover their tracks, they then conspire to tell their father that Joseph has fallen victim to a wild animal (Gen 37:25–33). Joseph is then sold as a slave to Potiphar, the captain of Pharoah's guard. Joseph is a handsome young man. Potiphar's wife attempts to seduce Joseph, but he refuses her advances. In retaliation, she falsely accuses him of attempted rape, leading to Joseph's imprisonment as a sex offender (Gen 39:1–19).

While in prison, Joseph interprets the dreams of two government officials, both of which come to pass exactly as Joseph has foretold (Gen 40:1–23). In a hopeful plea to the official who would be reinstated, Joseph asks, "Remember me, when it is well with you, and please do me the

kindness to mention me to Pharaoh, and so get me out of this house"
(Gen 40:14). Unfortunately, the chief cupbearer promptly forgets about
Joseph as soon as he is freed from prison (Gen 40:23). Joseph finds him-
self despised, rejected, and betrayed by his brothers, sold as a slave into
Egypt, wrongfully imprisoned for a crime he did not commit, and ulti-
mately forgotten by those he had helped.

While in prison, the word of the Lord tested Joseph (Ps 105:19).
What has happened to the dreams God gave Joseph? What has become
of God's promise? Had God really spoken to Joseph? If so, what was God
doing and why did all this happen to Joseph? To be tested (ṣārap) literally means to be "smelted." Smelting is the process of purifying metals by
subjecting ores, like silver or iron ore, to high temperatures and separating impurities from the metal. In the scriptures, the word describes the
process of purification and refinement within the hearts of individuals
(Isa 1:25; Jer 6:29; Zech 13:9; Ps 66:10). This smelting process unveils
the essence of God's divine action in testing his creation, serving as a
crucible wherein character and faith are examined (Judg 7:4; Jer 9:6; Isa
48:10; Zech 13:9; Pss 17:3; 66:10). The term also serves as a testament
to the proven, tried, and refined nature intrinsic to the word of God. It
signifies the enduring validity and reliability of God's divine utterances,
forged through the crucible of trials and tribulations (Pss 18:31; 119:140;
Prov 30:5).

Testing is God's way of refining, shaping, and purifying his creation
while emphasizing the unwavering nature of his divine word. Just as metal is extracted from ore in a furnace, so we are refined by God's word. The
rough parts of our personality, like crude materials, get put into the furnace of transformation. Through the convergence of faith and trials, our
character begins to shine like a precious metal. This is divine smelting.

It was in the dark prison of Egypt that the illuminating fire of God's
word smelted Joseph. The word burned in his heart, removing the dross
and waste lying deep within, leaving behind a clean and pure heart to see
God, and this clarified everything.

Joseph did not give way to bitterness, anger, and unforgiveness. The
word of the Lord was working in Joseph a profound transformation that
exceeded the confines of his external circumstances. It was an unseen
shaping, preparing him for a destiny far grander than his finite mind
could conceive. The refining fire of God's word burned away the impurities of rejection, betrayal, false accusations, the agony of being forgotten,
and the desolation of confinement. Joseph tenaciously held to God's word,

and it refined him. Then, when the appointed hour arrived, Joseph's journey took an astonishing turn; he went from the confines of prison to the spacious splendor of the palace. The transformative power of God's word had molded Joseph into a vessel ready to fulfill God's purpose.

Joseph guarded his heart above all things (Prov 4:23), and this developed within him a spiritual sensitivity that set him apart (Gen 37:2). He exemplified honor in the face of temptation, steadfastly resisting the allurements that sought to undermine his integrity (Gen 39:2–20). This aligns with Proverbs 23, 29, and 31. We see wisdom on display when Joseph was a slave in Potiphar's household, a prisoner in an Egyptian jail, and the second-in-command of all of Egypt. Joseph showcased wisdom in his administrative and managerial skills, embodying the essence of Proverbs 22:29: "Do you see a man skillful in his work? He will stand before kings; he will not stand before obscure men." Wisdom and prudence flowed from his lips and actions as he navigated Pharaoh's court (Gen 41:38–49). Amidst emotional turmoil, Joseph exhibited remarkable strength, concealing his identity until the opportune moment (Gen 43:29–31). With keen discernment, he recognized the hand of God orchestrating events for a greater purpose (Gen 45:7, 8). Joseph was a wise man and resourceful man, but he also had his moments of failure, as well shall discuss shortly. It involves the tragic irony that while Joseph used his power to save his people from famine, he also used his power to enslave the Egyptians (Gen 47:13–26). And it, too, becomes a lesson in wisdom.

Joseph's wisdom went beyond benefiting the Egyptian Pharaoh and nation; it also led to reconciliation and restoration within his own family (Gen 50:19–21). Despite the immense pain and suffering inflicted by his brothers, Joseph chose righteousness over vengeance. His act of forgiveness and reconciliation exemplified the pinnacle of Wisdom's goal to build leaders who pursue righteousness, justice, and integrity (Prov 1:2–7). It comes as no surprise that the writer of Hebrews refers to Joseph as a man of faith (Heb 11:22).

In Joseph's remarkable journey, we witness the transformative power of the divine Word, shaping his character and molding him into a vessel in the hands of God. As Joseph was honed through trials, the wisdom of God illuminated the path to his destined role in the tapestry of God's grand design. Though dead, he still speaks to us today. We are to surrender to the refining fire of divine truth, allowing it to mold us into vessels of honor, wisdom, emotional resilience, discernment, and forgiveness.

Joseph also teaches us another lesson, one that is both painful and powerful. It is a lesson that reminds us that God demonstrates his faithfulness and accomplishes his saving purpose in the midst of human imperfection, weakness, and sin. It is a lesson so important that Proverbs repeats it twice (14:12; 16:25), "There is a way that seems right to a man, but its end is the way to death."

As Genesis 47:13–26 describes, Joseph enacted a policy that resulted in the enslavement of the entire nation of Egypt. As the famine persisted, "Joseph gathered up all the money that was found in the land of Egypt and in the land of Canaan" and brought it into Pharoah's house (Gen 47:14). The people of the land were now starving and financially destitute. The people had no money to buy the grain held in reserve and stored during the years of abundance. In response, Joseph proposed that they exchange their livestock for food. The people agreed and gave their livestock, including horses, cattle, sheep, and donkeys, to Joseph in exchange for food. When this supply of food was exhausted, they had nothing left to offer except themselves and their land in exchange for food. Joseph accepted their offer, and the people became slaves to Pharaoh. Furthermore, Joseph established a law requiring farmers to give one-fifth of their produce to Pharaoh while keeping the rest as seed. This law endured even after the famine ended. Though Joseph had wisely prepared Egypt for the coming famine, his subsequent policies concentrated wealth and power in the hands of the elite while stripping the people of their possessions, land, and autonomy, reducing them to the status of Pharaoh's property.

Within both Jewish and Christian interpretations, conflicting evaluations of Joseph emerge. Some view him as a virtuous hero and role model, while others perceive him as a cunning politician. Reading Genesis might leave us uncertain about the moral judgment of Joseph's economic policies. The text portrays the Egyptians as willingly selling their land and themselves as slaves to Pharaoh and expressing gratitude for being saved (vv. 19, 25). However, it is important to recognize that their appreciation does not justify Joseph's ruthless policies, particularly when considering the broader context of the Hebrew Bible. We should consider how starvation and crisis, such as this famine, reduced these Egyptians to their primitive survival instincts. Scripture does not support Joseph's economic policies of a food monopoly, the enslavement of the Egyptians, and centralized landownership. Any oppression of humans by means of a monopoly of landownership and enslavement is an insult to the Lord (Prov 14.31).

Joseph was certainly God's instrument to save both the Egyptians and the Israelites. God used Joseph to deliver people from the famine, but that does not mean that God approves of his hard and heartless economic policies that resulted in servitude for the Egyptians as they became serfs to the Pharaoh.

This somber narrative serves as a poignant reminder that the success of a leader should never serve as justification for the abuse of power. It beckons us to glean wisdom from this tragic event, for it is an eternal truth that no matter how fruitful or capable a leader may be, their accomplishments do not grant them the license to exploit their authority.

In the case of Joseph, we witness a figure of immense wisdom and foresight whose actions played a pivotal role in saving lives during the famine. However, the subsequent implementation of his policies that led to the enslavement of the Egyptian people stands as a stark testament to the perils of unchecked power.

Through the implementation of Joseph's economic policies, an unsettling transformation took place. Pharaoh became the embodiment of an enemy of the common good, while Joseph inadvertently played a role in making this happen. We must also take heed of the ominous undertones present in Joseph's enslavement of the Egyptians, for it serves as a foreboding precursor of what lay ahead. When a new Pharaoh who did not know of Joseph rose to power, the Israelites, in turn, became slaves to him (Exod 1:8–14).

This story reminds us that even the most capable leaders must be guided by moral principles and mindful of the potential repercussions their policies may have on the well-being and freedom of others.[1] It is in the exercise of power with humility, compassion, and an unwavering commitment to the common good that true leadership emerges.

## Leadership for Such a Time as This: Esther and the Persian Empire

The book of Esther tells the story of a Jewish girl who becomes queen of Persia. Her cousin and guardian, Mordecai, uncovers a plot by a high-ranking official named Haman to exterminate all the Jews in the Persian empire. Esther, risking her life, uses her position to approach the king and reveal Haman's plan. The king is angered and orders Haman's execution.

1. Kilnam, "Economic Policies," 2016

The Jews are saved, and a celebration called Purim is established to remember this victory.

Virtually from the time of its composition, the book of Esther has
posed many problems for its readers. In antiquity, a number of Jews and
Christians contested its canonicity. Protestant reformer Martin Luther
denounced the book, "I am so hostile to this book [2 Maccabees] and
Esther that I could wish that they did not exist at all; for they judaize too
greatly and have much pagan impropriety."

Modern scholars have also been quite critical of the book's moral
tone. Paton, who has written one of the most detailed and comprehensive
commentaries on Esther in the English language, concluded: "There is
not one noble character in the book."[2] Other scholars have been almost
as severe, claiming that Vashti, the deposed queen, was the only honorable person in the entire story. Scholar and Rabbi Sandmel confessed that
he "should not be grieved if the book of Esther were somehow dropped
out of Scripture"[3] while the Israeli Ben-Chorin actually advocated that
Jews abandon both the book and its holiday, arguing, "Both festival and
the book are unworthy of a people which is disposed to bring about its
national and moral regeneration under prodigious sacrifice."[4] All this and
much more has been said about a biblical book which the great Jewish
scholar Maimonides (1135–1204) ranked as second only to the Torah
itself.[5]

In modern times, readers have been troubled primarily, though not
exclusively, by moral issues, and the book has been stigmatized by many
readers as "vengeful, bloodthirsty and chauvinistic in spirit."[6] However,
Shemaryahu Talmon provides a solution to the interpretive challenges of
the book of Esther when he argues that the book is a historicized wisdom
tale that portrays the application of wisdom to a very complex situation.
He contends that the outline of the plot and the presentation of the central
characters show the wise in action. The implication, though not explicitly
stated, is that their ultimate success derives from the proper execution of
wisdom as set forth in Proverbs—and, to a certain degree, Ecclesiastes.[7]

2. Paton, *Esther*, 96.

3. Sandmel, *Enjoyment of Scripture*, 44.

4. Ben-Chorin, *Kritik des Estherbuches*, 5.

5. Moore, "Esther," 2:635.

6. Gordis, "Esther," 359.

7. Talmon, "'Esther," 419–55.

The story revolves around three couples. The king and queen of Persia, Ahasuerus and Vashti; Esther and her cousin, Mordecai; and Haman and his wife, Zeresh. The three couples stand as living embodiments of the timeless wisdom triangle. It is a scene that resonates with echoes of the Ancient Near East wisdom tradition: the powerful but witless dupe, the upright and discerning sage, and the deceitful schemer who weaves intricate webs of manipulation.

Ahasuerus represents the classic image of the foolish king depicted in wisdom literature. As a ruler easily ensnared in deceit, he becomes the wellspring of corruption among his court officials (Prov 29:12). His gullibility breeds their wickedness. Unaware of his own folly, he swells with conceit, succumbing to irritability and impulsiveness. Dining in his presence is a treacherous affair for no one can predict his whims. Proverbs warns about the dangers of sharing a meal with this type of leader (Prov 23:1). Beware, for dire consequences shall follow when his wrath ignites, and woe betide the one who provokes it (Prov 20:2). His actions are swift, spontaneous, and later regretted. His anger blazes forth, and he acts with reckless haste. In his hastiness, he condemns an innocent man, only to regret his decision when clarity returns. This tumultuous tide of emotions, consistently attributed to Ahasuerus, finds its place among the annals of wisdom literature: he is the type of the wicked ruler.[8]

Mordecai possesses remarkable foresight and discretion. He keeps his thoughts and actions to himself, sharing them only with Esther, recognizing the importance of secrecy for someone in his position (Prov 12:23). He refuses to bow to Haman, but he does not explain his actions, avoiding further provocation of Haman's anger. Whatever feelings he may have experienced, Mordecai guarded his heart for it determines the course of life (Prov 4:23). Mordecai remains composed even in the midst of extreme distress. He plans meticulously and avoids impulsive actions, knowing that patience is more powerful than brute force (Prov 16:32). In the end, he achieves success by displaying wisdom, which carries more weight than the strength of ten rulers combined (Eccl 7:19).

Esther faced a critical situation where the lives of her people, the Jews, were at stake. Through careful discernment and strategic thinking, she navigated a hazardous path to save her people from destruction. When Mordecai informed Esther about Haman's plot to annihilate the Jews, she initially hesitated to intervene due to the risks involved. However, after

8. Talmon, "Esther," 442.

seeking guidance through prayer and fasting, she made the courageous decision to approach King Ahasuerus, even though it could forfeit her life (Esth 4:15–17). Her wisdom enabled her to recognize the urgency and take a bold step to protect her people (Prov 28:1).

Esther wisely planned her approach to King Ahasuerus (Prov 25:11). Instead of immediately revealing Haman's wicked plot, she invited the king and Haman to two banquets, skillfully setting the stage for her revelation at the opportune moment. This strategic planning allowed her to maximize her influence and present her case effectively (Prov 16:21, 23).

Esther demonstrated wisdom in her communication with the king. She approached him with respect, humility, and tact rather than accusing Haman directly (Prov 22:11). By revealing the truth gradually and appealing to the king's sense of justice (Prov 16:2), she successfully gained his support in thwarting Haman's scheme.

Esther exhibited wisdom in her timing and patience (Prov 25:15). She recognized that timing was crucial in executing her plan. She did not rush into action but waited for the right moment to reveal Haman's intentions, ensuring that her message would have the maximum impact. Esther's wise decision-making, strategic planning, diplomatic communication, and discerning timing all exemplify the practical wisdom emphasized in Proverbs.

The stories of Joseph and Esther share similar characteristics (compare Gen 40:22 and Esth 1:3; Gen 39:10 and Esth 3:4; Gen 41:37 and Esth 1:21; Gen 41:35 and Esth 2:3; Gen 41:42 and Esth 3:10; 8:2). Joseph and Esther, along with Daniel 1–6, express the possibility of harmonizing the challenges of the foreign court with loyalty to one's own people. Life could be rewarding and creative under foreign rule, in service to the rulers at court. Yet, the position could carry risks to one's own people (the Israelites) and religious identity (in covenant with God). The Joseph and Esther stories provided models for the Jews in their mode of life in the pagan environment of the diaspora.[9] The story provides enduring examples for us, as well, who live as "sojourners and exiles" in this world (1 Pet 2:11).

---

9. Moore, "Esther," 2:639.

## When Cultures Clash, Acts 6:1–7

While Joseph and Esther demonstrate wisdom at work in a pagan environment, Acts 6:1–7 will show wisdom at work in the household of faith when bigotry, prejudice, and discrimination make an unwelcome appearance in the early church. It happened right in the middle of miracles, signs and wonders, and as multitudes were coming to Christ. In a pivotal test of faith for the apostles, characterized by their boldness in enduring shame for Christ and fearlessly proclaiming the gospel amidst threats from authorities (Acts 5:17–42), a momentous evil began to surface within the church. While the threats of external adversaries held lesser weight, the internal danger proved more alarming as it originated from the very heart of the church itself. This internal evil emanating from within the ranks of its own members presented a far more formidable risk, in stark contrast to the avowed enemies outside. Despite the growing numbers embracing the gospel, this internal turmoil posed a significant and complex challenge: "A complaint by the Hellenists arose against the Hebrews because their widows were being neglected in the daily distribution" (Acts 6:1).[10]

The attitude of first-century CE Hebrew Jews towards Hellenistic Jews was complex and varied. Hellenistic Jews lived outside of the traditional Jewish homeland and were influenced by Greek culture and language. After Alexander the Great conquered the Persian Empire in the fourth century BCE, his generals divided his empire into several smaller kingdoms, which became known as the Hellenistic kingdoms. The Greeks ruled these kingdoms for over 200 years until the Romans took over in the first century BCE. The empire during the time of the early Jesus movement was Greco-Roman in culture. Jews living outside of Israel, in Asia Minor and other parts of the Greco-Roman world constituted the Jewish diaspora.[11] The Hellenists mentioned in Acts 6:1–7 were more than likely Jews from the Jewish dispersion who had settled in Jerusalem. Their language and ways were largely Greek. They had their

---

10. There is more going on in this passage than I can address here. Further insights into issues such as the respective roles in the community, the nature of the community, gender subordination, the dispute regarding "serving at table" versus "preaching the word," widows, and other issues, please consult commentaries such as Fitzmyer, *Acts*, 1998.

11. Diaspora refers to a people dispersed throughout a region outside of their homeland.

own synagogues (Acts 6:9); and funerary inscriptions excavated in Jerusalem attest to their extensive presence there.[12]

Some Hebrew Jews viewed Hellenistic Jews with suspicion and concern—as Jews far too influenced by foreign customs and beliefs. They were worried that Hellenistic Jews might compromise their Jewish identity and traditions. There were also Hebrew Jews, however, who embraced Hellenistic culture as an opportunity for intellectual exchange. They believed that Greek philosophy and language could enrich their understanding of the world and their own religious and intellectual development.

The relationship between Hebrew Jews and Hellenistic Jews was not uniform, and there were both tensions and points of connection between the two groups. The degree of acceptance or rejection of Hellenistic influences varied depending on the specific community and individuals involved. In the New Testament, particularly the book of Acts, there are accounts of conflicts between Hebrew Jews and Hellenistic Jews within the early Christian community. These conflicts were related to cultural and linguistic differences, but they were also part of the broader tensions between traditional Jewish practices and the influences of Hellenistic culture.[13] In Luke's account, the Hellenistic Jews from the diaspora found their own widows slighted, overlooked in the daily distribution of food to the weak and most vulnerable; this perceived insult lead to their discontent and protest. But this was far from a simple matter, for beneath the surface lies a complex reality where the subtextual becomes the textual.

The apostles follow a God who has broken open the binaries of honorable and dishonorable people, master and slave, us and them. Their differences and distance were collapsing in a community born of the Holy Spirit through the work of Christ. A new revelation was emerging around these apostles—a new worldview and way of living. Now a primary site of struggle for the new order began to appear in this dispute between the Hebrew and Hellenist Jews.[14] What revealed the threatening fissures within the newly forming community was the issue of caring for the weak and disadvantaged among the marginalized diaspora. These widows were the marginalized of the marginalized, those most vulnerable to the sway of power and influence. Luke's portrayal offers insights into the harsh realities of survival and support within patriarchal agrarian cultures, where widows and orphans depend on threads of mercy for their existence.

12. Polhill, *Acts*, 179.

13. Betz, "Hellenism," 3:127–35.

14. Jennings, *Acts*, 64.

Had I been in charge that day, I would have preached on the evils of bigotry and then recruited volunteers to collect day-old bread from local bakeries and appointed a few administratively gifted people to ensure the food would get distributed fairly. I am glad I was not there. I would have made a mess of things.

If the gospel was truly from God, it would have to confront the prejudice and discrimination that was present in the early church. The issue at hand was not food distribution, but rather the broken human impulse to dominate and discriminate against those who are different from us. Instead of addressing the prejudice directly, the apostles engaged in serving as the means of "overcoming evil with good." They asked the Hellenists and the Hebrews to select seven men from among themselves who were "of good repute, full of the Spirit and of wisdom" (v. 3). These men "from among them" had to be Spirit-filled, wise, and trusted because they were responsible for addressing the deep-seated issues of prejudice, bigotry, and discrimination that were present in the church. This was a radical act, as those with power typically repressed complaining minorities. In this case, however, the apostles handed the entire system over to those in conflict and called them to find a way forward in love and service.

In caring for those on the edge of survival, you often face the darkest parts of our humanity and the overwhelming lack of material resources. No wonder these men needed to be "of good repute, and full of the Spirit and wisdom." Wisdom was needed to establish righteousness, justice, and equity among them, and it must come from them, from their own, and not be imposed by others who may have their own agendas. These leaders needed to be known and trusted.

The spiritual impact was immediate; "the word of God continued to increase. . .the number of disciples multiplied greatly in Jerusalem, and a great many of the priests became obedient to the faith" (v. 7). Acts 6 powerfully illustrates that there is always more going on than meets the eye. Undercurrents, agendas, and human frailty are always mingling with the goodness and blessings of God. Like the disciples, we need men and women "of good repute, full of the Holy Spirit and wisdom" who can help us face our issues through generosity and radical welcome. The passage is an example of how wisdom can break spiritual and cultural strongholds that hold captive the people of God.

## Cultivating the Habits that Cultivate Your Heart

Wisdom is freely offered but not easily given. It is bestowed upon those who diligently search for it as though they are seeking hidden treasures of gold, silver, and precious stones. It demands a relentless pursuit, a quest of unwavering dedication (Prov 1:28; 2:1–15; 8:17; 25:2; 28:5; 29:26). It is for those desperate enough to ransack the storehouses of knowledge until they gain understanding that eventually leads to insight and culminates in wisdom. In the light of wisdom, illusions crumble, and the eternal is unveiled. It is in seeing God that we come to see everything else, not as it appears, but as it truly is.

The wise are not mere collectors of data, nor do they boast encyclopedic minds. They understand that the abundance of information alone does not satisfy the depths of their being, for true wisdom is not merely a collection of facts or clever insights but a deep communion with the source of all truth and understanding. Consequently, for the wise, it is not enough for the intellect to overflow with knowledge alone, for they grasp the truth: "Whoever trusts in his own mind is a fool" (Prov 28:26). The wise know that wisdom is not found in an intellect brimming with facts; rather, it is rooted in a heart shaped by the very hand of God. The heart attains wisdom through a life disciplined by the pursuit of knowing God. It is in seeking him, knowing him, and aligning one's path with him, that the soul gains wisdom. So, let us not be deceived by the allure of information alone, for wisdom transcends the mere accumulation of facts. It beckons us to embrace a deeper journey—a journey of the heart, where the touch of the Divine molds our being.

Among the verses of Proverbs, the heart emerges as central to gaining wisdom. The heart is mentioned at least seventy-five times in Proverbs. The Hebrew word for heart (*lēbāb*) appears a least seventy-five times in Proverb. *Lēbāb* is a term of depth and nuance that encompasses heart, mind, self, and inner person. It encompasses both the physical core and the intangible essence of our being—our emotions, desires, thoughts, motivations, and will. It is the inner sanctuary and wellspring of our life and the place where God wants to abide with us.

God longs to fill our hearts with wisdom, a treasure bestowed by the Almighty (Prov 2:10). Yet, this filling is not a passive affair. The heart must be cultivated with intention (Prov 4:23). Habits are those small daily choices that mold our inner landscape. Here lies the crux of the matter, to cultivate the habits that cultivate the heart. Notice how the following poem captures the power of habits.

> **WHO AM I?**
> *I am your constant companion.*
> *I am your greatest helper or heaviest burden.*
> *I will push you onward or drag you down to failure.*
> *I am completely at your command.*
> *Half the things you do you might just as well turn over to me*
> *and I will be able to do them quickly and correctly.*
> *I am easily managed—you must merely be firm with me.*
> *Show me exactly how you want something done and after a few lessons,*
> *I will do it automatically.*
> *I am the servant of all great people,*
> *and alas, of all failures as well.*
> *Those who are great, I have made great.*
> *Those who are failures, I have made failures.*
> *I am not a machine, though I work will all the precision of a machine*
> *plus the intelligence of a human.*
> *You may run me for profit or run me for ruin—it makes no difference to me.*
> *Take me, train me, be firm with me, and I will place the world at your feet.*
> *Be easy with me and I will destroy you.*
> *Who am I? I am habit!*[15]

Like ancient rites, these three habits bear the potential to cultivate within you a heart aligned with wisdom's cadence. These habits, like faithful companions, will guide you along the path of wisdom, lending strength and resilience to your pursuit. These habits will be familiar to you, for they have been woven throughout this book.

## Cultivate the Habit of Prayer

Leadership can feel overwhelming at times because it is. There is no way around it, leadership is demanding. Spiritual leadership is even more demanding, for not only does it require excellence in the craft of leading others, but it also requires integrity of heart before God. When you realize this, it makes you desperate for God, and this is OK, for prayer is no problem when you know how desperate you are.

Take the time each day to nurture and strengthen your personal relationship with God. It's important to customize the amount of time you

---

15. Author unknown

dedicate to this practice based on your unique role as a leader and your current life situation. If you are a leader who is also a mother of young children, your schedule will naturally differ from that of a leader without children in the home. The key is to discover the rhythms that effectively nourish your spiritual connection with God, regardless of the season of life you find yourself in. Cultivate your soul as a gardener cultivates the soil.[16]

As a leader, you will have plenty of things to worry about. I know worry doesn't fix anything, but I still have a whole list of things that I worry about. I have found the solution is to turn my worry list into a prayer list, just like it says in Philippians 4:6, "Don't worry about anything; instead, pray about everything" (NLT). It is a life-giving discipline to take everything I am concerned about as a leader and present it to God in prayer. I talk things over with him and ask for his wisdom and will in all these matters. I have found this practice essential for godly leadership.

I have also found praying the Psalms to be a powerful and meaningful practice. When I pray these ancient prayers and songs, I immerse myself in the emotions, praises, laments, and expressions of faith that have resonated with believers throughout history. I find in the Psalms a range of expressions that resonate with my own hopes, fears, regrets, complaints, experiences, and feelings. Through them, I experience a greater understanding of my own journey with God. They have become a constant companion, enriching my prayer life and fostering a deeper and more intimate relationship with God.

The daily practice of journaling helps me to slow my mind down so that I can listen to what I am thinking and feeling. I then submit those parts of myself to God through reflective prayer. I set forth before the Lord all the things I am dealing with, worried about, or hoping to achieve. I typically write everything out, and then I ask for wisdom to know what to do.[17] I do this until the peace of God fills my heart and mind. This is what the saints of old called "praying through." You pray not only about the problem, but you also pray "through it" to reach the other side. Pray through that list until the peace of God floods your heart and mind. You will then be in a better condition to hear from God. I realize journaling isn't for everyone. Find what works for you, then work it.

Prayer can also involve silence. There is a profound beauty in embracing silence. It is a restorative practice of being still in the presence of

16. Prov 1:7, 29; 2:5; 8:13; 9:10; 10:27; 14:26, 27; 15:16, 33; 16:6; 19:23; 22:4; 23:17; 29:25

17. Prov 2:3; 2 Chr 1:10; Ps 90:12; Eph 1:17; Col 1:9; Jas 1:5

God, without any expectations or words spoken. In the silence we can immerse ourselves in the pure joy of his presence, allowing this stillness to envelop us and foster a deep connection with him. Silence becomes a powerful language of the soul, where communion with God transcends words. The Psalmist said it is like a weaned child lying upon the mother's breast. There is no grasping, no fidgeting, no demanding, only lying calm and quieted in mother's presence, enveloped in love (Ps 131:2).

News reporter Dan Rather once asked Mother Teresa what she said during her prayers. She answered, "I listen." Dan turned the question and asked, "Well then, what does God say?" Mother Teresa smiled with confidence and answered, "Nothing. He just listens. And if you don't understand that, I can't explain it to you." Listen without speaking and without hearing, just being with him Who is Being Itself; this, too, is prayer.

## Cultivate the Habit of Listening

We grow in wisdom when we listen—listening not only to the divine voice of God (Prov 1:24) but also to the wisdom imparted by our parents (Prov 1:8; 3:1; 6:20), the counsel of Wisdom herself (Prov 6:23), the insight of the wise (Prov 13:14), the guidance of our spouse (Prov 31:26), the diverse perspectives of others (Prov 5:7; 8:32; 15:22), and yes, even the harsh words of our critics (Prov 13:1; 15:32). It is through the act of attentive listening that we nurture the soil of profound humility and an eagerness to learn—as fertile ground for the growth of prudence (Prov 15:5, 31, 32).

Listening, particularly to correction, criticism, instruction, and differing viewpoints, is no easy task. It demands effort and vulnerability. Yet, the rewards that spring forth from this labor are immeasurable. Perhaps this is why the call to listen appears at least twenty-one times in Proverbs. In *Life Together*, Dietrich Bonhoeffer tells us that in the realm of fellowship and love for others, there exists a fundamental service—one that begins with the act of listening.

Just as our love for God finds its inception in attentively hearing the word, our love for others is kindled by learning to listen to them. It is a reflection of God's boundless love for us that he not only imparts his word but graciously inclines his ear to our pleas.

When we lend our ears to others, we engage in God's work, offering a tangible display of love to our brothers and sisters. Yet, we often feel compelled to speak rather than listen, forgetting that listening can be a greater form of love and service than speaking.

We yearn for the sanctuary of an attentive ear, a space where we can be heard. Regrettably, we discover that such a haven can be scarce, for we often fill the void with our own words instead of providing receptive silence. We talk when we should listen. Bonhoeffer warns us that those who cannot listen to others will eventually find themselves incapable of listening to God as well. They become mere babblers in God's presence, disguising spiritual chatter and condescension as piety.

It is at this moment of deafness that the decline of spiritual life commences. It is an erosion of genuine communication, replaced by self-centered ramblings. Those who cannot listen patiently and attentively gradually lose their ability to speak meaningfully to others. If one believes their time is too precious to be spent in receptive silence, they will ultimately find no time for God or their fellow human beings but only for their own vain and trivial pursuits.

The essence of true fellowship and spiritual vibrancy resides in the humble art of listening—to God, to others, and to the quiet spaces where genuine connection can flourish. It is through the reverent act of listening that love finds its fullest expression, fostering a vibrant and authentic community of believers, bound together by the harmony of their shared understanding.[18]

Listening to others was hard for me as a young leader, and it can still be a challenge. For example, during one of our recent ministry team meetings, I did one of those questionnaires which probe your strengths and weaknesses and then produce a summary of the results. I did not like the results. I told our team, "I don't think this summary of me is correct. It says that because of how I process information and reach conclusions, I can tend to come across as arrogant or closed off to other opinions." Or some such nonsense! My whole team started laughing. "That is so true! We know, love, and trust you, but at times you do come across that way." I considered firing every one of them! Then I decided I should listen instead. I began to pay attention to how I come across in conversations. Proverbs tells us, "The way of a fool is right in his own eyes, but a wise man listens to advice" (Prov 12:15). And: "Cease to hear instruction, my son, and you will stray from the words of knowledge" (Prov 19:27). Through

---

18. Bonhoeffer, *Life Together*, 97–98.

listening, we break through our current limitations and perspectives, and we avoid the snares of death (Prov 13:14).

## Cultivate the Habit of Intentionality

To grow in wisdom also requires intentionally guarding how you live. Proverbs 4:1–27 instructs us to intentionally guard our heart, lips, eyes, ears, hands, and feet. To become wise, you must station a guard at all the gateways of your soul. The words you hear, the words you say, the things you see, the places you go, and the things you do—these plant seeds in your heart that shape your character. "Above all else, guard your heart, for everything you do flows from it" (Prov 4:23, NIV). These questions are helpful

- Are my words honoring of God and others?
- Are my words gracious and merciful, or are they harsh and judgmental?
- Have I allowed myself to look upon things that are destructive, defiling, or demeaning to myself or others?
- Have I listened to gossip, slander, profanity, or coarse language that hardens my heart against God and others?
- Are my hands working for justice and righteousness toward others?
- Am I walking with others in mercy, truth, and transparency?
- What is happening in the interior life of my being?
- Am I generous or greedy?
- Do I have anger, unforgiveness, bitterness, or hatred toward someone else?

Cultivating wisdom means being intentional about your companions. Proverbs 13:20 tells us, "Whoever walks with the wise becomes wise, but the companion of fools will suffer harm." Choose your friends carefully because you will become like them. Seek out people who are wiser, more experienced, and more knowledgeable than you are. You may only be a few friend upgrades away from your next breakthrough in life. Build relationships with people who have a growth mindset, who are always listening, learning, and growing. Surround yourself with people who inspire you to become more like Christ. Seek out people who challenge your thinking, have a different perspective, and are smarter than you. Remember: If you are the smartest person in the room, you are in the wrong room. Walk with the wise, and you too will become wise (Prov 13:20; 20:26).

Intentionality in all areas of life is the key. "The wise are cautious and turn away from evil, but the fool throws off restraint and is careless" (Prov 14:16, NRSVue). The wise have learned to watch their paths and to avoid "a thorny, treacherous road" (Prov 22:5, NLT). Wise leaders are intentional about their companions and careful about their paths. So, choose both carefully, for they will determine your character and your destiny.

## Spend Time in Wisdom's Dwelling

Our journey together now draws to a close. As we part ways, may we heed the call that resonates within our souls and that has kept us together through these many pages—to seek wisdom with hearts ablaze and minds focused—to follow wisdom and lead wisely.

May we embrace the discipline of the quest, knowing that the pursuit of God and his ways holds the key to unlocking the treasures of wisdom. It is through this pursuit that our eyes are enlightened, enabling us to discern truth from falsehood and navigate the path of wisdom with grace, elegance, and purpose.

Throughout our time together, I have shared with you some of the most important leadership lessons I have gleaned from my daily exploration of Proverbs for over three decades. Yet, we have but barely scratched the surface of the vast riches contained within this timeless book of wisdom. There are depths yet unexplored; insights awaiting your arrival as you take your rightful place at Wisdom's table, eagerly listening to her voice and walking upon her paths.

As we part ways, may the lessons learned on our shared journey resonate within you, propelling you forward on the path of wisdom. May your leadership be marked by the presence of God, the illumination of truth, and the gentle voice of Wisdom herself. Go now as a beacon of light in this world, a testament to the transformative power of wisdom. This generation yearns for leaders adorned with wisdom, and I pray that you are an answer to this cry.

# Discussion Questions

## Chapter 1: A Book for Leaders

1. The World Economic Forum asked, "What skills do leaders need to win back the confidence of their populations?" What are the two most essential skills you believe are needed for the cultural context you are currently serving?

2. The basic meaning of Proverbs is "a comparison" because a proverb typically seeks to instruct by making a comparison. Many of Solomon's proverbs are comparisons or contrasts. Comparisons are often indicated by the word "like," and contrasts are often indicated by the word "better." Considering leadership in the present-day world, what are two or three comparisons or contrasts you can draw when comparing leadership styles today?

3. The book of Proverbs invites you to unleash the power of God's word in your leadership. What are specific areas of your leadership where you would like to see the power of the Bible unleashed right now?

## Chapter 2: Wisdom and Folly

1. Through reading Proverbs, we can begin to see wisdom in numerous pathways, Wisdom will *protect* (Prov 2:1–12), *direct* (Prov 3), and *perfect* (Prov 4:1–9). As you think about these three directives, which one do you feel you need the most improvement in as a leader, and why?

2. No one is born wise; we all start at the place with folly locked in our hearts. And yet, our ability to obtain wisdom comes from a life of disciplined obedience. Wisdom is freely given, yet it does not come free. How would you describe your journey of obtaining wisdom and removing folly? What has it cost you to reach the point you are at today?

3. Humility is to clothe leaders like *humus* clothes the soil. Just as *humus* cultivates healthy soil, humility cultivates healthy leadership and culture. What has been your experience with humble leaders? How have they brought health to your organization or community? In what ways has their behavior caused you to want to follow them or not?

## Chapter 3: Wise and Foolish Leaders

1. Where you start is not as important as where you finish. You can move from folly to wisdom or wisdom to folly. What actions and attitudes are you choosing to ensure that you position yourself to "finish well?"

2. A foolish leader is unteachable because he will only listen to himself and those who agree with him (Prov 12:15). In your experiences as a leader, how have you dealt with a leader who is unteachable? How did it affect your relationship with this person(s)? How did you navigate the situation?

3. No one is born wise. However, we can choose to become wise. Wise leaders choose:

   - *To fear of the Lord*
   - *To guard their heart*
   - *To cry out for wisdom*
   - *To practice self-discipline*
   - *To listen and learn*

   Which of these do you find as a strength? Which of these should you focus on at this season of your growth as a leader? What do you need to adjust, change, or start doing?

## Chapter 4: The Intoxicating Attraction

1. Why do you think Proverbs spends so much time and effort talking about sexual temptations?

2. Sexual integrity is essential for godly leadership. Building this integrity requires intentionality and discipline, especially in the highly sexualized world we live in today. The good news is that the Bible offers a clear and simple solution: RUN! Based on what you have just read, and in your own words, what does it mean to run from sexual temptation? What practices do, or should, you have in place to help protect yourself in the area of sexual temptation?

3. While sexual sin is destructive, sex within the boundaries established by God is a wonderful gift. What are two or three ways you can cultivate a healthy celebration of the gift of sex?

## Chapter 5: Husbands and Wives

1. While marriage can be awesome, it can also be miserable if laden with misconceptions. These misconceptions create tremendous pressure, unrealistic expectations, and false obligations. Of the five misconceptions listed below what are one or two that you have wrestled with personally, and how would you describe your struggle?

   - *Is "Biblical Marriage" Biblical?*

   - *Is "Normal" Normal?*

   - *Is Something wrong with her?*

   - *Does this church focus on my family?*

   - *Does this church make me look fit?*

2. Disagreements and conflicts are common to all human relationships. However, marriage takes it to a whole other level by digging into the deepest levels of human identity, worth, pride, and self-centeredness. The digging removes the dirt within us and reveals the gold. If you are married, what does the process of digging for "gold" look like right now? What areas of your marriage need to be opened to this digging process? Do you have any areas in your relationship that you have said, "No digging allowed?" If yes, why?

If you are single, What relationships do you have that help you "dig through the dirt?" What is your experience navigating conflicts and disagreements with those close to you?

3. At the wedding, the husband and wife begin a lifetime of choosing "I do." Your daily choices are the incremental steps that eventually build a good marriage. Growing old is inevitable, growing up is a choice. Based on the *Noble Choices for a husband and a wife*, what are one or two areas that you can identify as places of growth in your marriage? What is the next step you need to take to grow in these areas?

## Wives—

- *Chooses to be the crown of glory in her marriage.*
- *Chooses to build her husband up.*
- *Chooses to embrace her beauty.*
- *Chooses to be content.*

## Husband—

- *Chooses to cherish his wife.*
- *Chooses to be wise rather than foolish child.*
- *Chooses to be responsible.*
- *Chooses self-control rather than controlling others.*

## Chapter 6: Parents and Children

1. Proverbs elevates the status of the family when guided by the wisdom of God as the ideal place for human flourishing. What were two or three key points in this chapter for you? Why?

2. Parenting and leadership are easily linked together because your priorities as a parent are pretty much the same as your priorities as a leader. This chapter identifies eight priorities of parents and leaders. After reviewing the list below, can you identify specific ways these

priorities have been strengthened or neglected in your parenting and leadership?

- *Wise Parents and Wise Leaders Pursue Shalom*
- *Wise Parents and Wise Leaders Protect from Dangers*
- *Wise Parents and Wise Leaders Provide Security*
- *Wise Parents and Wise Leaders Nurture Life*
- *Wise Parents and Wise Leaders Equip for Wise Living*
- *Wise Parents and Wise Leaders Create Culture*
- *Wise Parents and Wise Leaders Know Their Limits*
- *Wise Parents and Wise Leaders Persevere*

3. We read that "the family you grew up in is the place where you typically learn to become who you are and where you first learn your values and beliefs." Have you taken the necessary time to examine your family of origin and its influence on your thinking and behavior? If yes, what did you discover? If not, what is one next step you could take in discovering this new reality?

## Chapter 7: Friends, Foes, and Neighbors

1. As a leader, you do not get to choose those who follow you. However, when it comes to friends, you do get to choose. Proverbs tells us, "The righteous choose their friends carefully, but the way of the wicked leads them astray" (Prov 12:26). How has your leadership role changed the landscape of your personal relationships? How do you choose your friends? What steps have you taken as a leader to choose your friends wisely?

2. As a leader, you will have people angry with you. It is inevitable. Sometimes, they become your enemy. What insights did you receive from this chapter for dealing with foes? In what ways are you learning to walk in love towards those who have decided to be your enemy?

3. How are you learning to love your neighbor in thought, word, and deed?

## Chapter 8: The Lazy and the Diligent

1. Finishing well means different things to different people. What does finishing well mean to you? Can you describe what finish well looks like for you? What do you need to set in place for you to finish well?

2. Lazy leaders idly dream of someday or someplace that will be different, never realizing "the eyes of a fool are on the ends of the earth" (Prov 17:24), but "the soul of the diligent is richly supplied" (Prov 13:4). How can you cultivate greater diligence in your life right now?

3. The Church Fathers considered faintheartedness the greatest danger of the soul. When your heart grows faint, you can become despondent, you are unable to see the light or even to desire it. What is your experience with faintheartedness?

## Chapter 9: The Wise Leader's Use of Money

1. How has mammon influenced your life and ministry? What adjustments do you need to make?

2. Has your management of finances ever come into question? If so, how did you navigate the situation? What acts of accountability and transparency do you need set in place to ensure the financial integrity of the resources entrusted to you by God?

3. How are generosity and compassion growing in you as an individual and as a leader?

## Chapter 10: The Wise Leader's Use of Words

1. The author confessed, "I did a lot of damage to a lot of people that I love. Some of the damage has been healed. Some of the damage has left scars. Some is still present." Death and life are truly in the power of the tongue. Have you hurt others with your words? How did you heal or correct the situation? Have you been hurt by the words of others? If so, how are you finding healing, forgiveness, and growth?

2. Proverbs 20:12 states, "*The hearing ear and the seeing eye, the LORD has made them both.*" Take this to heart, your first job as a leader is not to lead but to listen. On a scall of 1–10, how would you rate your

ability to listen? How would your spouse rate your ability to listen? How would those you lead rate your ability to listen? What is one step you could take today to make you a better listener?

3. *"The way of a fool is right in his own eyes, but a wise man listens to advice."* (Prov 12:15). If you only listen to those with whom you already agree, you are not learning anything new, you are only having your opinion reinforced. If you listen to those who see and think differently, then you are learning and growing. What conversations are you having with those who might see things differently than you do? What is one action step can you take to broaden your perspective?

## Chapter 11: Righteous and Wicked Leaders

1. "Noah found favor in the eyes of the Lord." (Gen 6:8). We know nothing about Noah's ability as a carpenter, nor do we know of his skills in animal husbandry, nor his ability to navigate the waters of the flood. All we know of him is his character, showing us once again that character is destiny. How would you describe the current condition of your character? What practices do you have in place that will build your character over time?

2. What were your reactions to the stories about Pastor Hank and Pastor John? Have you witnessed similar acts of violence by respected leaders? Can you identify times when you have been tempted to use, or justify, acts of violence in leadership?

3. To be called to lead God's people is a serious responsibility—the great pantheon of leadership retains a vacant seat for a single good person; the wise leader who embodies righteousness, justice, and integrity. Of these three biblical traits defined in this chapter, which one is most needed in your ministry leadership? And what course corrections need to be made today?

## Chapter 12: Cultivating the Habits that Cultivate the Heart

1. Wisdom beckons us, her children, to open our hearts, heed her voice, and follow her ways with unwavering devotions. To those

who diligently seek her, who wait at her threshold, life's richness and Gods favor shall be their reward. First, what part of wisdom have you come to realize has truly taken root in your life in your ministry and leadership from Proverbs? And second, what is one or two pearls of wisdom that have you received that you desire to implement into your leadership?

2. As we read through the story of Joseph, we witness the transformative power of God's word in shaping his character. We also saw the perils of unchecked power and the cruel consequences of Josh's economic policies. How has power affected your leadership and ministry? What are some observations you have regarding the story of Joseph? How can you apply what you have learned in this chapter to your leadership?

3. The chapter ends with the challenge to cultivate the *Habit of Prayer, the Habit of Listening, and the Habit of Intentionality*. Which of these habits need to be strengthened, implemented, or completely overhauled in your life and leadership? What steps can you take to cultivate these habits that cultivate your heart?

# Bibliography

Aitken, Kenneth T. "נָשִׂיא (nāśîʾ I) chief, king (#5954) < נָשָׂא (nāśāʾ) lift up." In VanGemeren, Willem, ed., *New International Dictionary of Old Testament Theology & Exegesis* (Grand Rapids, MI: Zondervan, 1997), 171–72.

Allen, David. *Getting Things Done.* New York: Penguin, 2015.

Alter, Robert. *The Art of Biblical Poetry.* New York: Perseus, 2011.

Andreassen, Cecilie Schou. "Workaholism: An Overview and Current Status of the Research." *Journal of Behavioral Addictions* 3, no. 1 (2014): 1–11. https://doi.org/10.1556/jba.2.2013.017.

Archer, Gleason L. "1015 כָּסַף," In *Theological Wordbook of the Old Testament*, ed. R. Laird Harris, et al. Chicago: Moody, 1999.

Arendt, Hannah. *Eichmann in Jerusalem: A Report on the Banality of Evil.* London: Penguin, 2006.

Aristotle, and Reeve C D C. *Politics: A new translation.* Indianapolis, IN: Hackett, 2017.

Asad, Sarosh, and Eugene Sadler-Smith. "Differentiating Leader Hubris and Narcissism on the Basis of Power." *Leadership* 16, no. 1 (February 2020): 39–61. https://doi.org/10.1177/1742715019885763.

Ball, R. Glenn, and Darrell Puls. "Frequency of Narcissistic Personality Disorder in Pastors: A Preliminary Study." http://www.darrellpuls.com/images/AACC_2015_Paper_NPD_in_Pastors.pdf.

Balz, Horst Robert and Gerhard Schneider, *Exegetical Dictionary of the New Testament.* Grand Rapids, Mich.: Eerdmans, 1990.

Barna Group, in partnership with World Vision, "82% of Young Adults Say Society Is in a Leadership Crisis," October 30, 2019.https://www.barna.com/research/leadership-crisis/.

Barth, Karl. *Church Dogmatics.* Peabody, MA: Hendrickson Pub, 2010. III.4.

———. *The Word of God and the Word of Man.* New York, NY: Harper and Row, 1957.

Belcher, Richard P. *Finding Favour in the Sight of God: A Theology of Wisdom Literature.* Downers Grove, IL: IVP Academic, 2018.

Bellezza, Silvia, Neeru Paharia, and Anat Keinan. "Conspicuous Consumption of Time: When Busyness and Lack of Leisure Time Become a Status Symbol." *Journal of Consumer Research*, 2016. https://doi.org/10.1093/jcr/ucw076.

Bellis, Alice Ogden. *Helpmates, Harlots, and Heroes: Women's Stories in the Hebrew Bible.* Louisville, KY: Westminster John Knox, 2007.

Bellis, Alice Ogden, et al. *Proverbs.* Collegeville, MN: Liturgical, 2018.

Berlin, Adele. "Parallelism." In *The Anchor Yale Bible Dictionary.* New York: Doubleday, 1992.

Bertram, Georg. "Ὕβρις, Ὑβρίζω, Ἐνυβρίζω, Ὑβριστής." In *Theological Dictionary of the New Testament,* ed. Gerhard Kittel, et al. Grand Rapids, MI: Eerdmans, 1964. 8:294–307.

Betlyon, John W. and Mark Allan Powell, "Money," in *The HarperCollins Bible Dictionary (Revised and Updated),* ed. Mark Allan Powell. New York: HarperCollins, 2011.

Betz, Hans Dieter. "Hellenism." In *The Anchor Yale Bible Dictionary,* ed. David Noel Freedman. New York: Doubleday, 1992.

Bonhoeffer, Dietrich. *Life Together.* New York: Harper & Row, 1954.

Bowling, Andrew. "1071 לָבַב (lābab) ravish." In *Theological Wordbook of the Old Testament,* ed. R. Laird Harris, et al. Chicago: Moody, 1999.

Brown, Francis, Samuel Rolles Driver, and Charles Augustus Briggs, *Enhanced Brown-Driver-Briggs Hebrew and English Lexicon.* Oxford 1977.

Brown, William P. "Proverbs 8:22–31." *Interpretation,* (2009). https://doi.org/10.1177/002096430906300308.

———. *Wisdom's Wonder: Character, Creation, and Crisis in Bible's Wisdom Literature.* Grand Rapids, MI: Eerdmans, 2014.

———. "The Pedagogy of Proverbs 10:1—31:9." in *Character and Scripture: Moral Formation, Community, and Biblical Interpretation,* edited by William P. Brown, 150–82. Grand Rapids, MI: Eerdmans, 2002.

Bruckner, J. K. "Ethics." In *Dictionary of the Old Testament: Pentateuch,* ed. T. Desmond Alexander and David W. Baker. Downers Grove, IL: InterVarsity, 2003.

Butcher, Pat. "Athens Marathon Record Broken by Nearly Two Minutes: News: World Athletics." worldathletics.org. https://www.worldathletics.org/news/news/athens-marathon-record-broken-by-nearly-two-m.

Byrley, Chris. "Healing." In *Lexham Theological Wordbook,* ed. Douglas Mangum et al., Lexham Bible Reference Series. Bellingham, WA: Lexham, 2014.

Carney, Dana R. et al. "People with Power are Better Liars." Columbia University (2009). https://wwwo.gsb.columbia.edu/mygsb/faculty/research/pubfiles/3510/Power.Lying.pdf

Carr, G. Lloyd. "2401 שָׁלֵם (šālēm)," In *Theological Wordbook of the Old Testament,* ed. R. Laird Harris, et al. Chicago: Moody, 1999.

Cavelos, Jeanne, *The Science of Star Wars.* New York: St. Martin's Griffin, 2000.

Chesterton, G. K. "The Drift from Domesticity." Essay. In The Collected Works of G.K. Chesterton. Volume 3. Prunedale, CA. Ignatius, 1990.

Chesterton, G. K. *Orthodoxy.* London: Hodder & Stoughton. 1999.

Clinton, Robert J. "Finishing Well—Six Characteristics." (2007): http://storage.cloversites.com/missouristateassociationoffreewillbaptists/documents/Finishing-Well-Six-Characteristics.pdf

Collins, Raymond F. "Golden Rule." In *The Anchor Yale Bible Dictionary,* volume 2. ed. David Noel Freedman. New York: Doubleday, 1992.

Covey, Stephen R. *The 7 Habits of Highly Effective People: Powerful Lessons in Personal Change.* New York: Simon & Schuster, 2020.

Dayton, Howard. "The Bible on Money." 2021. https://compass1.org/the-bible-on-money/

Dershowitz, Alan. *Abraham: The World's First (but Certainly Not Last) Jewish Lawyer.* New York: Nextbooks/Schocken, 2015.

DigitalHubUSA. "Average American Worries about Money Six Times a Day." digitalhub US. https://swnsdigital.com/us/2022/01/average-american-worries-about-money-six-times-a-day/.

Dunham, Kyle C. "Structure and Theology in Proverbs: Its Function as an Educational Program for Novice Leaders in Ancient Israel," *Bulletin for Biblical Research 29, no. 3 (2019) 361–88.*

Dweck, Carol S. *Mindset: The New Psychology of Success.* New York: Ballantine, 2016.

Einstein, Albert. *The World as I See It.* New York. Barnes & Noble, 2007.

Elwell, W. A. & P.W. Comfort. "Poetry, Biblical." In *Tyndale Bible Dictionary.* Wheaton, IL: Tyndale House, 2001.

———. "Weights and Measures." in *Tyndale Bible Dictionary.* Wheaton, IL: Tyndale, 2001.

Elwell, Walter A. and Barry J. Beitzel, "Patience," in *Baker Encyclopedia of the Bible.* Grand Rapids, MI: Baker, 1988.

———. "Righteousness," in *Baker Encyclopedia of the Bible.* Grand Rapids, MI: Baker, 1988.

Enns, Peter. *How the Bible Actually Works: In Which I Explain How an Ancient, Ambiguous, and Diverse Book Leads Us to Wisdom Rather than Answers-and Why That's Great News.* New York. Harper, 2020.

Estes, Daniel J. *Hear, My Son: Teaching and Learning in Proverbs 1–9.* Leicester: Apollos, 2003.

Fee, Gordon D., and Douglass Stuart, *How to Read the Bible for All Its Worth.* Grand Rapids, MI: Zondervan, 2014.

Fisher, Milton C. "1393 נפל." In *Theological Wordbook of the Old Testament*, ed. R. Laird Harris, et al. Chicago: Moody, 1999.

Fiske, Alan Page, and Tage Shakti Rai. *Virtuous Violence: Hurting and Killing to Create, Sustain, End, and Honor Social Relationships.* Cambridge: Cambridge University Press, 2015.

Fitzmyer, Joseph A. *The Acts of the Apostles. The Anchor Yale Bible Commentaries.* New Haven: Yale University Press, 1998.

Gaventa, Beverly Roberts. *Our Mother Saint Paul.* Louisville: Westminster John Knox, 2007.

Gesenius, Wilhelm, and Samuel Prideaux Tregelles, in *Gesenius' Hebrew and Chaldee Lexicon to the Old Testament Scriptures.* Bellingham, WA: Logos Bible Software, 2003.

Goldingay, John. *Do We Need the New Testament? Letting The Old Testament Speak for Itself.* Downers Grove, IL: IVP Academic, 2015.

———. *The First Testament: A New Translation.* Downers Grove, IL: InterVarsity, 2018.

———. *Genesis for Everyone, Part 1: Chapters 1–16.* Louisville, KY: Westminster John Knox, 2010.

———. *Proverbs, Ecclesiastes, and Song of Songs for Everyone*, Old Testament for Everyone. Louisville, KY: Westminster John Knox, 2014.

Goodwin, Doris Kearns. *Team of Rivals: The Political Genius of Abraham Lincoln.* New York: Simon & Schuster, 2006.

Gordis, Robert. "Religion, Wisdom and History in the Book of Esther—A New Solution to an Ancient Crux," *JBL* 100 (1981) 359.

Guenther, Lisa. *Solitary Confinement: Social Death and Its Afterlives.* Minneapolis: University Of Minnesota Press, 2013.

Hall, Christopher A. *Living Wisely with the Church Fathers*. Westmont, IL: IVP Academic, 2017.

Hamilton, Victor P. "299 גָּאָה (gā 'â)." In *Theological Wordbook of the Old Testament*. ed. R. Laird Harris, et al. Chicago: Moody, 1999.

———. "Marriage: Old Testament and Ancient Near East," in *The Anchor Yale Bible Dictionary*, ed. David Noel Freedman. New York: Doubleday, 1992.

Harrison, R. K. *Leviticus: An Introduction and Commentary*. Downers Grove, IL: InterVarsity, 1980.

Hauck, Friedrich. "Μαμωνᾶς." In *Theological Dictionary of the New Testament*, edited by Gerhard Kittel, et al. Grand Rapids, MI: Eerdmans, 1964.

Hayes, E. R. "Justice, Righteousness." In *Dictionary of the Old Testament: Prophets*, ed. Mark J. Boda and Gordon J. McConville. Downers Grove, IL: IVP Academic, 2012.

Healey, Joseph P. "Peace: Old Testament." In *The Anchor Yale Bible Dictionary*, volume 5. ed. David Noel Freedman. New York: Doubleday, 1992.

Heschel, Abraham. *Wisdom of Heschel*. New York: Farrar, Straus and Giroux, 1985.

Hildebrandt, Wilf. *An Old Testament Theology of the Spirit of God*. Eugene, OR: Wipf & Stock, 2019.

Hirschfeld, Mary L. *Aquinas and the Market: Toward a Humane Economy*. London: Harvard University Press, 2018.

Jennings, Willie James. *Acts*. Louisville, KY: Westminster John Knox, 2017.

Johnson, Marguerite. *Sexuality in Greek and Roman Society and Literature: A Sourcebook*. New York, NY: Routledge Taylor & Francis Ltd, 2022.

Jorgenson, Kiara A., and Alan G. Padgett. *Ecotheology: A Christian Conversation*. William B. Eerdmans, 2020.

Kierkegaard, Søren, Howard V. Hong, and Edna H. Hong. *Works of love*. Princeton, NJ: Princeton University Press, 1998.

Kilnam, Cha. "Joseph's Unjust Economic Policies in Genesis 47:13–26," *Leaven* 24. 4 (2016): Article 6.

Kittel, Gerhard, Gerhard Friedrich, and Geoffrey William Bromiley, *Theological Dictionary of the New Testament, Abridged in One Volume*. Grand Rapids, MI: W.B. Eerdmans, 1985.

Knight, George W. *The Pastoral Epistles: A Commentary on the Greek Text*, New International Greek Testament Commentary. Grand Rapids, MI: W.B. Eerdmans, 1992.

Kruse, Colin G. *The Letters of John*. Grand Rapids, MI: W.B. Eerdmans, 2000.

Lange, John Peter, et al., *A Commentary on the Holy Scriptures: Proverbs*. Bellingham, WA: Logos Bible Software, 2008.

Langford, Justin. "Friendship." In *Lexham Theological Wordbook*, ed. Douglas Mangum et al., Bellingham, WA: Lexham, 2014.

Law, T. M. *When God Spoke Greek: The Septuagint and the Making of Western Civilization*. Oxford University Press, 2013.

Lewis, C. S. *The Abolition of Man*. New York: Touchstone, 1996.

———. *The Four Loves*. San Francisco: HarperOne, 2017.

———. *Letters to Malcolm, Chiefly on Prayer*. New York: HarperOne, 2017.

———. *The Problem of Pain*. London: HarperCollins, 2002.

———. *The Weight of Glory and Other Addresses*. New York: HarperOne, 2001.

Lipman-Blumen, Jean. *The Allure of Toxic Leaders: Why We Follow Destructive Bosses and Corrupt Politicians—and How We Can Survive Them*. Oxford: Oxford University Press, 2006.

Livingston, G. Herbert. "2222 רָשַׁע (rāša ') be wicked, act wickedly." In *Theological Wordbook of the Old Testament*, ed. R. Laird Harris, et al. Chicago: Moody, 1999.

Longman III, Tremper. "Fear of the Lord," ed. Peter Enns, *Dictionary of the Old Testament: Wisdom, Poetry & Writings*. Downers Grove, IL: IVP Academic, 2008.

———. *Proverbs*. Ada, MI: Baker Academic, 2006.

Lookadoo, Jonathon. "Body." In *Lexham Theological Wordbook*, ed. Douglas Mangum et al. Bellingham, WA: Lexham, 2014.

Lu, Francis G., ed. *Diagnostic and Statistical Manual of Mental Disorders, Fifth Edition Text Revision: DSM-5-TR*. Washington, DC: American Psychiatric Association, 2022.

Malory, Thomas, and Dorsey Armstrong. *Sir Thomas Malory's Morte Darthur a New Modern English Translation Based on the Winchester Manuscript*. West Lafayette, Ind: Parlor, 2009.

Marsden, George M. *Jonathan Edwards: A Life*. New Haven, CT: Yale University Press, 2004.

Martens, Elmer A. "1971 צָרַע (ṣāra') be diseased of skin, leprous."In *Theological Wordbook of the Old Testament*, ed. R. Laird Harris, et al. Chicago: Moody, 1999.

Mathews, K. A. *Genesis 1–11:26*, vol. 1A, The New American Commentary. Nashville: Broadman & Holman, 1996.

Maximus, and George C. Berthold. *Maximus Confessor: Selected Writings*. New York: Paulist, 1985.

Maxwell, John C. *Developing the Leader Within You 2.0*. Nashville: HarperCollins Leadership, 2019.

May, Simon. *Love: A History*. New Haven, CT: Yale University Press, 2012.

McCarraher, Eugene. *The Enchantments of Mammon: How Capitalism Became the Religion of Modernity*. Cambridge: Belknap, 2019.

McComiskey, Thomas E., "137 אָנֹשׁ, (issa)" In *Theological Wordbook of the Old Testament*, ed. R. Laird Harris, et al. Chicago: Moody, 1999

McKnight, Scot. *The Blue Parakeet: Rethinking How You Read the Bible*. Grand Rapids, MI: Zondervan, 2018.

Merrill, Randall. "Authority." in *Lexham Theological Wordbook*, ed. Douglas Mangum et al. Bellingham, WA: Lexham, 2014.

Meyendorff, John. *Marriage: An Orthodox Perspective* (St. Vladimir's Seminary Press, 2000).

Moisés Silva, ed., *New International Dictionary of New Testament Theology and Exegesis*. Grand Rapids, MI: Zondervan, 2014.

Mojola, Aloo Osotsi. "The Power of Bible Translation." In *Priscilla Papers*, vol. 33, no. 2 (Spring 2019) 3–7.

Moon, Ruth. "Founder of World's Largest Megachurch Convicted of Embezzling $12 Million," *Christianity Today*, February 24, 2014. https://www.christianitytoday. com/news/2014/february/founder-of-worlds-largest-megachurch-convicted-cho-yoido.html.

Moore, Carey A. "Esther, Book of." In *The Anchor Yale Bible Dictionary*, ed. David Noel Freedman. New York: Doubleday, 1992.

Moore, James D., "Ishtar." In *The Lexham Bible Dictionary*, ed. John D. Barry. Bellingham, WA: Lexham. 2016

Mounce, W.D. *Mounce's Complete Expository Dictionary of Old & New Testament Words*. Grand Rapids, MI: Zondervan. 2006.

Murphy, Roland E. *Proverbs*. Word Biblical Commentary. Dallas: Thomas Nelson, 1998.

Myers, Allen C. "Marriage." In *The Eerdmans Bible Dictionary*. Grand Rapids, MI: Eerdmans, 1987.

———. "Poetry." In *The Eerdmans Bible Dictionary*. Grand Rapids, MI: Eerdmans, 1987.

Nettelhorst, R. P. "Love." In *Lexham Theological Wordbook*, ed. Douglas Mangum et al., Lexham Bible Reference Series. Bellingham, WA: Lexham, 2014.

———. "Wisdom." In *Lexham Theological Wordbook*. Bellingham, WA: Lexham, 2014.

Niebuhr, Reinhold. *Reinhold Niebuhr: Major works on religion and politics*. New York, NY: The Library of America, 2015.

Oswalt, J. N. "God." In *Dictionary of the Old Testament: Wisdom, Poetry & Writings*, ed. Tremper Longman III and Peter Enns. Downers Grove, IL: IVP Academic, 2008.

Paton, Lewis Bayles. *A Critical and Exegetical Commentary on The Book of Esther*. New York: T. & T. Clark, 1976.

Philo. *The Works of Philo: Complete and Unabridged*. Translated by Charles Duke Yonge. Peabody, MA: Hendrickson, 1995.

Piketty, Thomas, and Arthur Goldhammer. *Capital in the Twenty-first Century*. Cambridge, MA: Belknap, 2017.

Polhill, John B. *Acts*, vol. 26, The New American Commentary. Nashville: Broadman & Holman, 1992.

Raine, Susan, and Stephen Kent, "The grooming of children for sexual abuse in religious settings: Unique characteristics and select case studies," *Aggression and Violent Behavior*, vol. 48 (Sept–Oct 2019) 180–89.

Ratner, Gerald. *Gerald Ratner: The Rise and Fall—and Rise Again*. Chichester: Capstone, 2008.

Redding, Jonathan D. "Violence," in *Lexham Theological Wordbook*, ed. Douglas Mangum et al. Bellingham, WA: Lexham, 2014.

Reeves, Ryan M., and Charles E. Hill. *Know How We Got Our Bible*. Grand Rapids, MI: Zondervan, 2018.

Reyburn, William David, and Euan McG. Fry, *A Handbook on Proverbs*. New York: United Bible Societies, 2000.

Roberts, Alexander, et al. eds., "Remains of the Second and Third Centuries: Melito, the Philosopher," in *Fathers of the Third and Fourth Centuries: The Twelve Patriarchs, Excerpts and Epistles, the Clementina, Apocrypha, Decretals, Memoirs of Edessa and Syriac Documents, Remains of the First Ages*, trans. B. P. Pratten, vol. 8, The Ante-Nicene Fathers. Buffalo, NY: Christian Literature Company, 1886.

Robertson, Ian H. "Petraeus, Sex and the Aphrodisiac of Power." *Psychology Today*, November 13, 2012. https://www.psychologytoday.com/us/blog/the-winner-effect/201211/petraeus-sex-and-the-aphrodisiac-power-0

Ben-Chorin, Kritik S. *des Estherbuches: Eine theologische Streitschrift* (Jerusalem:1938), 5.

Sacks, Jonathan. *Lessons in leadership: A weekly reading of the Jewish Bible*. New Milford, CT: Maggid, 2015.

———. *Leviticus: The Book of Holiness*. New Milford, CT: Maggid, 2015.

Sandmel, Samuel. *The Enjoyment of Scripture*. New York: Oxford University Press, 1972.

Schmemann, Alexander. *Great Lent: Journey to Pascha*. New York: St. Vladimir's Seminary Press, 2001.

Schneiders, Sandra M. *The Revelatory Text: Interpreting the New Testament as Sacred Scripture*. Collegeville, MN: Liturgical, 1999.

Scullion, J. J. "Righteousness: Old Testament," in *The Anchor Yale Bible Dictionary*, ed. David Noel Freedman. New York: Doubleday, 1992.

Shakespeare, William, Barbara A. Mowat, and Paul Werstine. *The Tragedy of Macbeth*. New York: Simon & Schuster Paperbacks, 2013.

Skinner, John. "Righteousness in OT." In *A Dictionary of the Bible: Dealing with Its Language, Literature, and Contents Including the Biblical Theology*, ed. James Hastings et al. New York: Charles Scribner's Sons, 1912.

Smalley, Stephen S. *1, 2, 3 John*. Dallas: Word, 1984.

Spicq, C. & J. D. Ernest, *Theological lexicon of the New Testament*. Peabody, MA: Hendrickson, 1994. vol. 3, 359.

Swanson, James. "9514 תִּפְאֶרֶת (tip̄·ʾě·rěṯ)," *Dictionary of Biblical Languages with Semantic Domains: Hebrew: Old Testament*. Oak Harbor, WA: Logos Research Systems, 1997.

———. "9514 תִּפְאֶרֶת (tip̄·ʾě·rěṯ)," *Dictionary of Biblical Languages with Semantic Domains: Hebrew: Old Testament*. Oak Harbor, WA: Logos Research Systems, 1997.

Talmon, Shemarayahu. "'Wisdom' in the Book of Esther," *Vetus Testamentum* 13, no. 4 (1963) 419–55. https://doi.org/10.2307/1516862.

Tocqueville, Alexis de, Harvey C. Mansfield, and Delba Winthrop. *Democracy in America*. Chicago: University of Chicago Press, 2000.

Tolkien J. R. R., *The Lord of the Rings*. Boston: Houghton Mifflin, 2005.

Tucker Jr., W. D. "Psalms 1: Book Of." In *Dictionary of the Old Testament: Wisdom, Poetry & Writings*. Nottingham, England: IVP Academic, 2008.

Waltke, Bruce K. *The Book of Proverbs, Chapters 1–15*. Grand Rapids, MI: Eerdmans, 2004.

———. *The Book of Proverbs, Chapters 16–31*. Grand Rapids, MI: Eerdmans, 2005.

Waltke, Bruce K., and Ivan De Silva. *Proverbs: A Shorter Commentary*. Grand Rapids, MI: Eerdmans, 2021.

Weber, Max, Peter R. Baehr, Gordon C. Wells, and Max Weber. *The Protestant Ethic and the "Spirit" of Capitalism and Other Writings*. New York: Penguin, 2012.

Wenham, Gordon J. *Numbers: An Introduction and Commentary*. Downers Grove, IL: InterVarsity, 1981.

Westmoreland-White, Michael. "Golden." In *Dictionary of Scripture and Ethics*, ed. Joel B. Green et al. Grand Rapids, MI: Baker Academic, 2011.

White, Ellen. "No, No, Bad Dog: Dogs in the Bible." Biblical Archaeology Society, March 29, 2022. https://www.biblicalarchaeology.org/daily/ancient-cultures/daily-life-and-practice/dogs-in-the-bible/.

Whybray, R. Norman. *Wealth and Poverty in the Book of Proverbs*. Sheffield: Sheffield Academic, 2009.

Wilder, James. *The Pandora Problem: Facing Narcissism in Leaders and Ourselves*. Carmel: Deeper Walk International, 2018.

Wilder, Jim. *Escaping Enemy Mode*. Chicago: Moody, 2022.

Williams, William A. "Agriculture." In *Lexham Theological Wordbook*, ed. Douglas Mangum et al., Lexham Bible Reference Series. Bellingham, WA: Lexham, 2014.

Wink, Walter. *The Powers That Be: Theology for a New Millennium*. New York: Doubleday, 1999.

Winship, A.E. *Jukes-Edwards. A Study in Education and Heredity*. Harrisburg, PA. R.L. Meyers, 1900.

Wiseman, Donald J. "930 יָשַׁר." In *Theological Wordbook of the Old Testament*, ed. R. Laird Harris, et al. Chicago: Moody, 1999.

Wood, Leon J. "547 זִיד (zîd), זוּד (zûd)." In *Theological Wordbook of the Old Testament*. ed. R. Laird Harris, et al. Chicago: Moody, 1999.

Workaholism. "Workaholism: It's Not Just Long Hours on the Job." American Psychological Association, 2016. https://www.apa.org/science/about/psa/2016/04/workaholism.

World Economic Forum, "Outlook on the Global Agenda: 2015," Trend 3: Lack of Leadership. http://reports.weforum.org/outlook-global-agenda-2015/top-10-trends-of-2015/3-lack-of-leadership/?doing_wp_cron=1541243910.4283349514007568359375.

Wuest, Kenneth S. *Wuest's Word Studies from the Greek New Testament* volume 11. Grand Rapids, MI: Eerdmans. 1997.

Milton Keynes UK
Ingram Content Group UK Ltd.
UKHW030653120324
439302UK00015B/975